SANTIMALS

Carving with Tom Wolfe

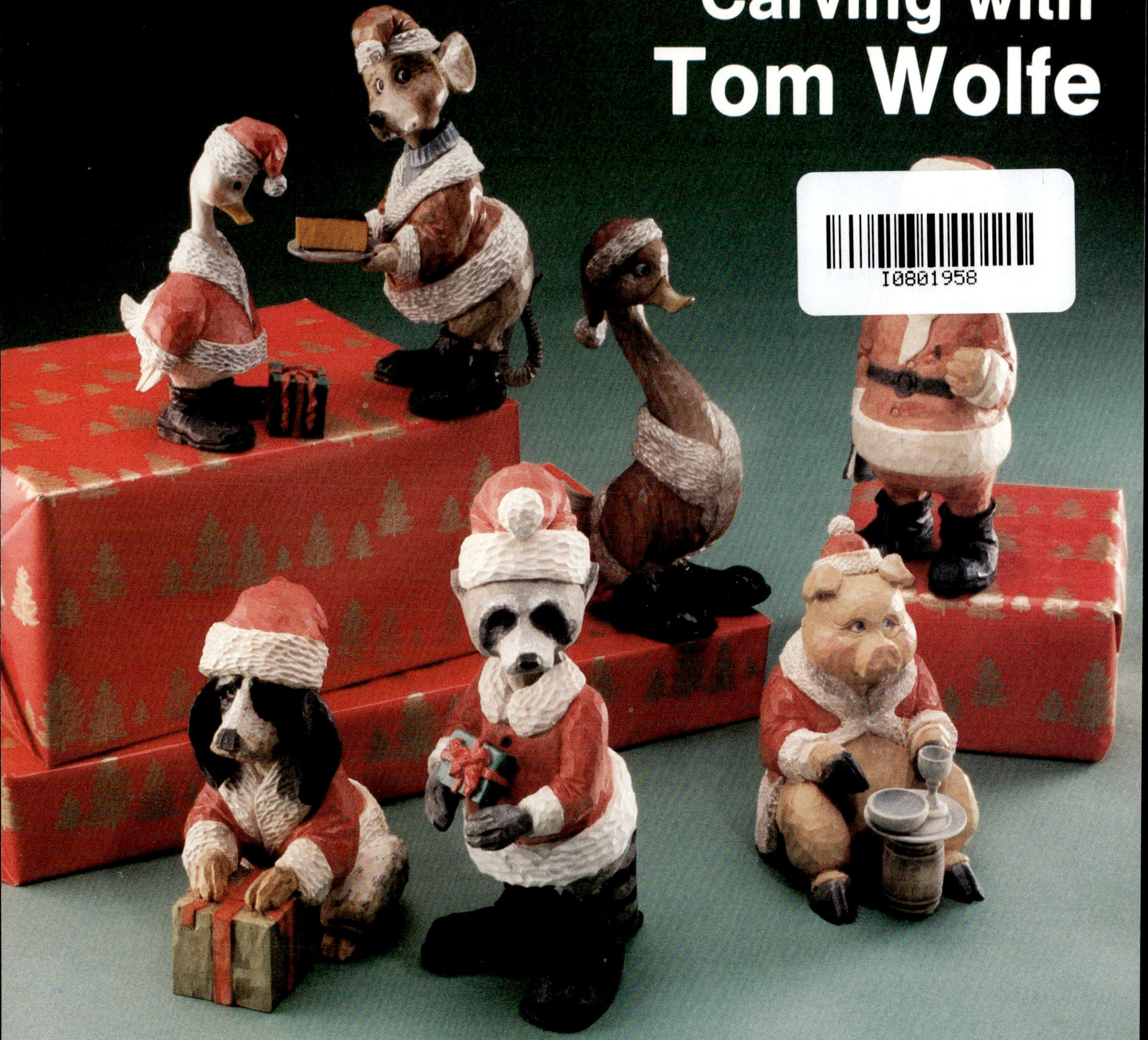

Schiffer Publishing Ltd

1469 Morstein Road, West Chester, Pennsylvania 19380

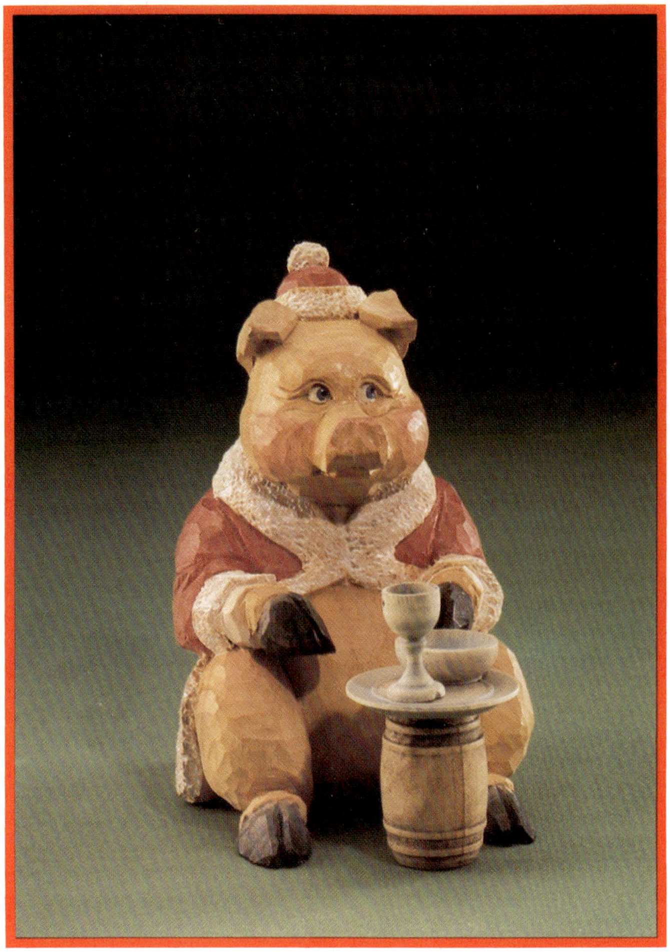

Contents

Library of Congress Catalog Number: 92-60696.

Printed in the United States of America.
ISBN: 0-88740-440-5

We are interested in hearing from authors with book ideas on related topics.

Published by Schiffer Publishing, Ltd.
1469 Morstein Road
West Chester, Pennsylvania 19380
Please write for a free catalog.
This book may be purchased from the publisher.
Please include $2.95 postage.
Try your bookstore first.

Photography by and text written with
Douglas Congdon-Martin

Introduction

The Story of the Santimals

Until now the story of the Santimals has been known only to Santa Claus, Mrs. Claus, and a few elves. Santa has agreed that it can be shared with you because everyone knows wood carvers don't give away their secrets!

It happened one Christmas several years ago. About a week before Christmas Santa came down with a terrible case of the flu. He blamed it on the week he spent at that trade show in Miami in early December, but whatever the cause, it sent him to bed and put the whole North Pole on edge. No one said anything out loud, but everyone was wondering if Santa Claus would be well enough for his Christmas Eve trek.

Raccoon loved the trash cans behind Santa's workshop. He would find all kinds of goodies there: broken candy canes, fruit cakes still in their wrappers, half eaten plates of Christmas cookies, and much more. The day before Christmas he was searching deep in one of the cans when two elves came from the workshop and looked carefully around. They didn't see Raccoon and began to whisper.

"I don't see how he's going to make it," said one. "Tomorrow is Christmas, and he hasn't been out of bed in a week. This is very bad."

"Maybe we should begin to make other plans. We don't want to disappoint the children." piped the other.

"Other plans? What other plans? It's Christmas Eve. Everyone's gone home early." the first elf squeaked in frustration.

The other elf thought for a while. It was true. There was no one who could deliver all the packages in time. There weren't enough overnight delivery people in the whole world to handle this job, even if they were working tonight. Finally he suggested softly and without much conviction, "Maybe we could deliver the presents."

"What? You want us to deliver them? You must be outta your mind! You'll never get me to fly in that rickety old sled. Besides I'm allergic to reindeer.", the first elf grumbled, shoving his small hands deep in his pockets and kicking at a pile of snow.

"But what about the children?"

"They'll just have to wait until Santa gets better."

"You mean we're going to postpone Christmas?"

"Afraid so, unless you've got a better idea."

The other elf didn't, so they went inside to tell the others.

Well, Raccoon couldn't believe what he had heard. He stuffed two or three candy canes into his cheeks and began to shake the can back and forth until it fell to the ground with a crash. He scampered into the woods where he called all the other animals together to tell them what he had heard.

"That's the story," said Raccoon as he finished.

"It's terrible," honked Goose.

"Where did you get the candy canes?" grunted Pig.

"We must do something," suggested Bear in a deep thoughtful rumble, and they all were quiet for awhile as they thought about the problem. The only sound to be heard was Pig's stomach rumbling at the prospect of candy canes.

"I have an idea." A wee voice broke the silence. Everyone turned toward Mouse. "We can make Santa's deliveries for him."

"What do we know about delivering presents?" snorted Pig.

"Not much, I'll admit." answered Mouse. "But how much do we have to know? The elves have the list and the reindeer could fly the route blindfolded. All we have to do is get the gifts into the houses and under the tree. If we work together it should be a cinch."

"I like it," said Bear.

"Me too," agreed Raccoon, and one by one they endorsed Mouse's plan. Until they got to Pig.

He sat there for a long time before he spoke. "I really don't think we should do this. Except for Goose and Duck, none of us has any experience flying. And besides, it's dangerous on those roofs. Count me out."

A sigh spread among the others. Perhaps it was disappointment that Pig would not join them, or maybe it was a twinge of fear that he just might be right. But before the fear could undo their resolve, Mouse spoke up.

"You know, Pig, I've been in houses on Christmas Eve. And I've seen a most wonderful thing happen. Every child in the world leaves a plate of cookies and fruit and other wonderful things for Santa to eat. It would be a shame for you to miss such a feast."

"Is that true?" Pig asked the others.

"I've seen it too," confirmed Dog. And the others just nodded their heads, though, of course, they had never been in a house on Christmas Eve or any other time.

"Well, perhaps I will join you then," said Pig. "Besides, of all of us, I will look best in Santa's uniform."

They made their way at once to Santa's workshop. Raccoon knocked on the door. One of the elves opened it and called the others to see the unlikely band of visitors. "Can we help you?" the startled elves asked.

"Actually," answered Raccoon, "we've come to help you. We know that Santa is quite sick, and we'd like to deliver the toys for him."

The elves looked at one another in disbelief. They began to whisper in an animated way. Occasionally one of them would laugh out loud. Finally, they turned to the animals and one of them, the most senior elf, began to speak officiously. "We appreciate the offer, but we don't really think that..."

Before he could finish, he was interrupted by a booming voice coming from somewhere deep in the workshop. "Who's at the door?"

"It's just some animals, Santa."

"What do they want?"

"They want to save Christmas."

"Is that so?" Santa was silent for a while. "That's a very interesting idea. Send them in."

The animals made their way through the workshop packed with toys and gifts, all neatly wrapped and ready to be loaded on the sleigh. At the back of the shop was a big red door, and through that door they found a great red bed with Santa lying in his night shirt and propped up by pillows.

"I'm glad you're here," he said. "I've been looking for some way out of this horrible fix, and you just might be it. Do you really think you can do it?"

"We think so," said Mouse, "but do you?"

"Well..." he paused for a few moments. A slow smile spread across his face. "Well, yes I do. Let's get at it." In a burst of energy Santa began to direct activities from his bed. The elves fitted each animal with its own Santa suit. The bags were loaded onto the sleigh and the reindeer placed in their harnesses. Santa double checked the list and handed it over to Bear.

Finally he leaned back on his pillows and smiled. "I think you are ready now. Are there any last minute questions?"

The only one who spoke was Pig. "Is it true about the food?"

"How do you think I got so round?" asked Santa, and for the first time in many days, he let out a deep belly laugh. "The only thing left to do is to give you a name. Let's see...I've got it. You shall be my Santimals."

And so the Santimals were off to every corner of the world, spreading Christmas joy and love. They saved Christmas that year, and ever since at least one of them has gone along with Santa on his annual ride.

We hope you enjoy carving these figures, and that they will find a special place in your home or the homes of your friends and loved ones.

The Raccoon

The Tools and Patterns

The tools needed for the Santimals project include a simple set of palm gouges, a turned-down blade and a turned-up blade, and some eye punches or nailsets for the eyes and buttons. The wood I use is bass, and it is probably the best for these figures. It carves and takes the paint nicely.

The patterns are reproduced at their actual size. You may use them as they appear or enlarge or reduce them on a photocopying machine. While you are at the copying machine, print several copies so you can cut them apart as needed to help in the drawing of the various parts.

I do not use a full-frontal pattern because I find it leads to more trouble than its worth. People tend to try to follow it too exactly and find that at some point they have cut off something they're going to need later. Besides, if everything is laid out too completely it limits the creativity that comes in the carving. The photographs in the book are designed to give plenty of guidance without overdoing it. I have included full-size frontal photographs of each figure so you can use it as an accurate guide.

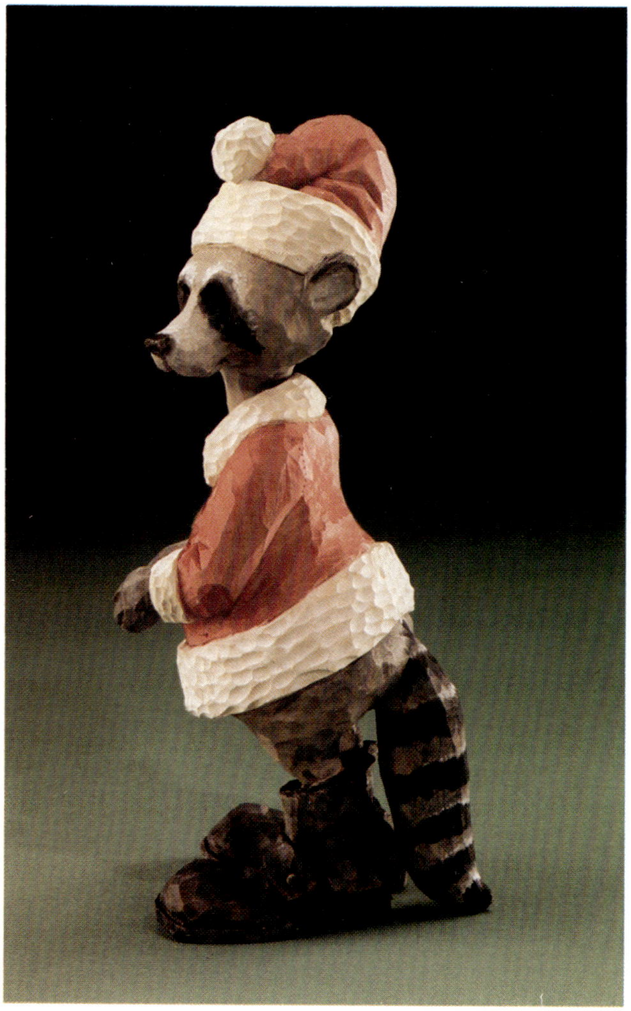

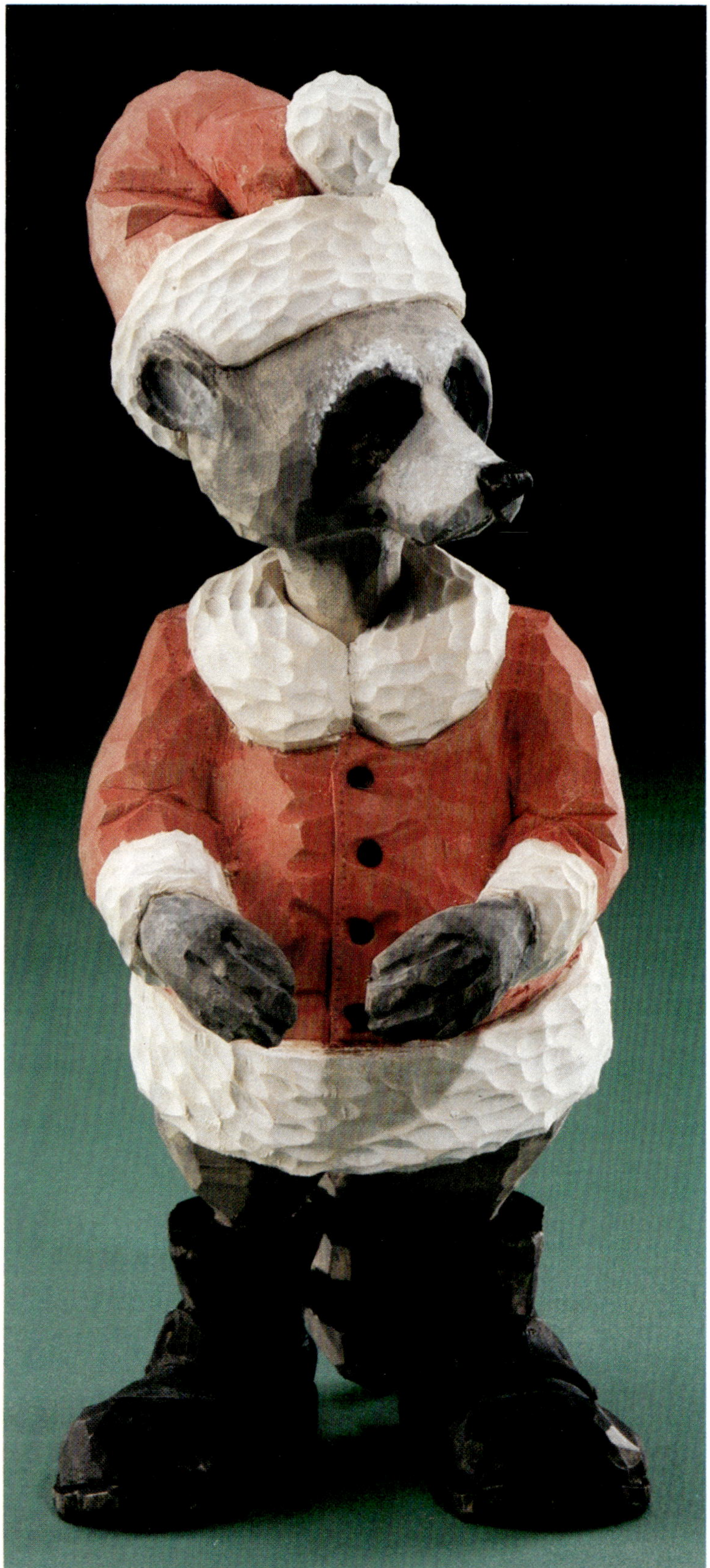

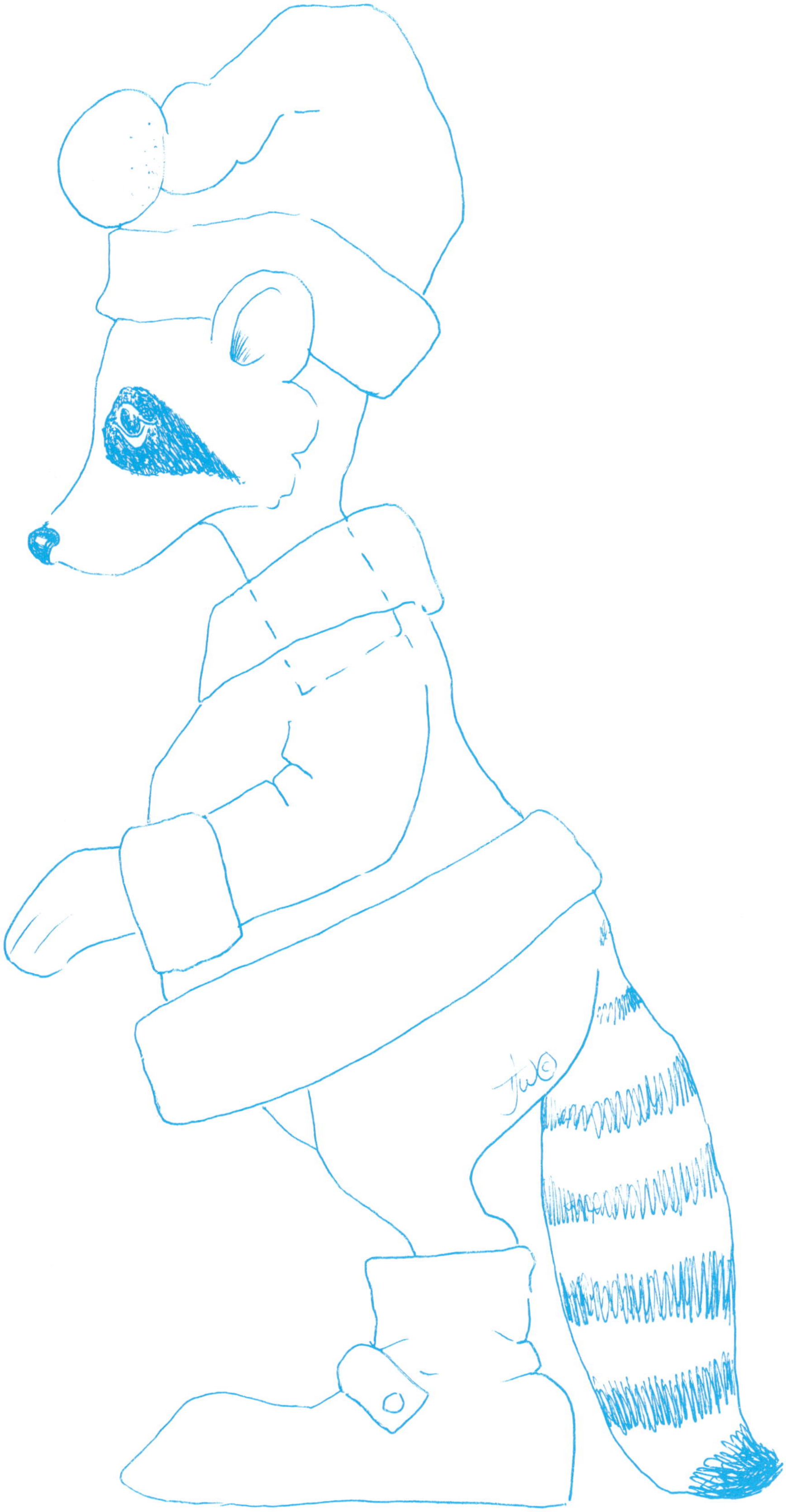

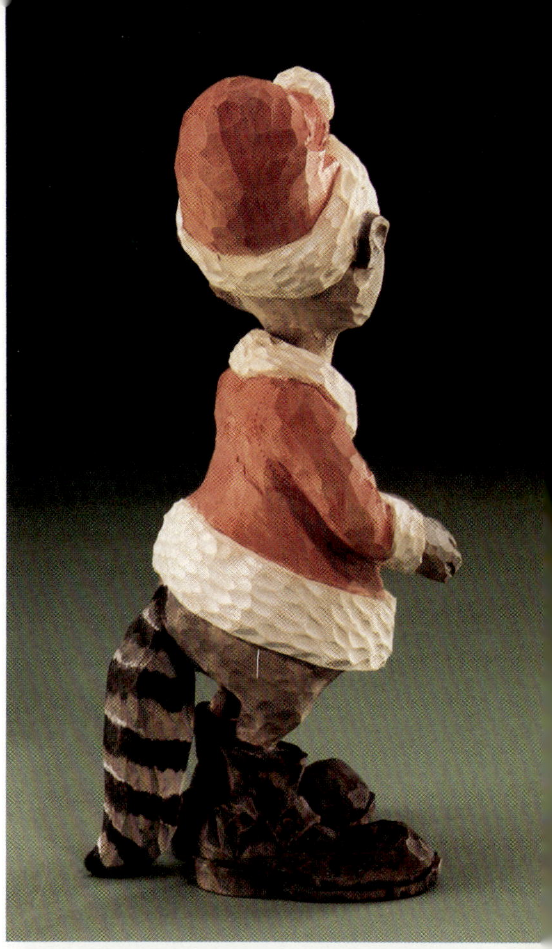

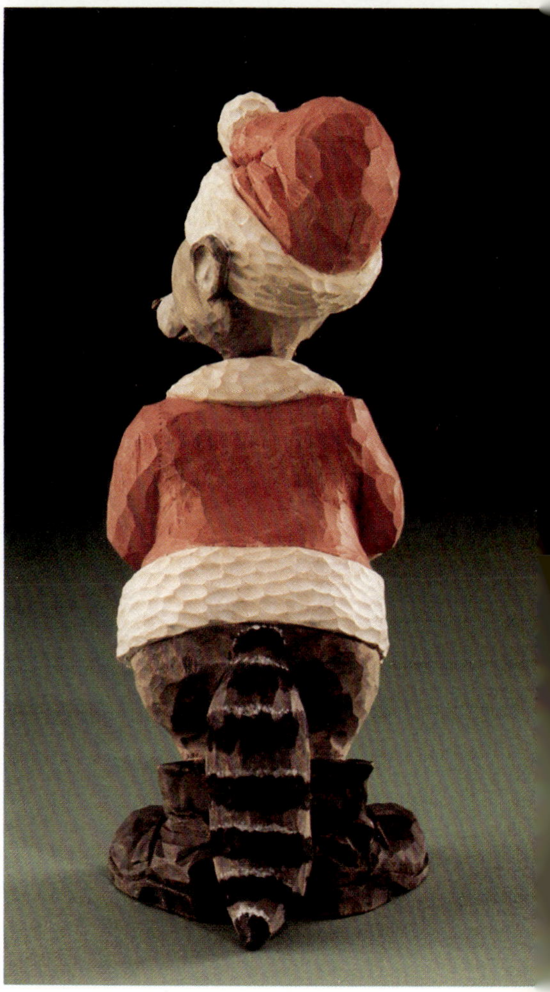

Carving the Raccoon

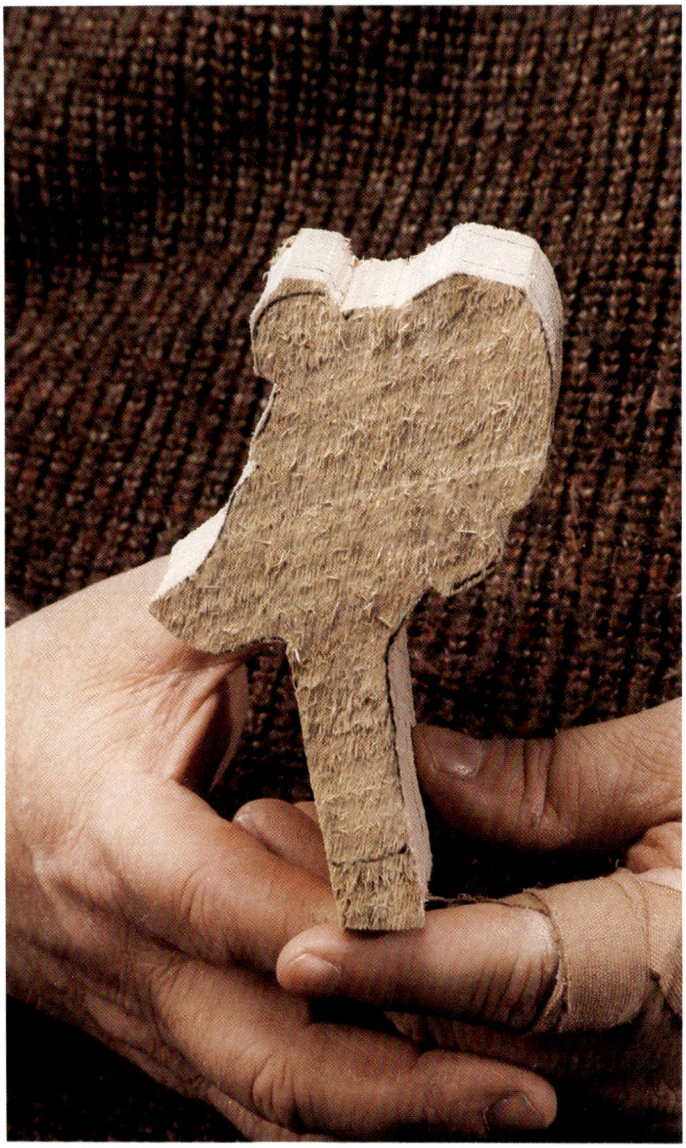

When working in this size, I use four inch stock for everything I do. Of course, if you reduce or enlarge the pattern you can use any size of wood you want or have available. This is the head pattern cut out on the band saw.

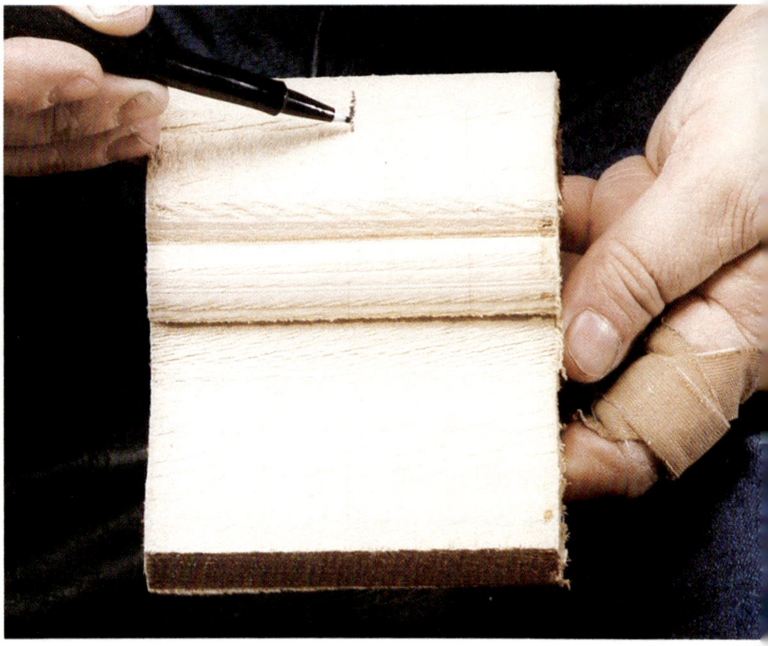

After laying out the patterns and cutting them on a bandsaw, find the center of the head and mark it.

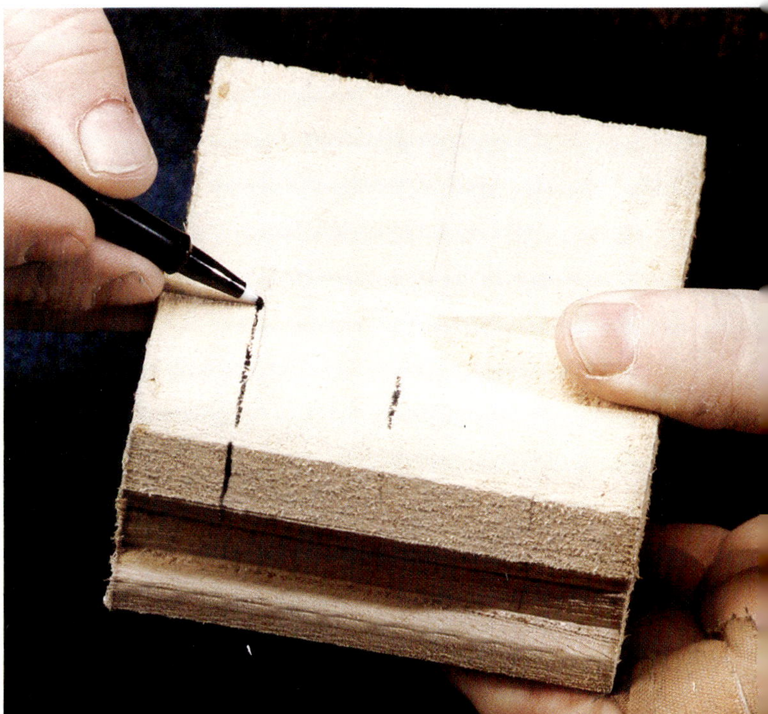

I want the head to be about ½″ narrower than the shoulder on each side, so I mark one side first...

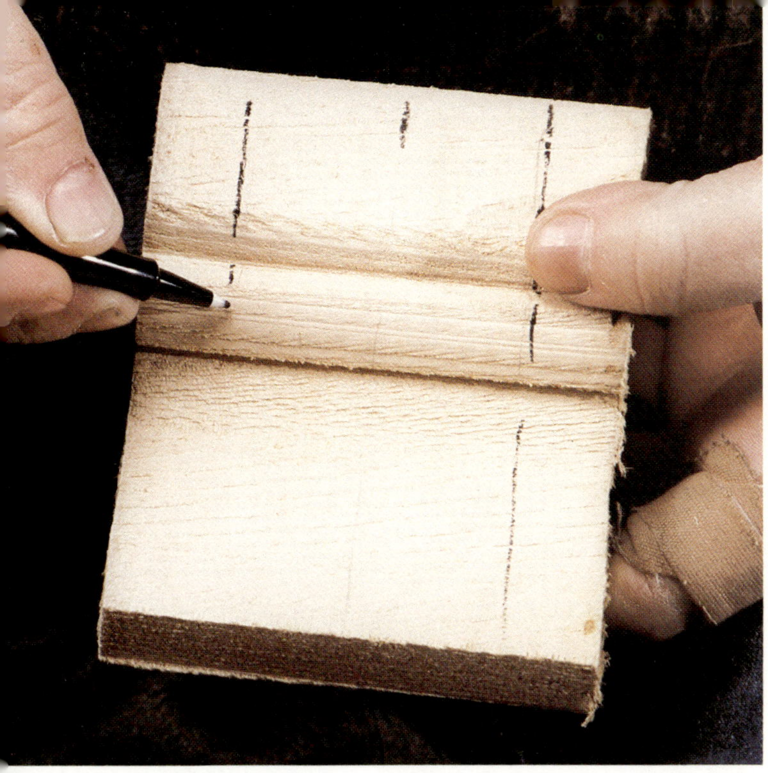

and then, holding my fingers in the same position to create a depth gauge, I mark the other side.

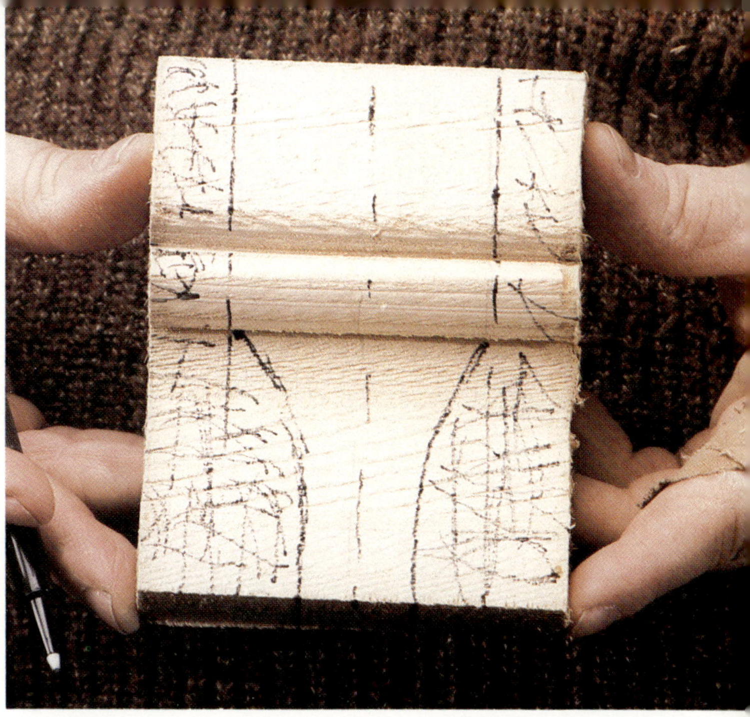

Bring the line up the neck making it wider as you go toward the bottom of the head. You must do this freehand, because if you try to lay down a frontal pattern, the contour of the wood will just throw you off.

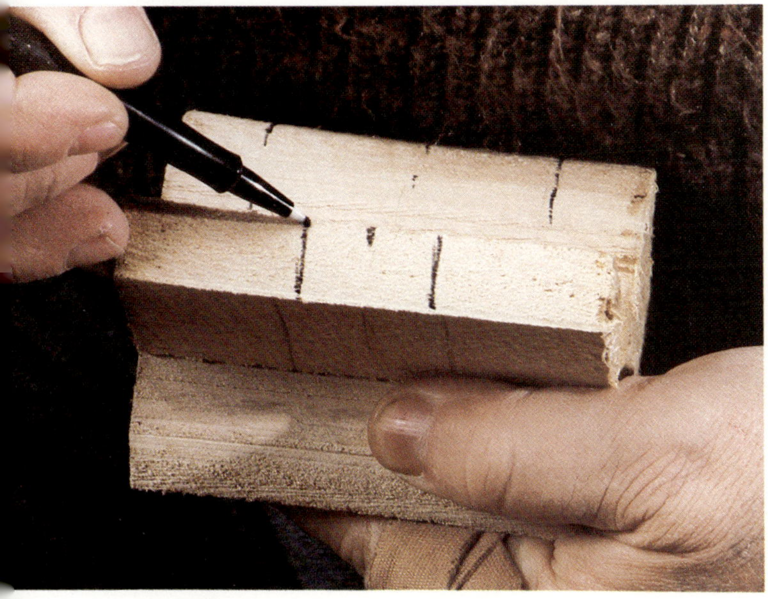

The neck will be round, so, starting from the center, mark either side.

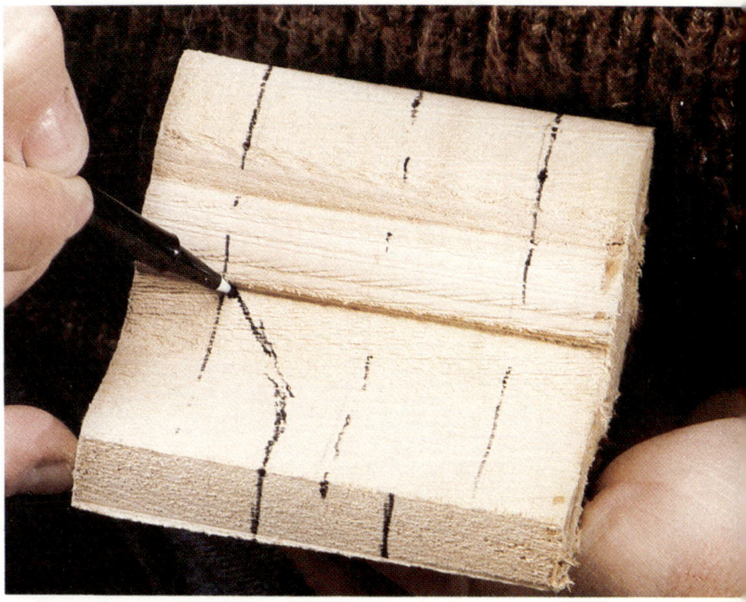

Mark the area to be removed.

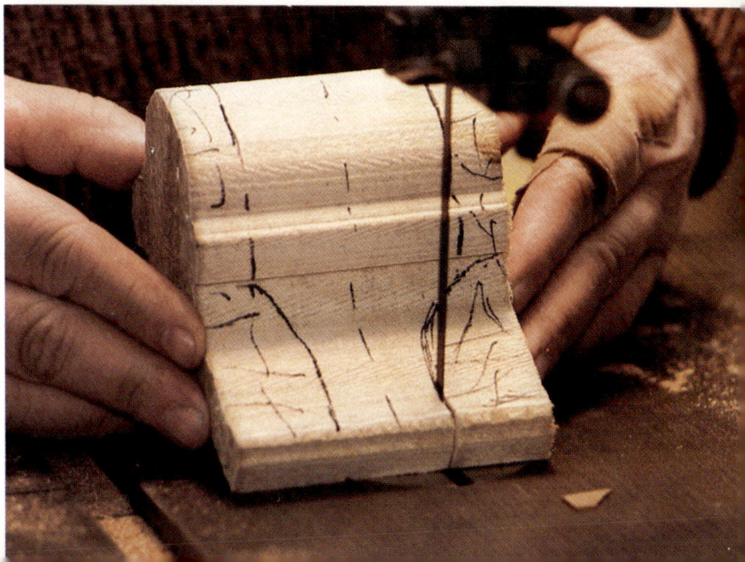

Cut the head out. You can do this by carving, but a coping saw or band saw makes a tedious job go much more easily.

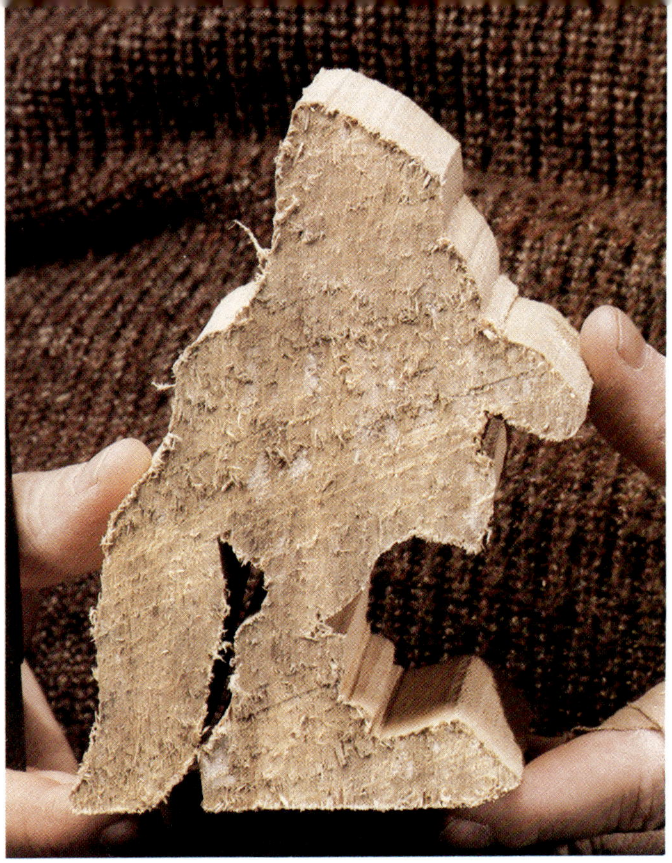

This is the cut out body in profile.

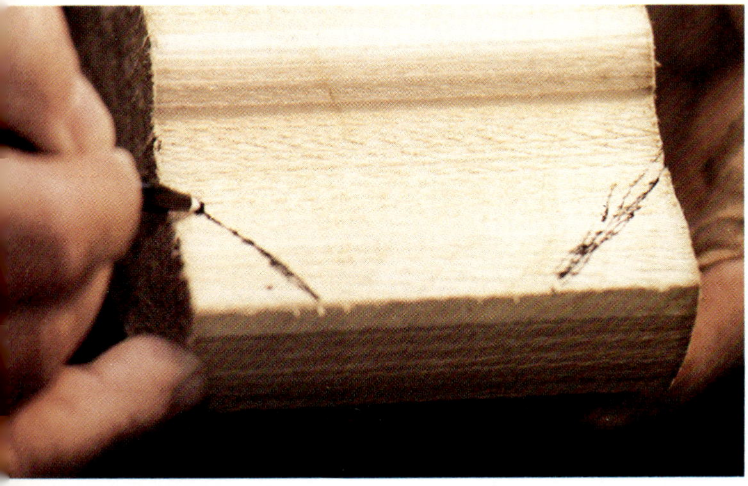

Mark the shoulders...

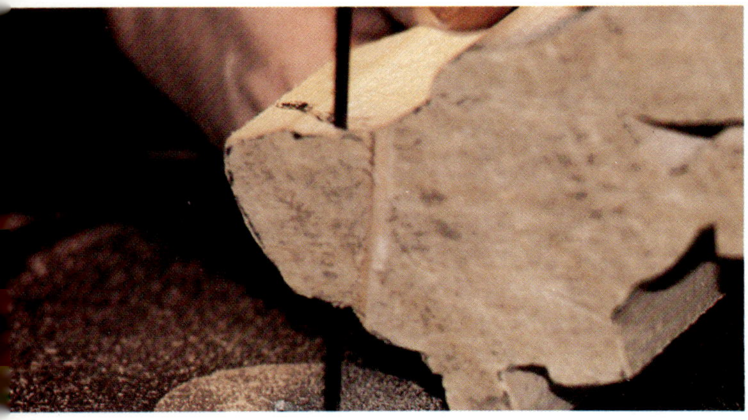

and cut them off with the band saw or a coping saw.

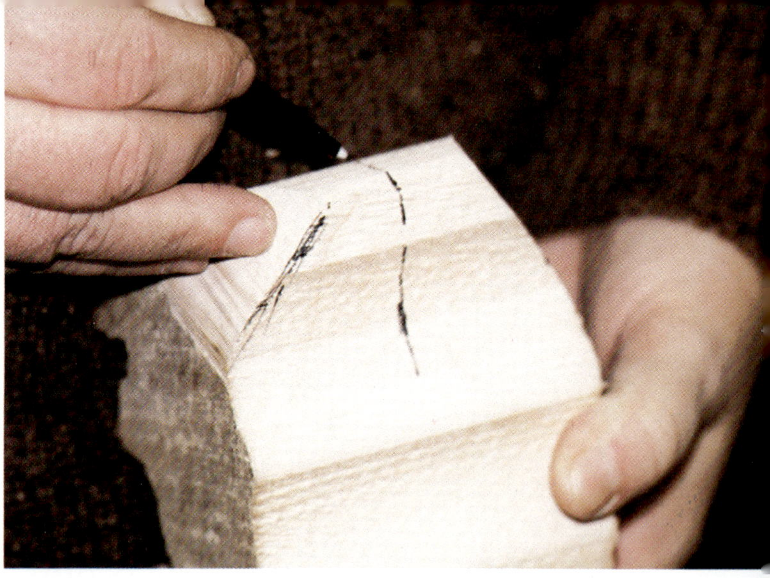

Mark the center of the body up over the shoulders and the neck.

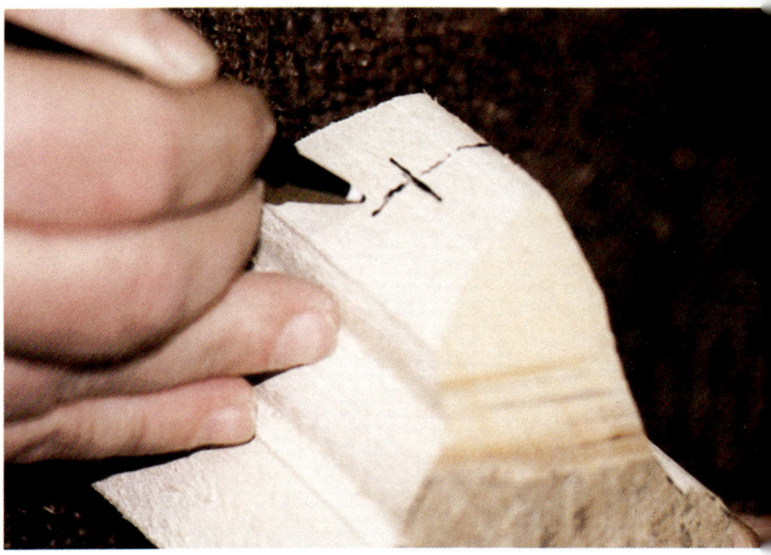

Mark across the center of the neck.

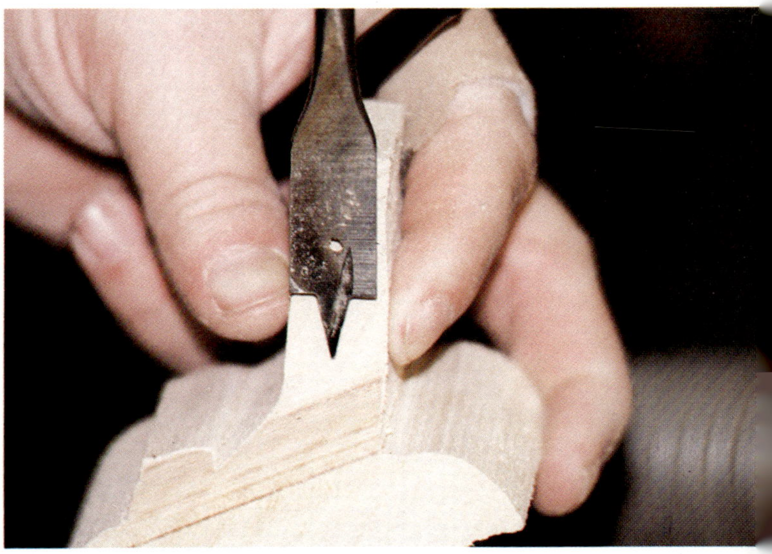

Find a square bit that matches the width of the neck. If you can't find one that is exact, it is better to go too small than too large.

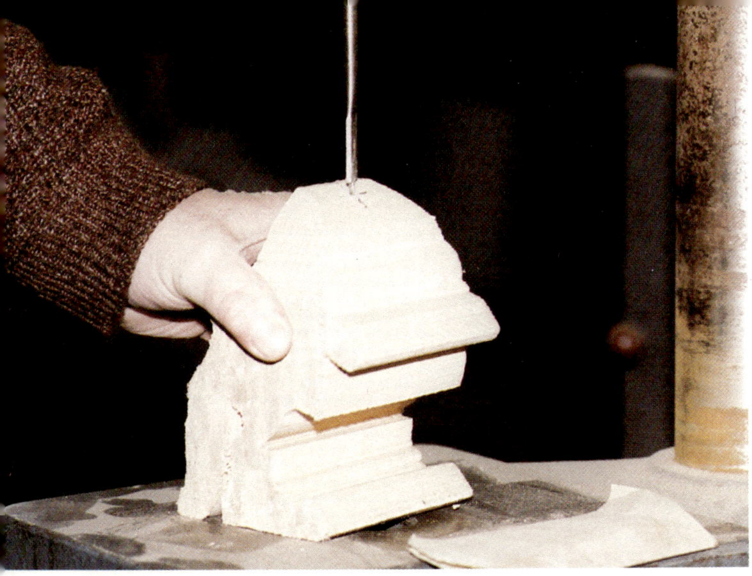

With the body standing on the table of the drill press, drill straight into the wood. You can angle it a little to get a certain attitude, but be careful not to drill through the body.

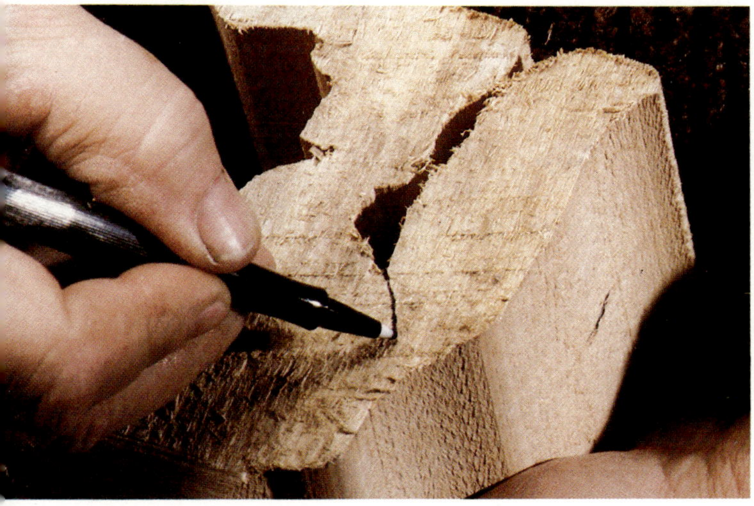

Mark the line of the rump on both sides.

Mark the center line of the tail.

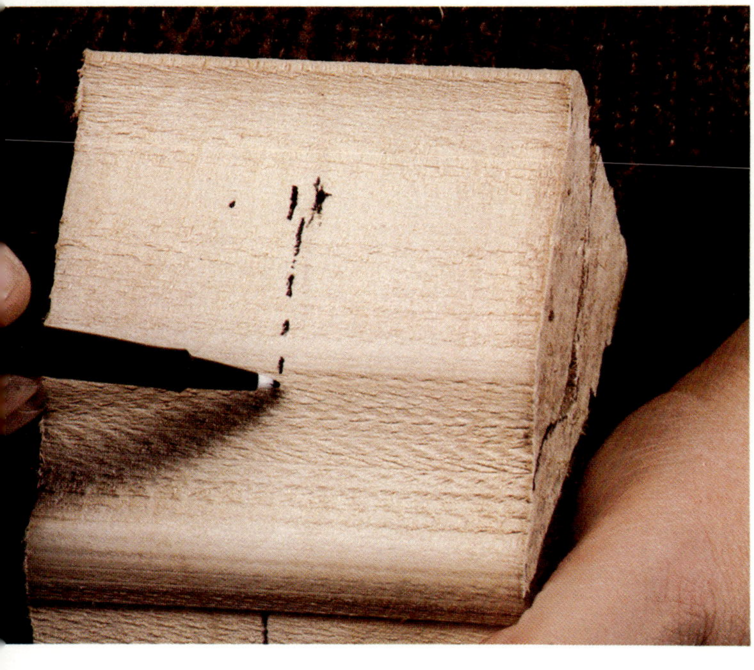

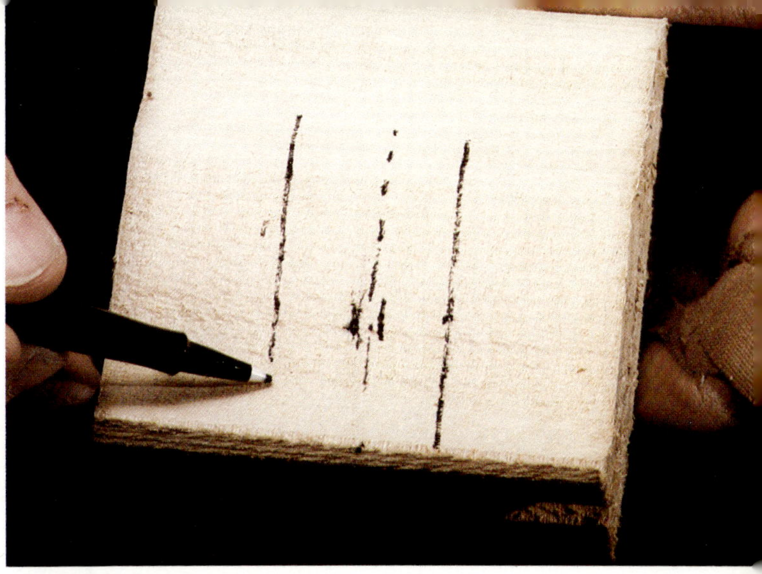

Using your fingers as a depth gauge, mark the outside of the tail.

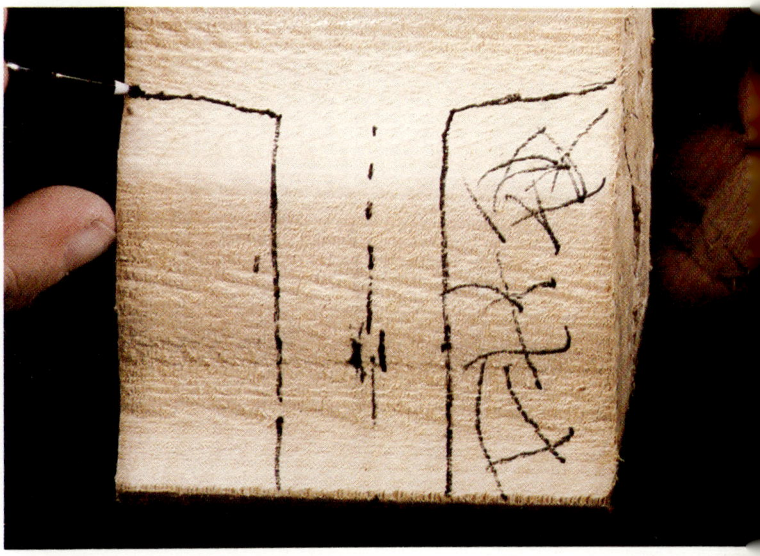

Mark the area to be removed.

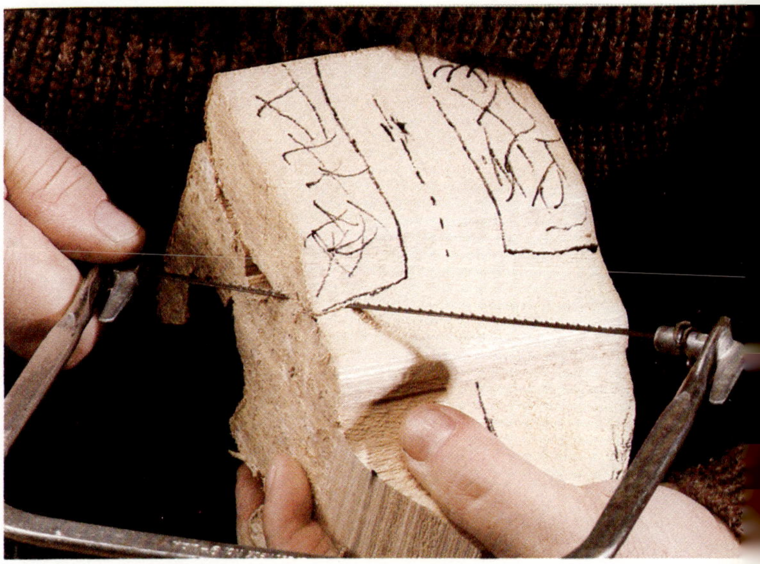

Use a coping saw with the blade reversed (so the pulling stroke does the cutting), cut along the rump on either side of the tail. This gives you a little head start on the carving.

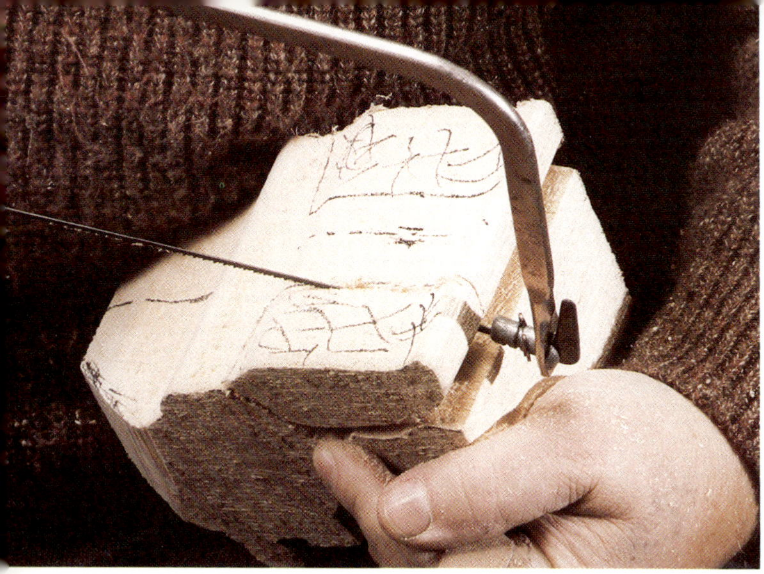

Turn the piece and cut up the sides of the tail.

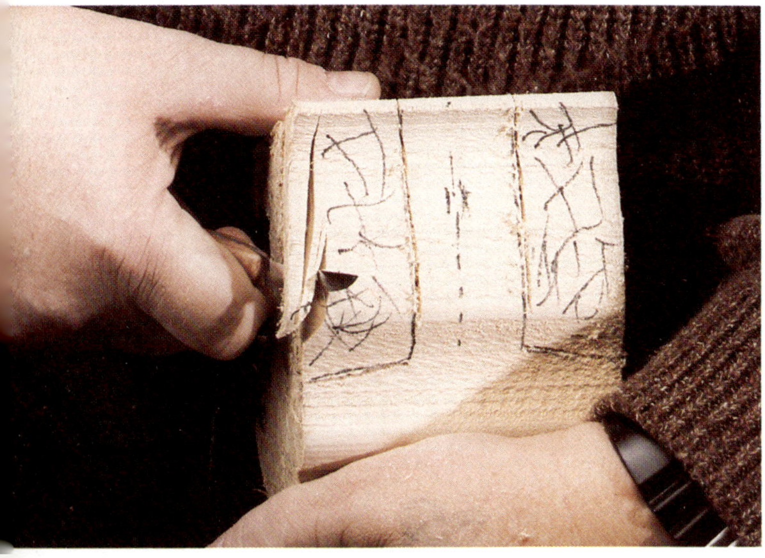

Because of the coping saw cuts and the direction of the grain, it is easy to pop off the excess wood beside the tail. You'll need a strong blade for this, so you can twist it and use it to pry the wood free.

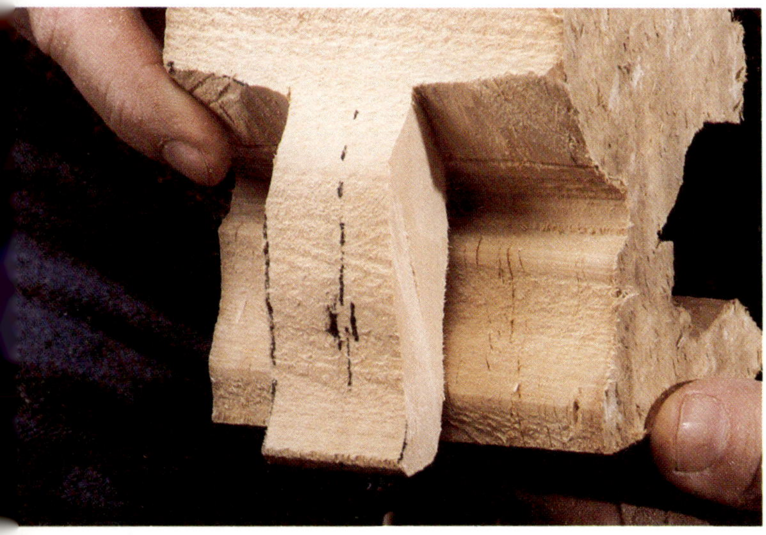

The tail defined.

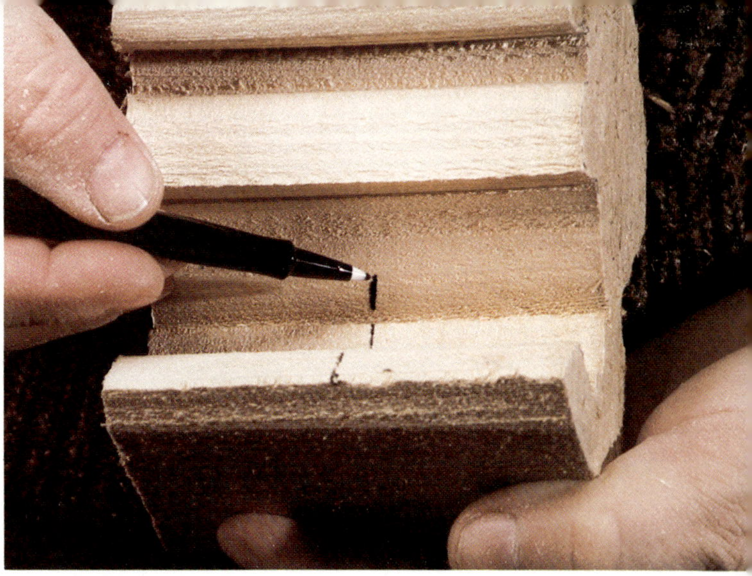

Turning to the front, mark the line between the legs. Be careful not to make the crotch too high.

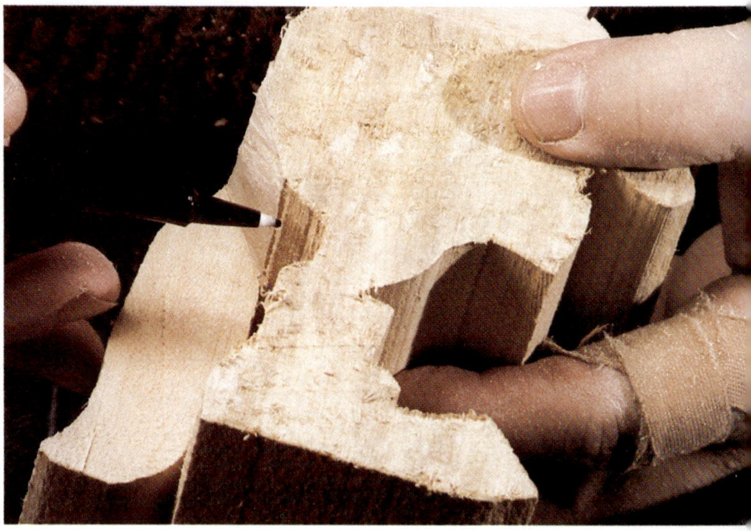

To guard against this look at the profile and line the crotch up with the bottom of the rump.

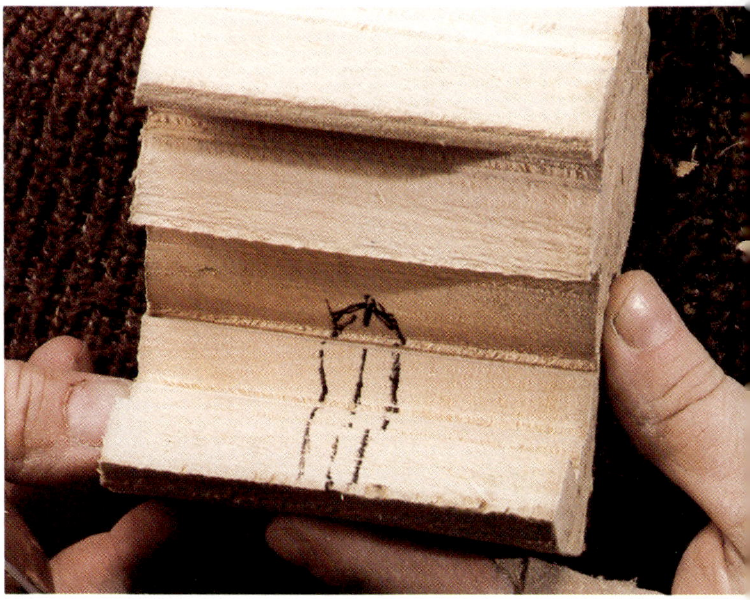

Draw in the space between the legs.

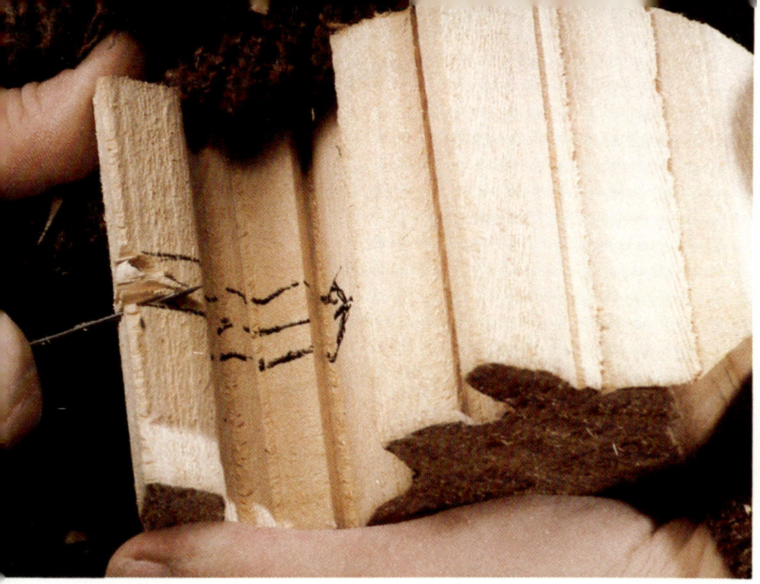

Using the narrowest knife you have, chip away the excess between the legs. You could use a coping saw here, but it is likely to lead to mistakes.

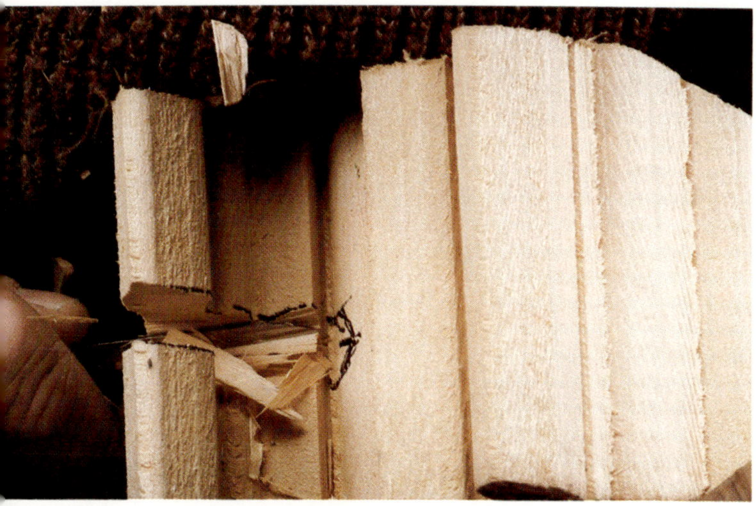

Start with the feet and work your way back to the legs.

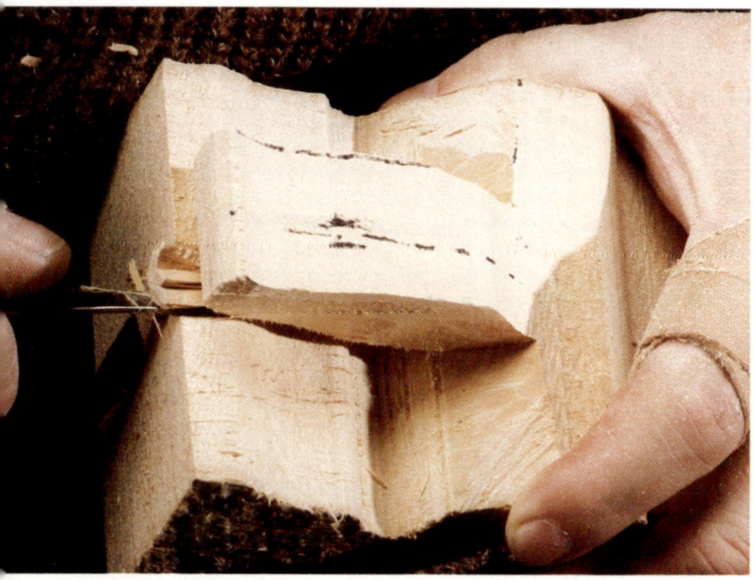

At some point you'll want to turn the piece over and work from the heels. The objective is to open the legs up all the way through.

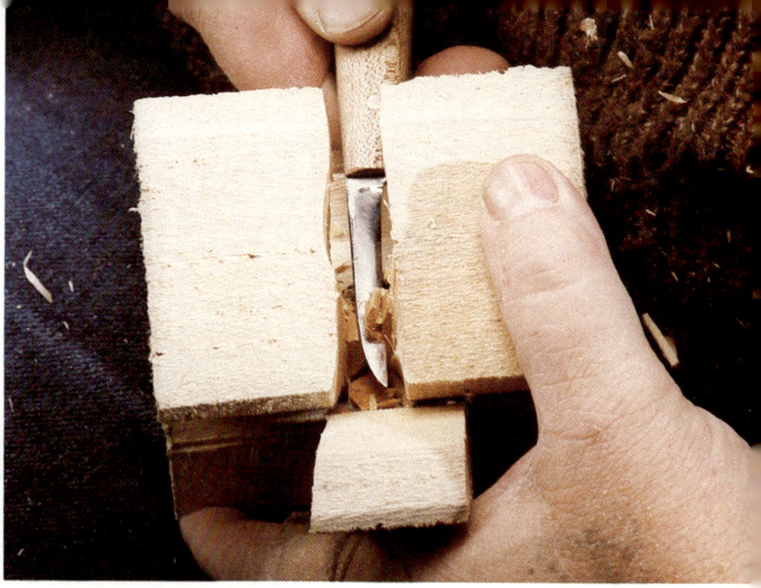

Continue up to the crotch.

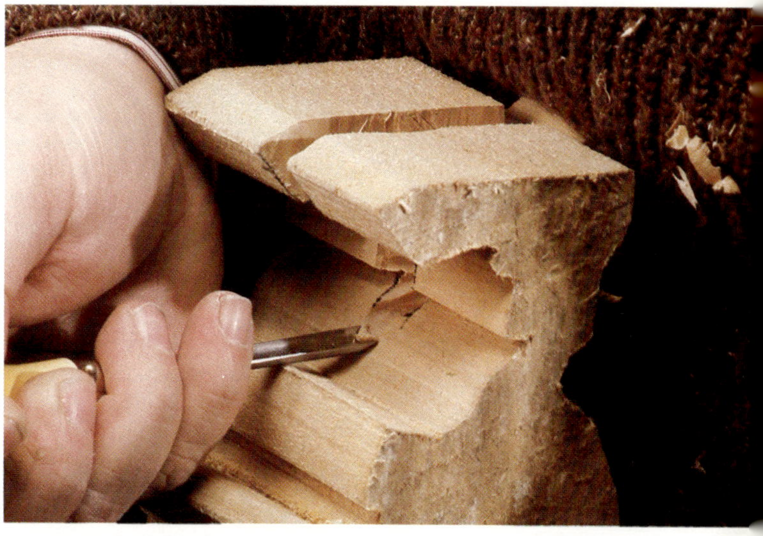

Clean up between the legs with a gouge. This area is tough to work because the two legs and the tail are always getting in each other's way, so be patient and keep at it. It will get easier as you go.

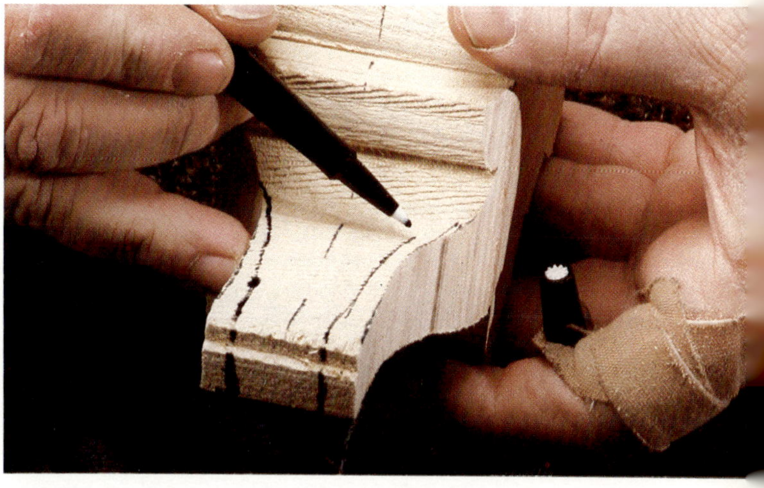

Move to the head now to fit the neck. Begin by marking the neck. You want the width and depth of the base to be equal.

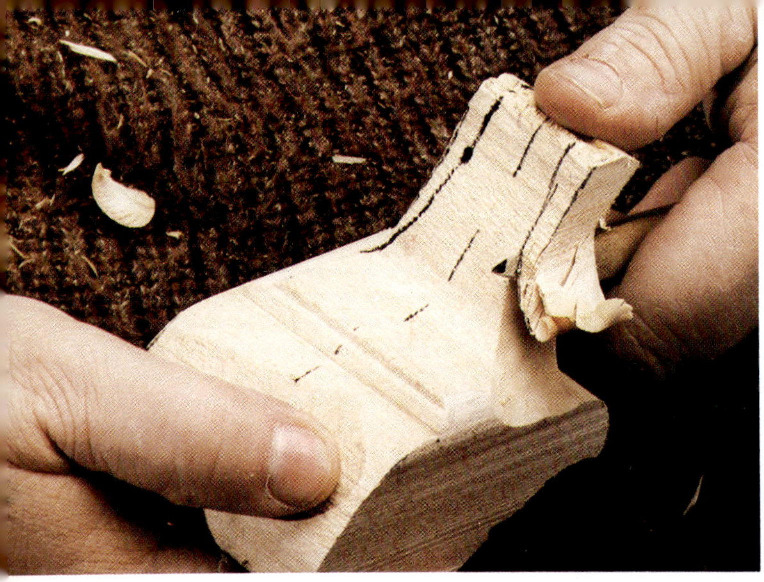

Trim the sides, keeping them square. If you start to round too soon, the carving will tend to be square with rounded edges. I first carve it square, then octagonal, and finally round. When you're pulling the knife toward you like this, keep the thumb hidden or get a good thumb guard.

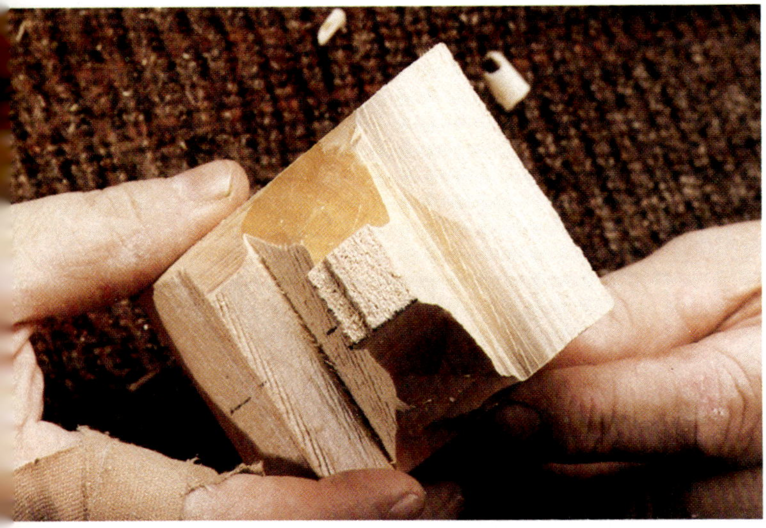

This is the neck at the square stage.

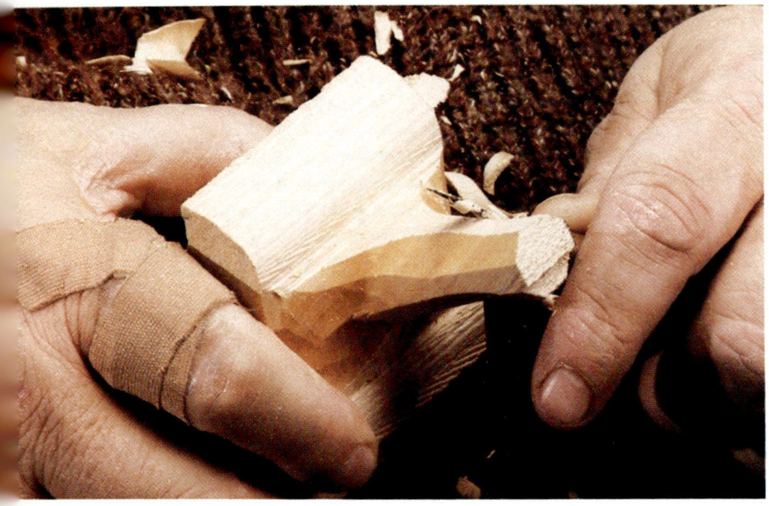

Next, I take off the corners of the neck to form this octagonal shape.

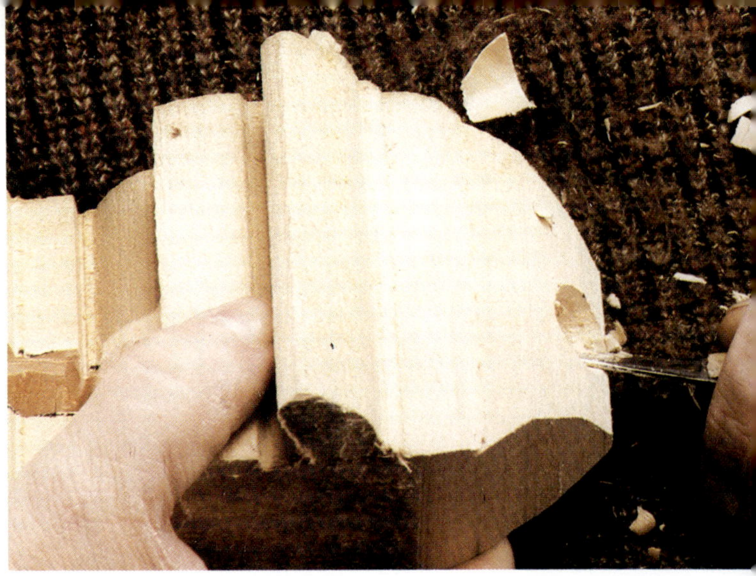

The neck is way too long, but if we begin fitting it at the bottom, it will fit all the way up. Begin by flanging the hole in the body a little bit. Just barely do the top of the hole, so it doesn't get out of round.

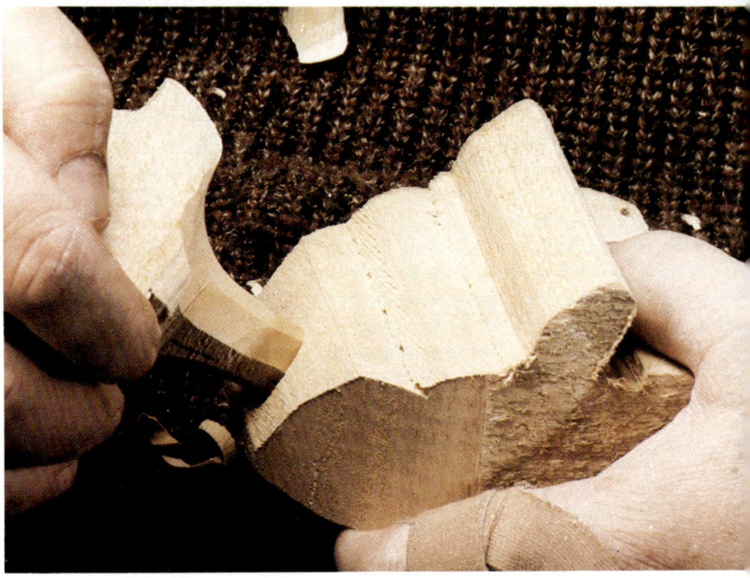

Place the neck in the hole and twist it around, applying pressure as you turn.

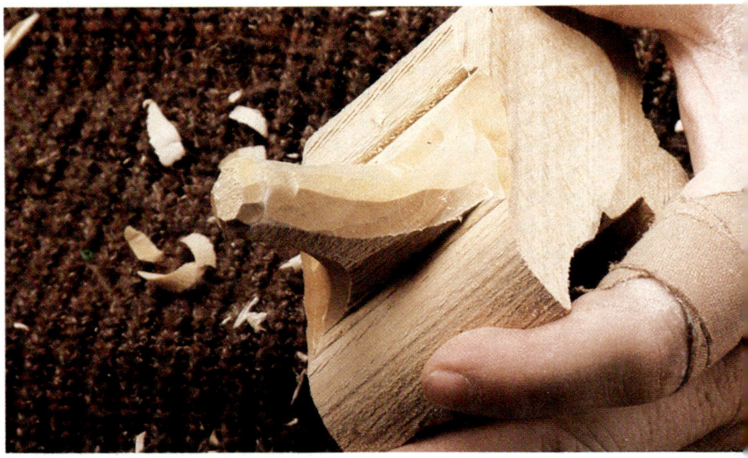

By this twisting those high spots that need to be removed will be made shiny. Trim away the high spots and repeat this process until the neck fits in the hole.

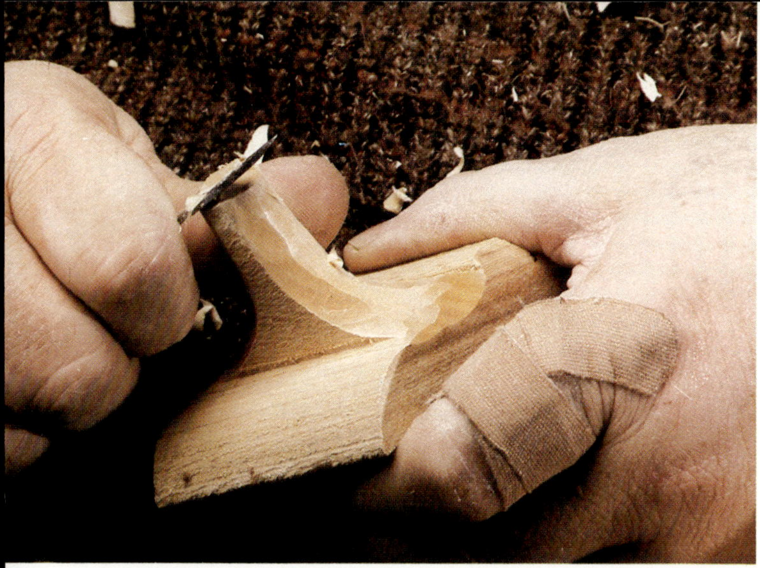

As the neck reaches the bottom of the hole, cut a little bit off the end and repeat the process until the head fits as you want it.

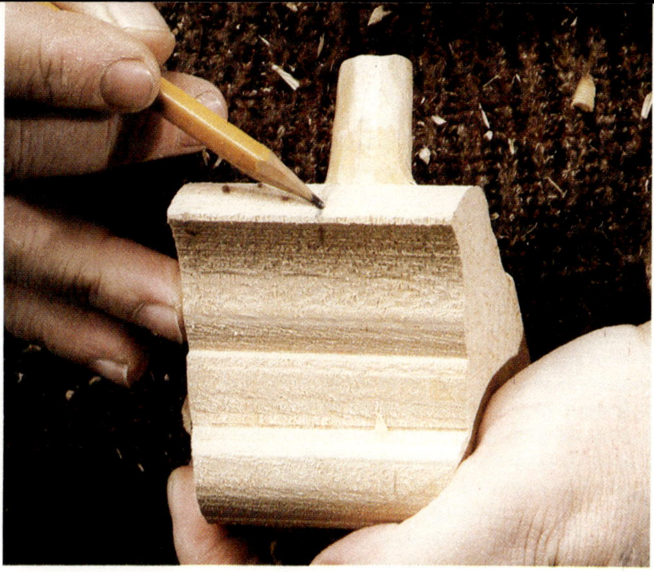

Using the neck as a guide, draw a center line for the face. When I cut out the neck, it was a little off-center. This step helps us get everything right again.

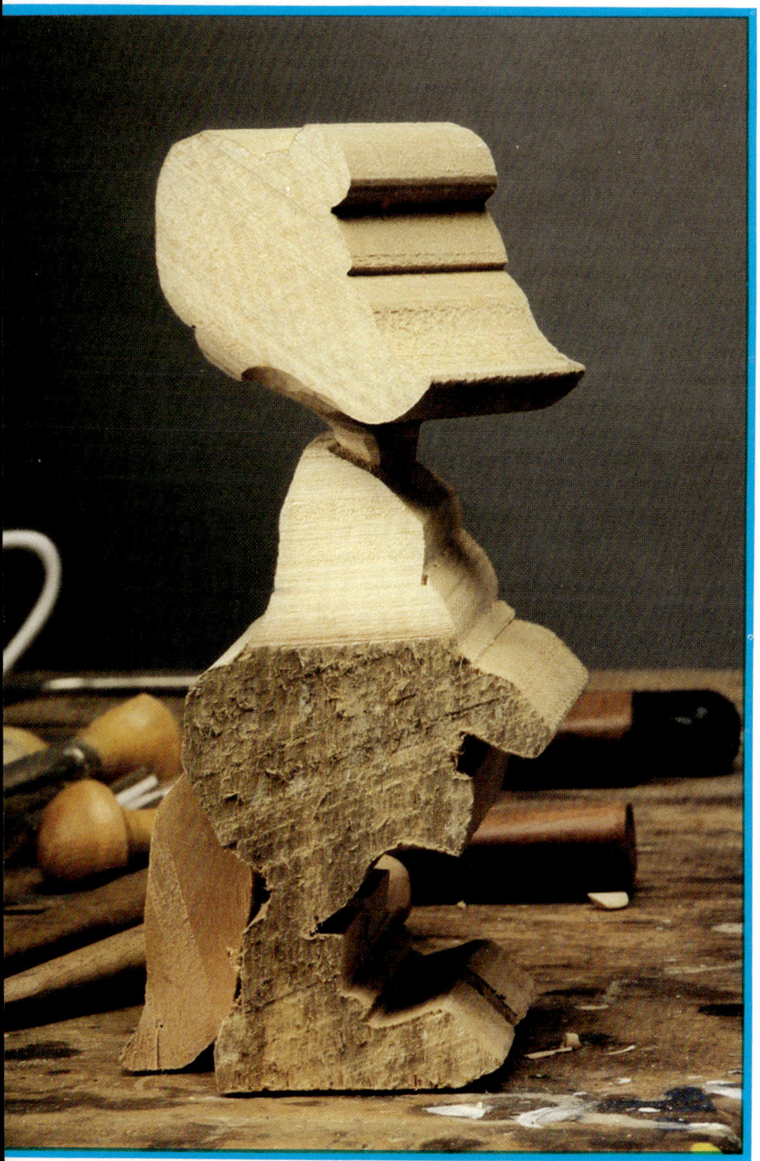

The fitted head. Notice that by doing the head this way it is possible to turn it in various positions, giving it different attitudes.

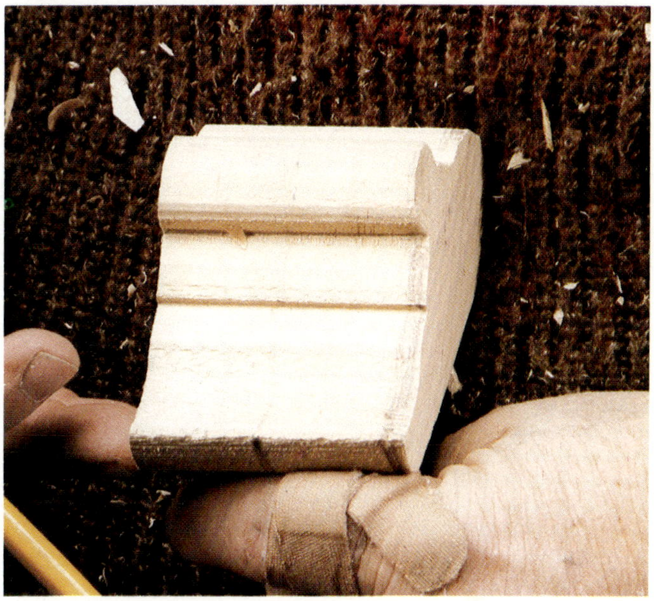

Now I can see how much I need to remove from the side to make everything balanced.

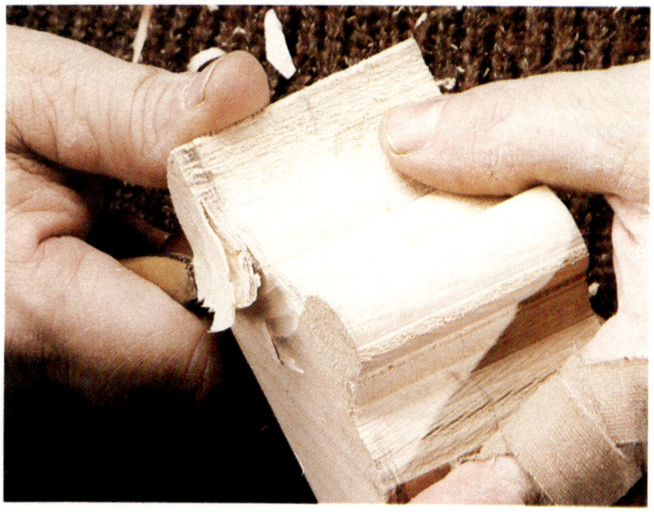

Remove the excess with the knife.

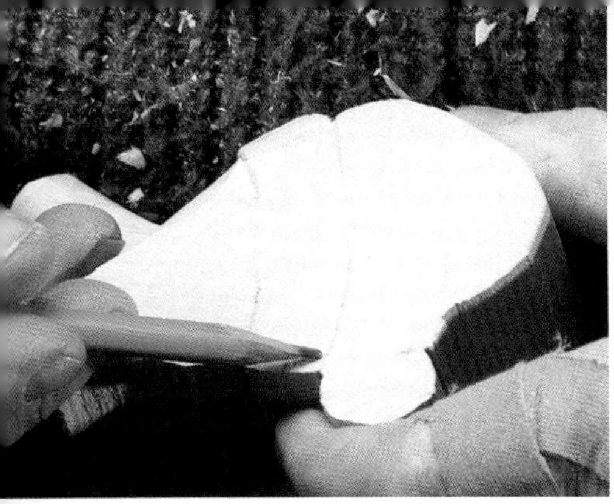

I am going to draw the hat and ears freehand, but you may wish to make copies of the patterns, cut them out and lay them on the piece as a guide. Start with the hat band.

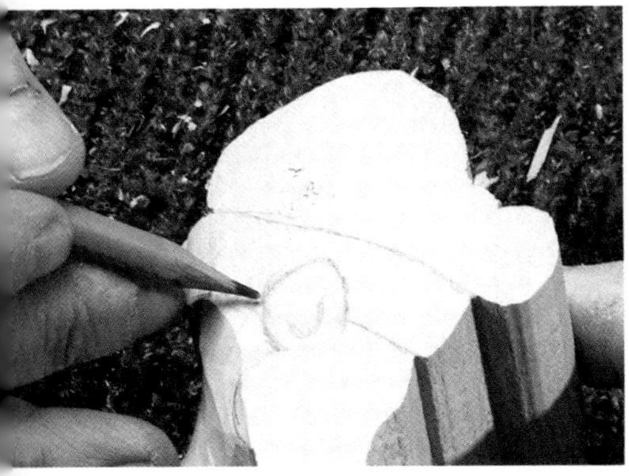

To situate the ears, align them with the point where the jawbone would meet the skull. This is common to all animals, and will bring a touch of realism to your carvings. This is important, even if the creatures are imaginary, like Santimals. It will make them believable.

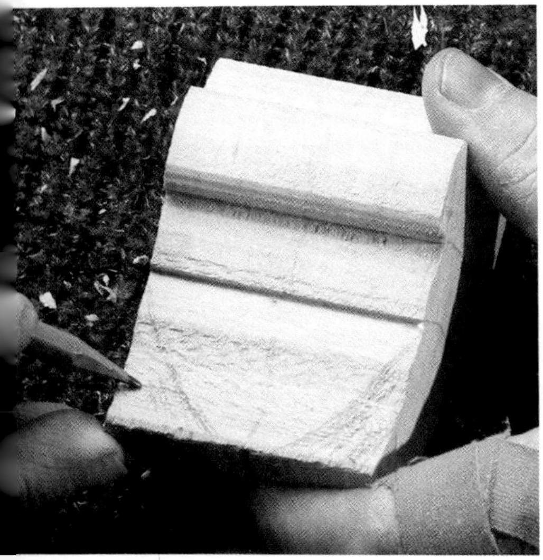

Mark the sides of the muzzle and darken the area to be removed.

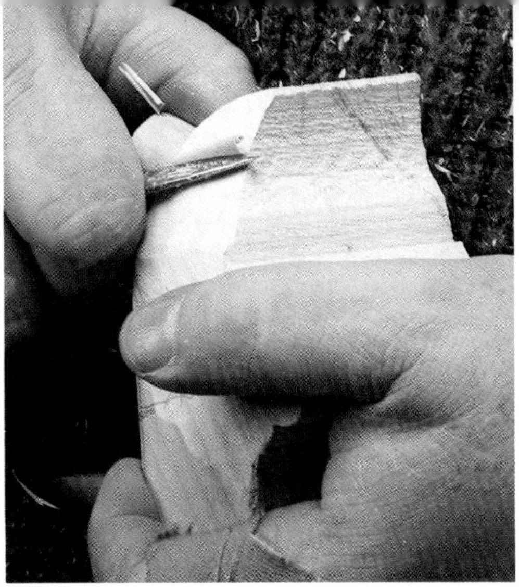

Use a knife to shape the muzzle.

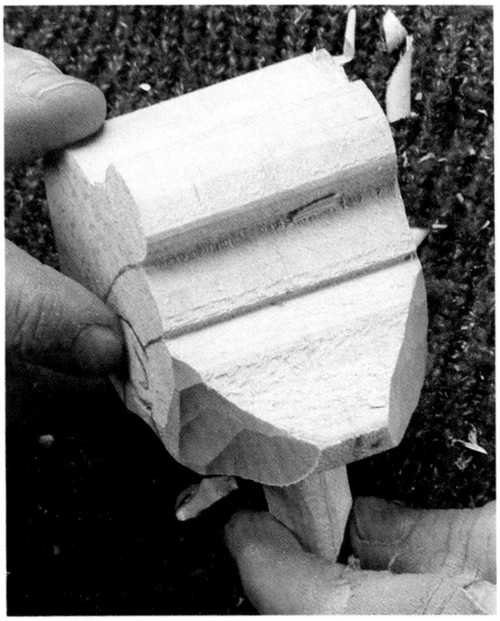

The roughly shaped muzzle.

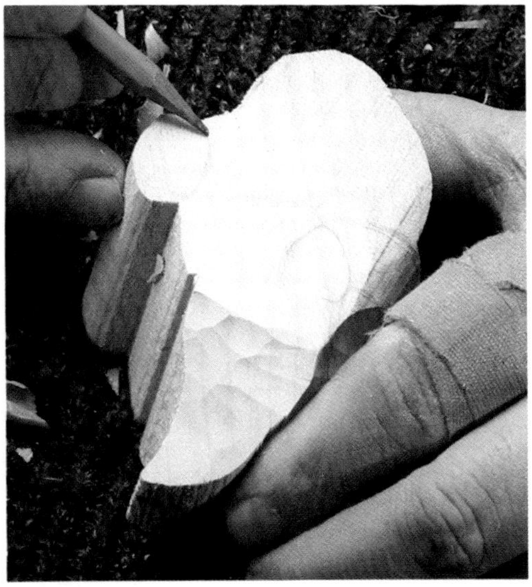

Mark the ball of the hat on the sides...

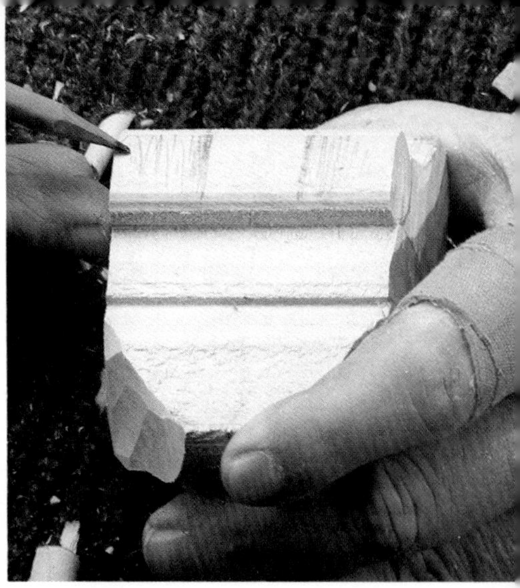

and on the front. Darken the area to be removed.

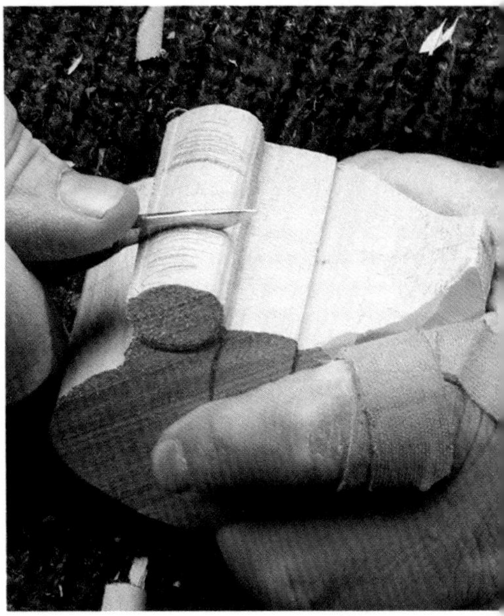

Cut a stop on both sides of the ball by rocking your knife back on forth.

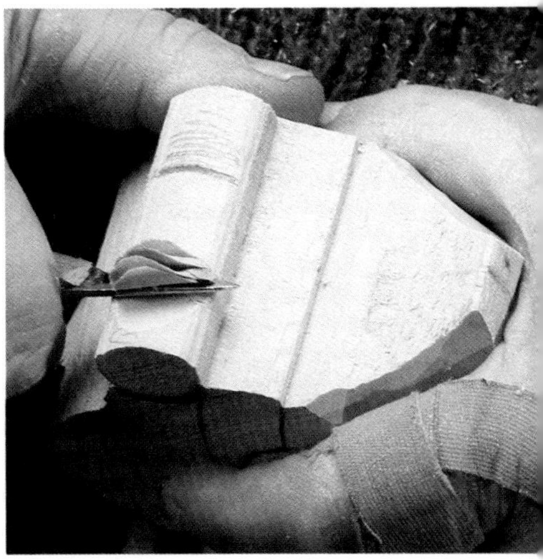

Cut back to the ball from sides.

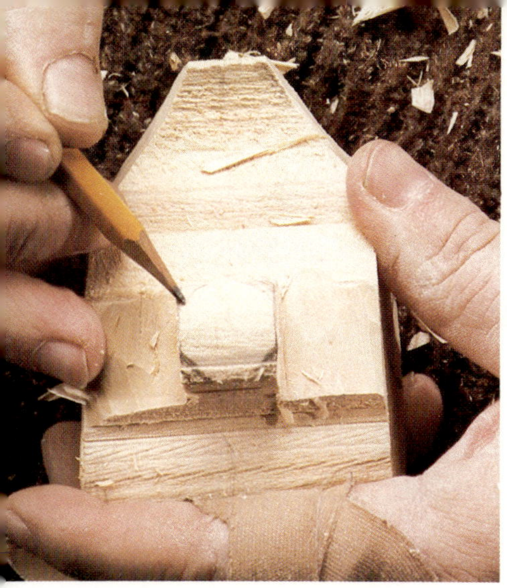

When you've trimmed it to square, mark the corners for removal.

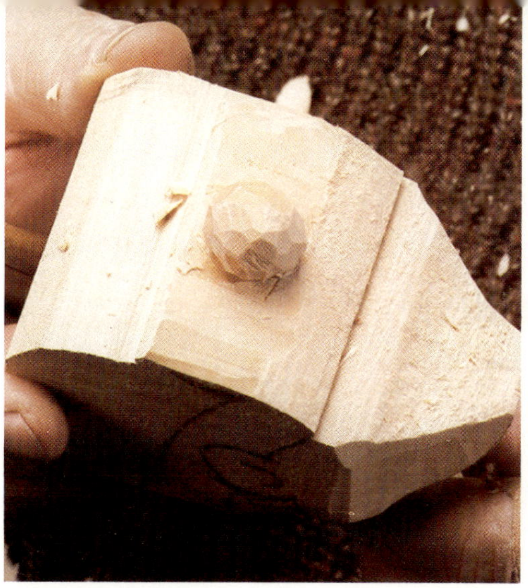

round it into ball.

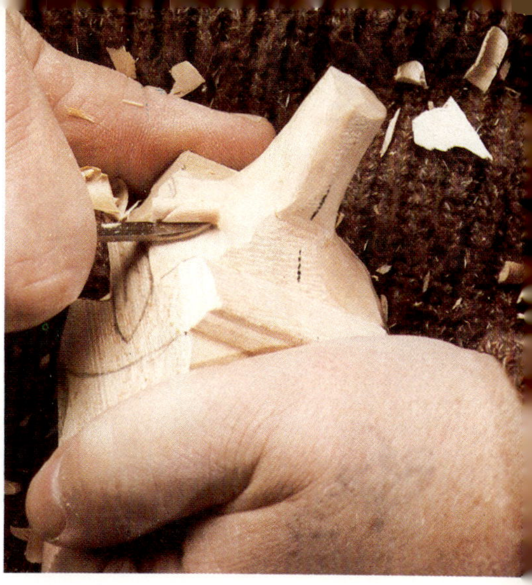

Take off the corners of the head under the cap and back to the ears.

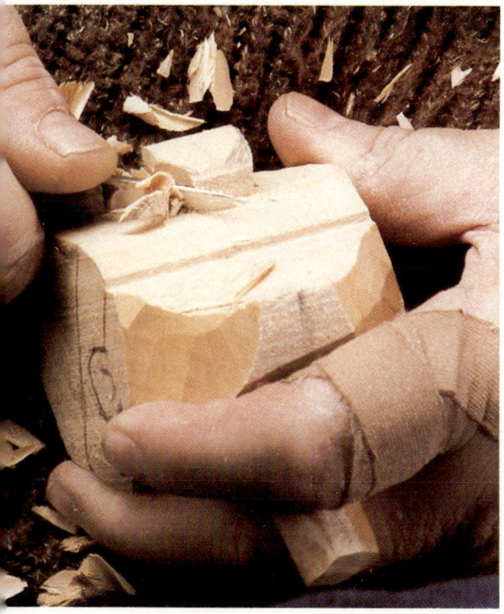

Cut straight down to trim the ball into an octagon.

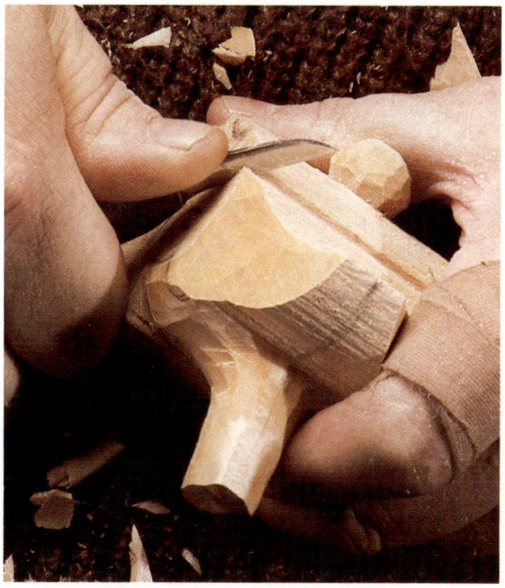

Cut stops all around the fur trim of the cap, starting on the corners. Cut in...

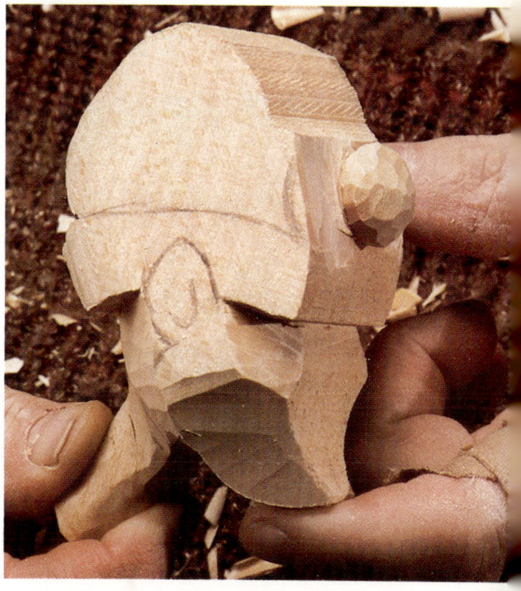

This should bring you to this point.

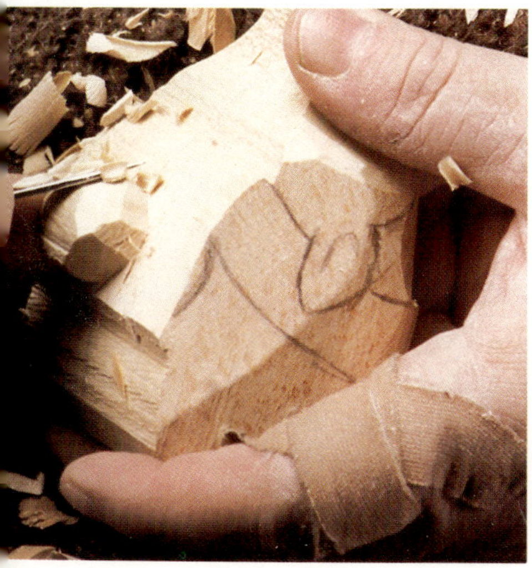

After you've gotten to the octagon shape...

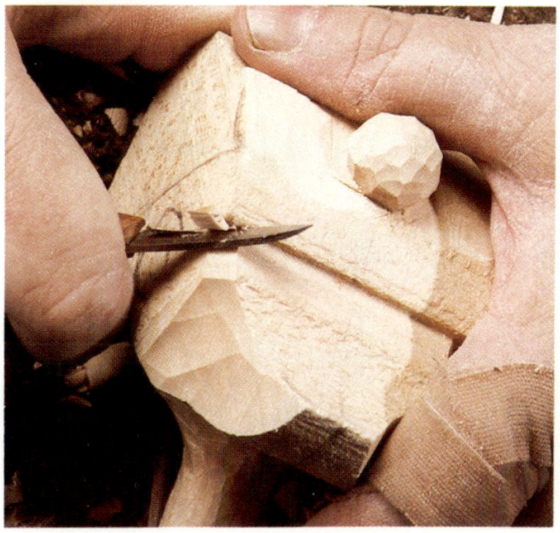

then come back from the head to pop it off.

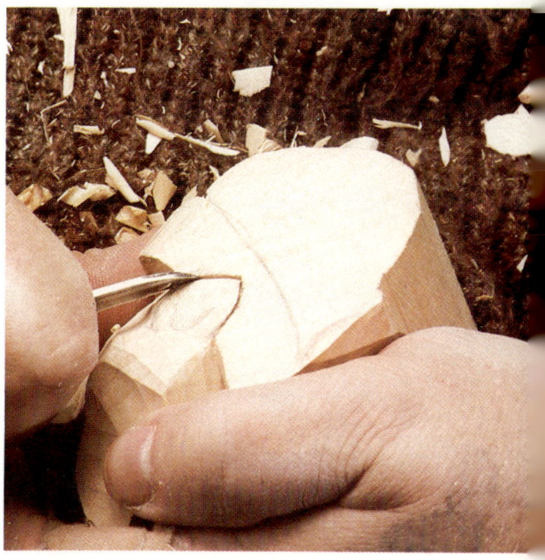

Cut a stop all the way around the ear.

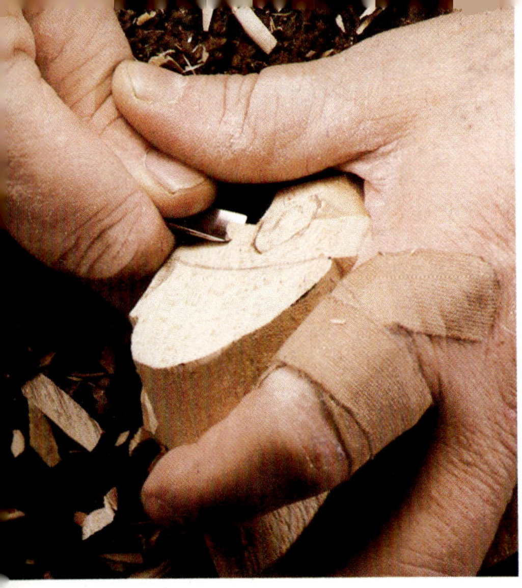

Take the excess off with a flat gouge. The thumb on the blade gives it the movement. The other thumb acts as a stop to keep you from going too far.

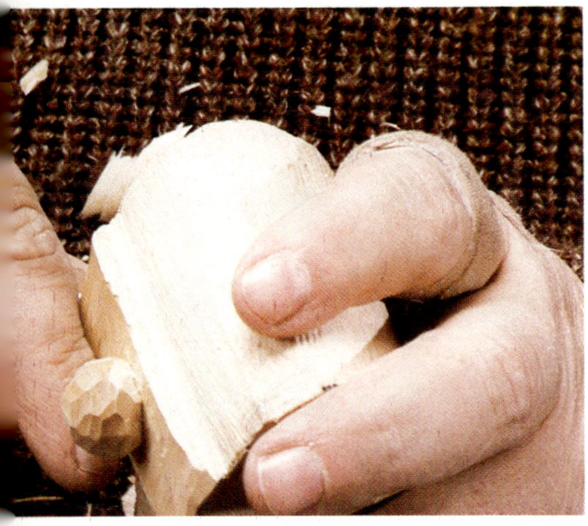

The forefinger of the hand holding the tool is firmly against the carving, giving you another safety stop.

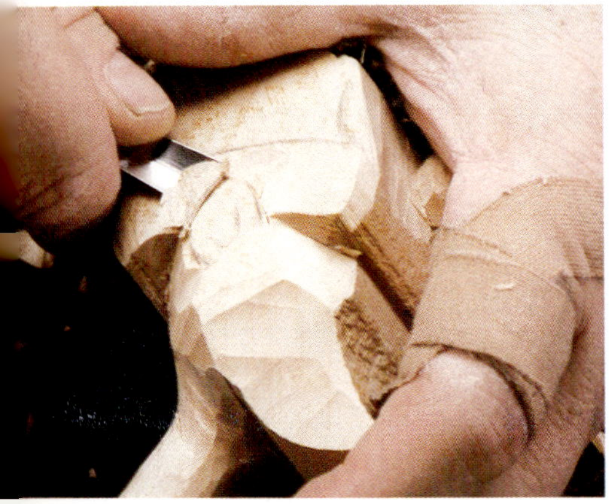

With your fingers in the proper position, carve back toward the ear. You may need to recut your stops as you go.

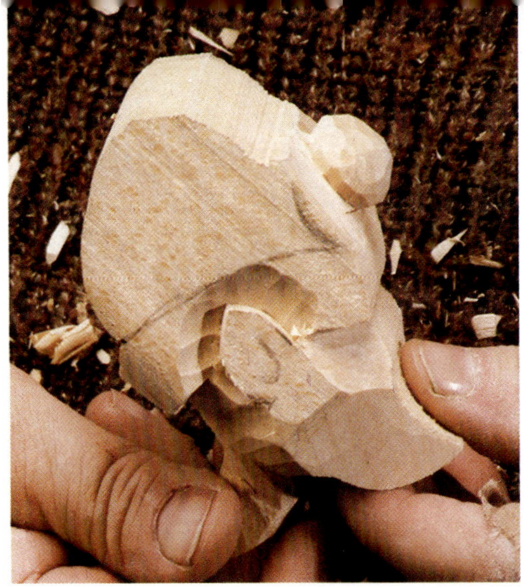

This is the result.

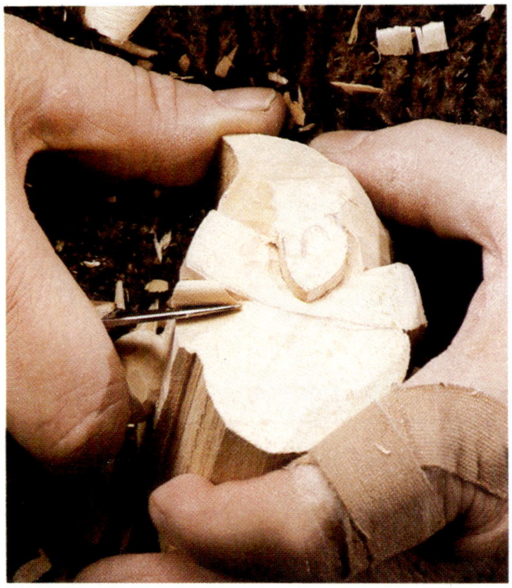

Starting at a corner, define the top of the fur trim. Cut a stop, then trim back to it. Repeat on each corner.

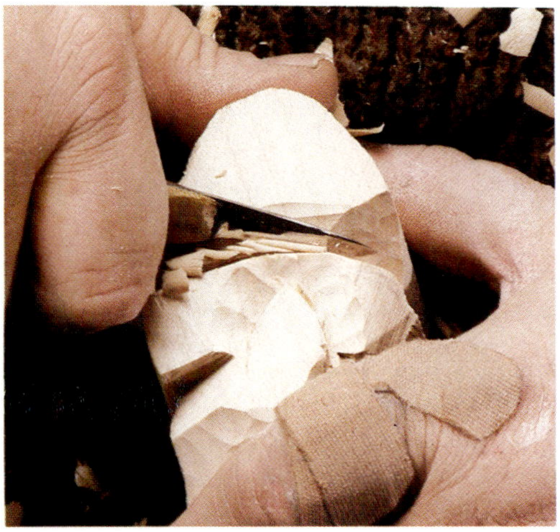

Continue removing wood from around the top of the fur trim.

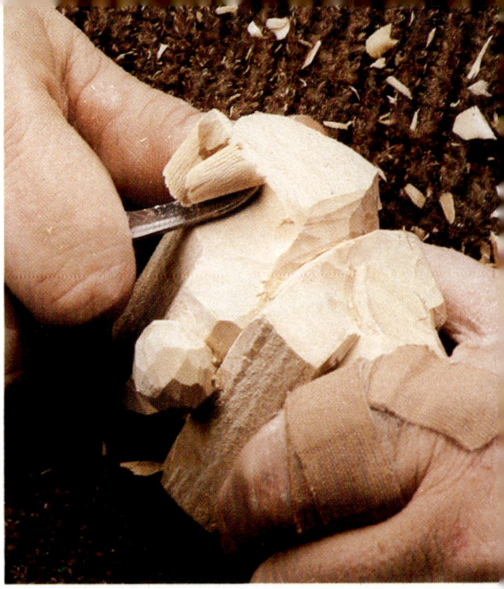

Knock the corners off the cap.

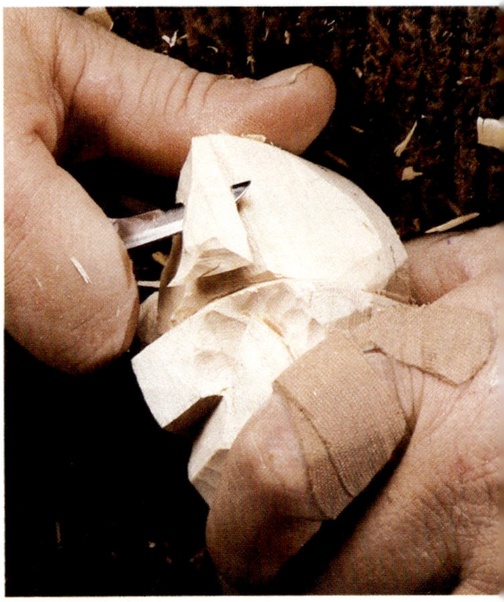

Round the sides of the cap.

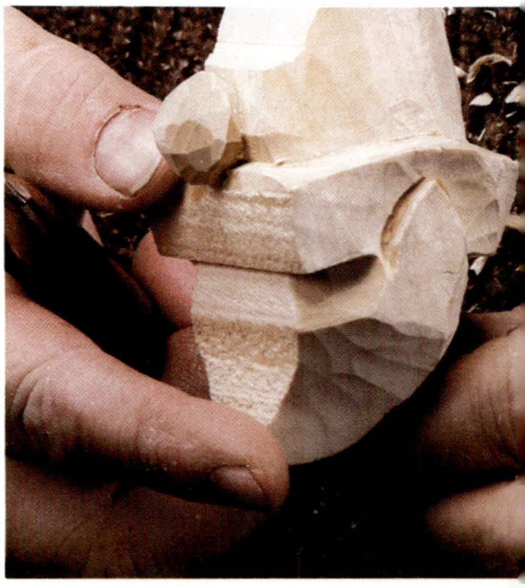

Trim the cap down until it looks like it will realistically fit on the head, not too small, not too large.

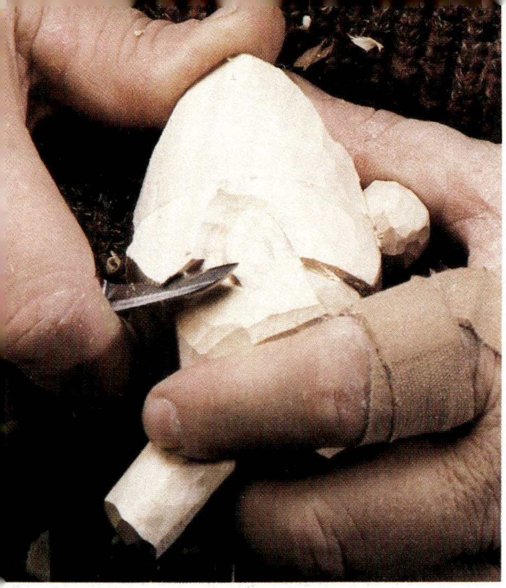

When the cap is fitted, I can carve the fur trim to the correct size. I begin by knocking off the corners.

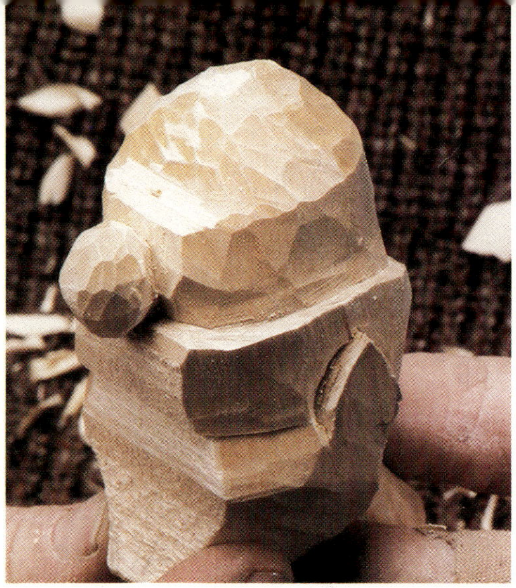

The rounded cap.

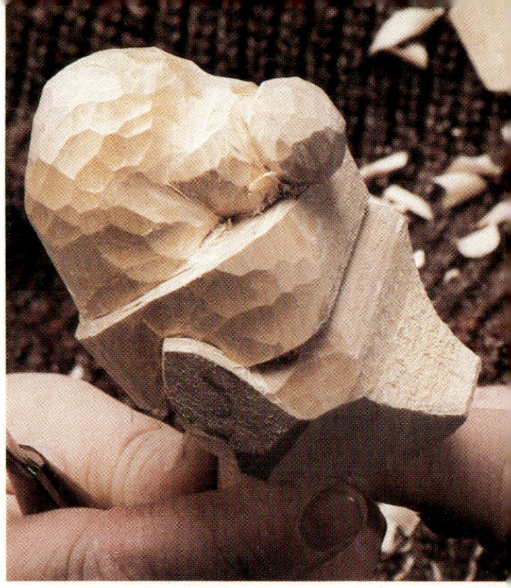

The shaped cap.

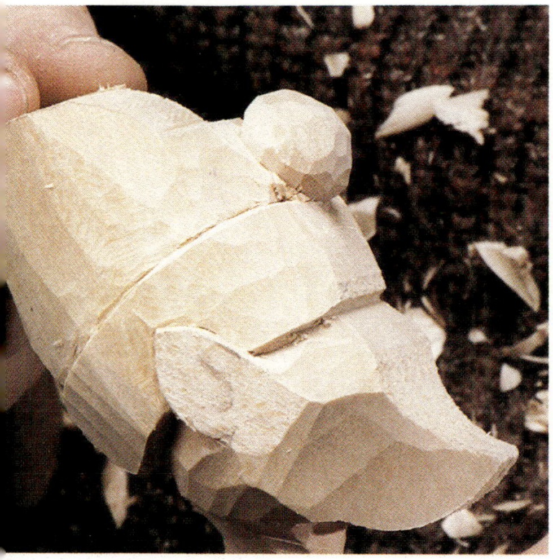

Continue to shape the sides, front and back, working your way around the ears.

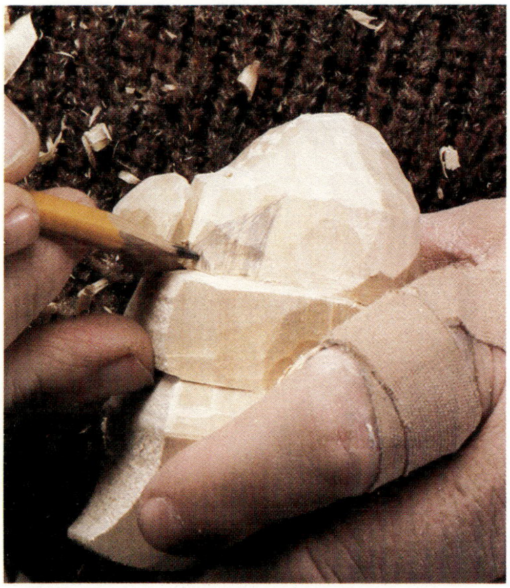

The cap will be folded over to the front, so, on each side, mark the folds and the area to be removed.

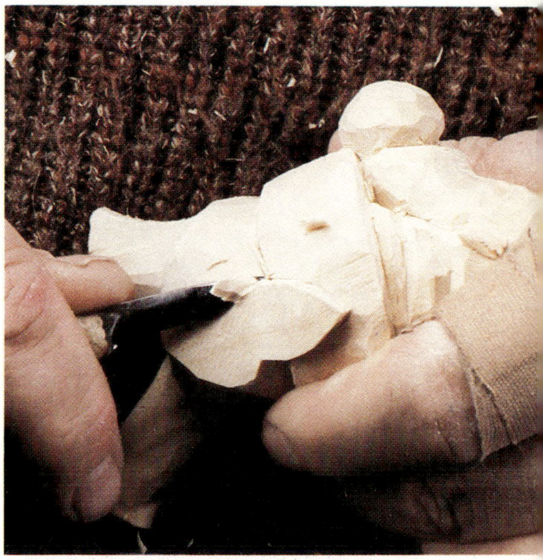

Go back over the figure and make refinements and corrections. I see that the area in front of the ear needs to be a little deeper to look like it goes under the hat.

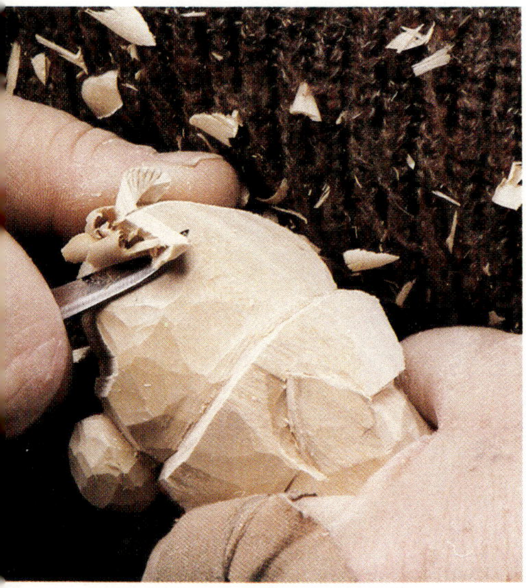

Round the cap over.

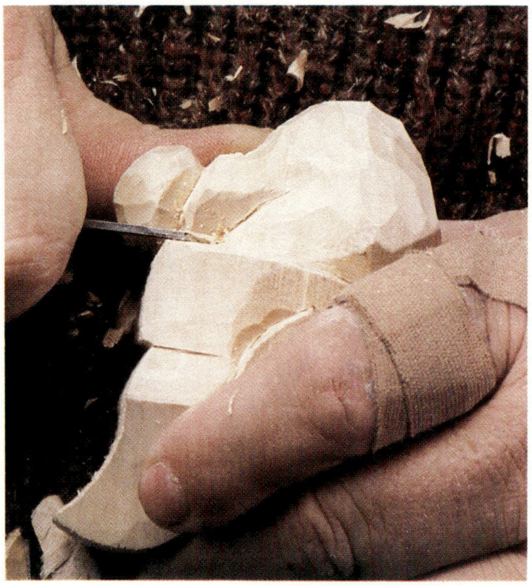

With a knife, shape the foldover.

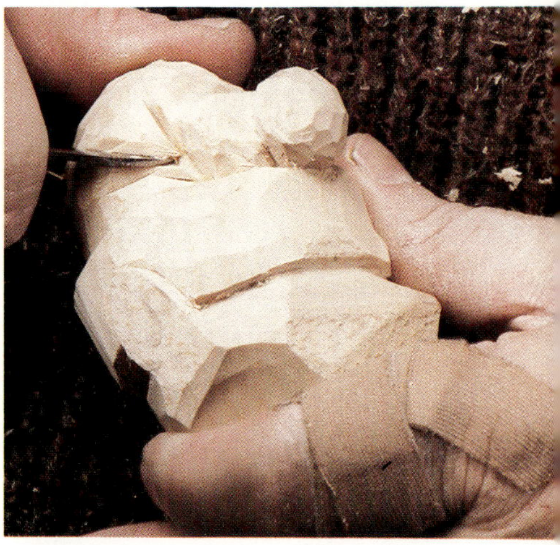

Make grooves in the sides of the cap. This is done simply by cutting one way and the other along a line.

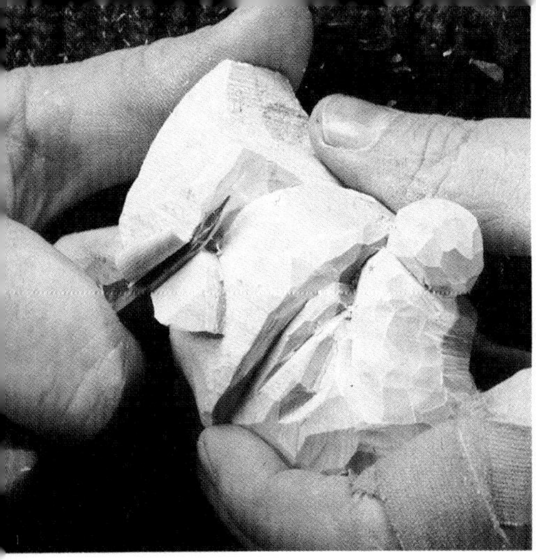

Starting at the top of the ear, narrow the jaw. This will make the ear seem to protrude.

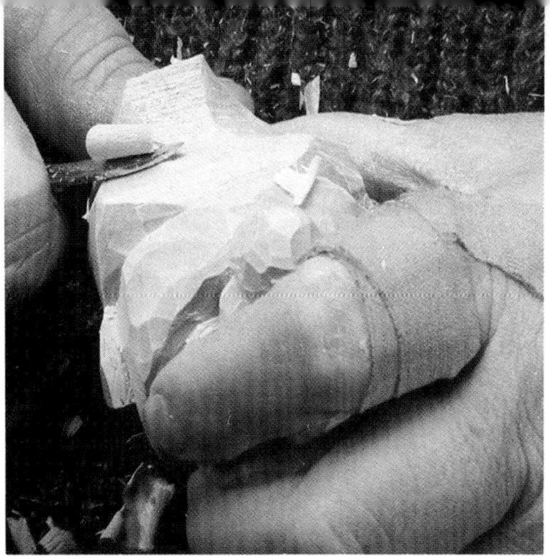

and form the eye socket at the same time.

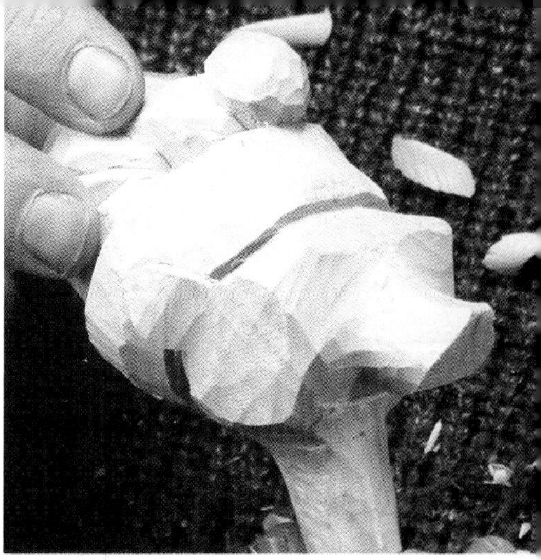

The head so far.

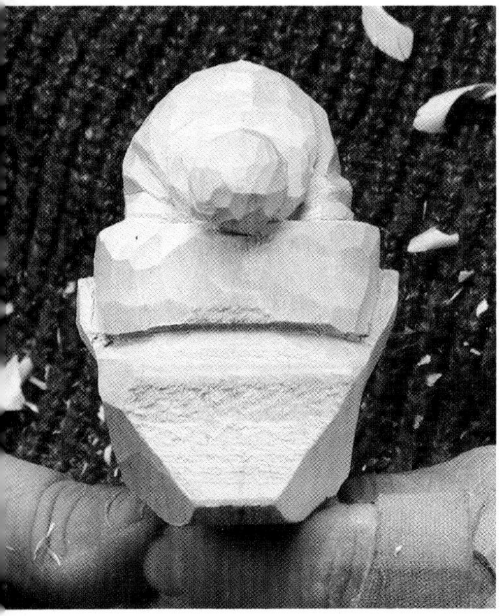

The tapered jaw gives the look of the raccoon.

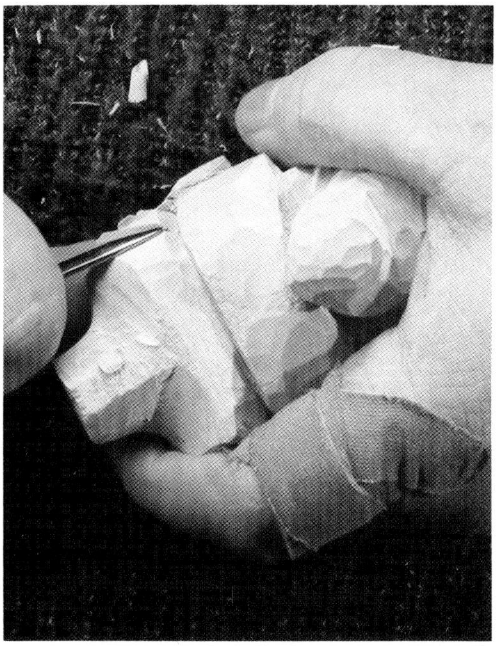

Go all around the muzzle.

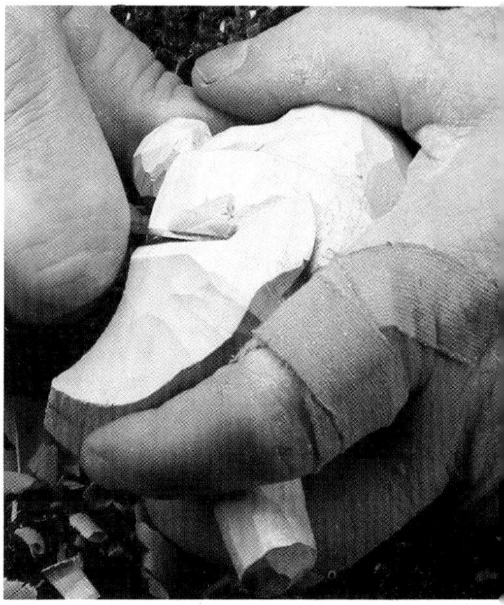

Round out the eyebrows and continue back to the front of the ears.

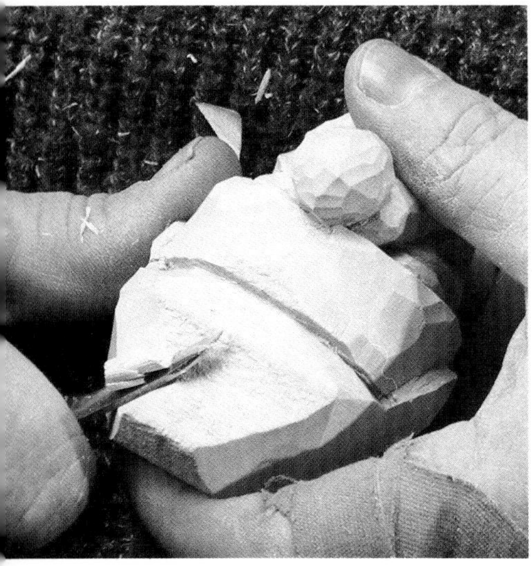

Carve the top edges of the muzzle, to shape it...

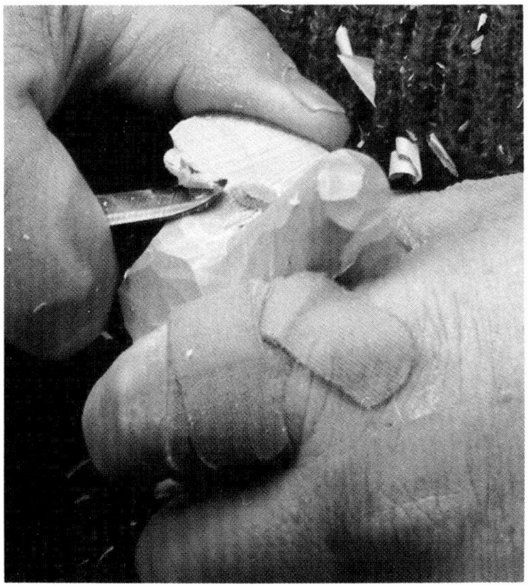

Continue under the muzzle.

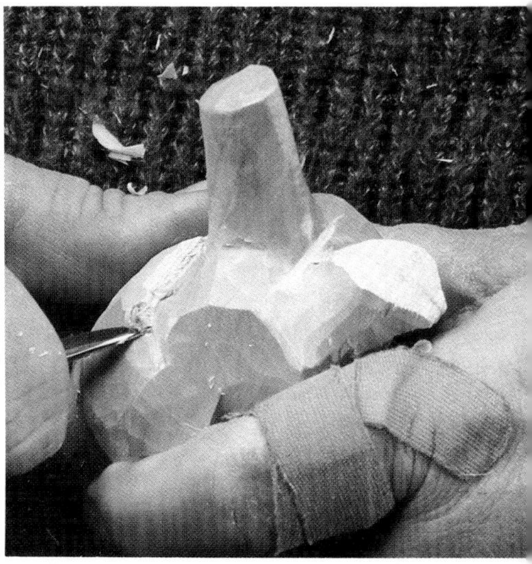

Round off the bottom edge of the fur trim on the cap.

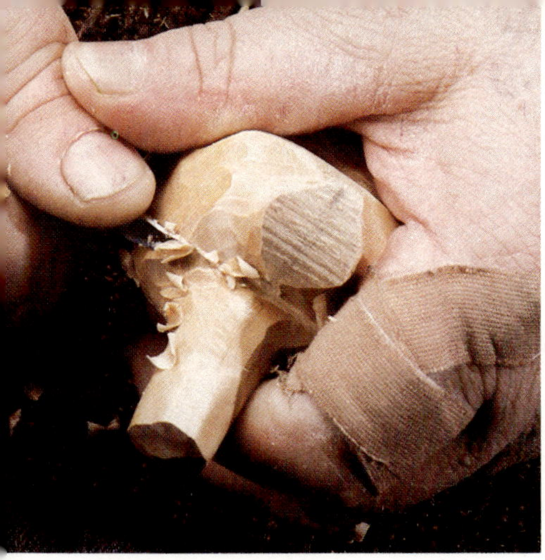

Round the cheeks.

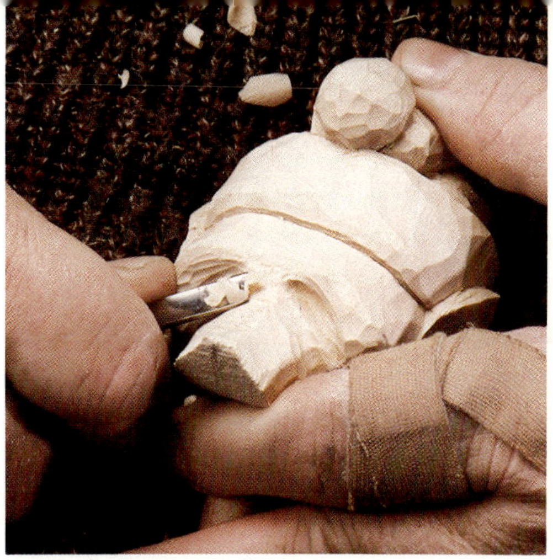

Use a flatter gouge to clean up the eyesockets.

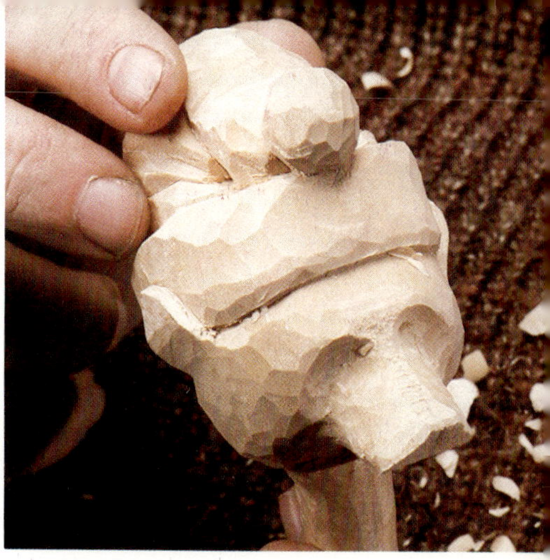

This makes it look more like a 'coon and less like a bear.

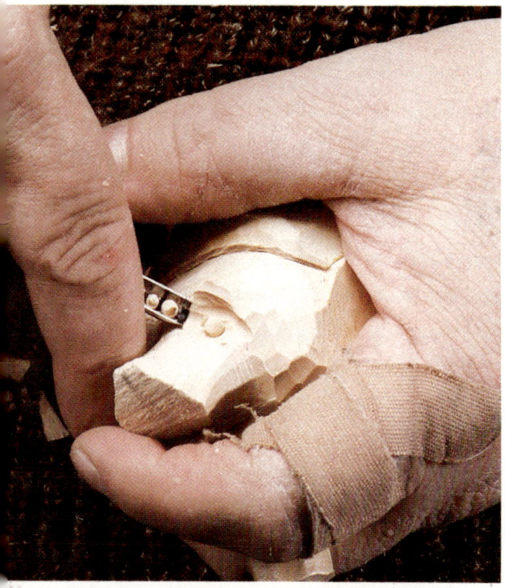

To create the cup for the eye sockets use palm gouges. Start with a half round #9 gouge. Start at the bridge of the nose and carve toward the outside.

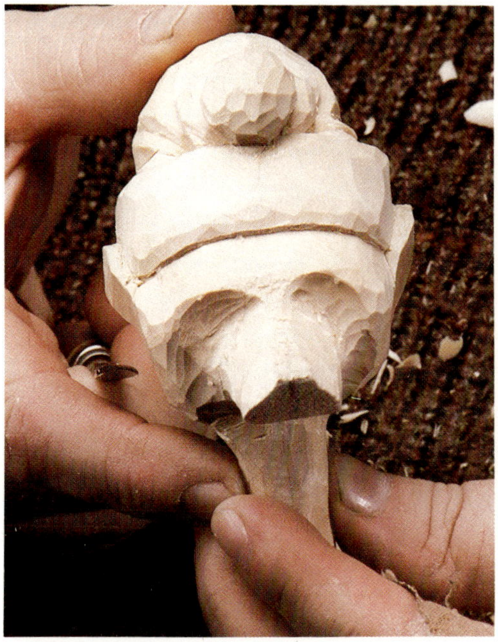

The eyesockets and the face so far.

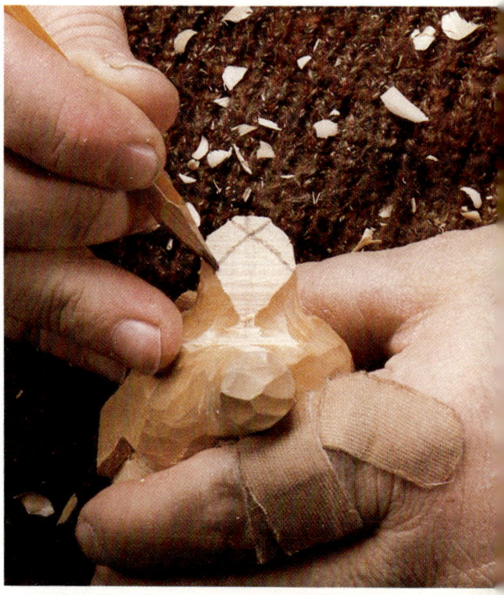

Mark an X on the front of the muzzle to form the nose and the mouth.

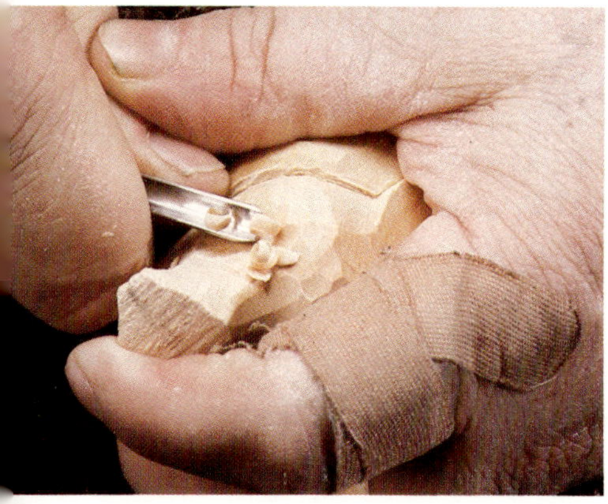

The cup should follow the contour of the muzzle, going down and out from the bridge. The raccoon's eyes seem to look better if they come down on the sides. Repeat on the other side.

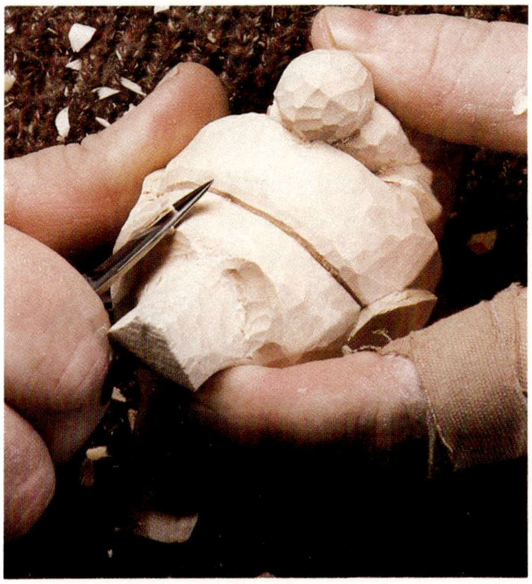

Round off the heavy eyebrow.

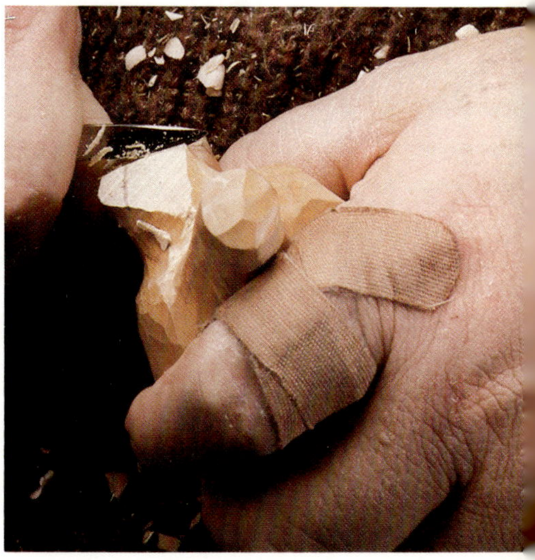

Make a groove along the lines using a knife...

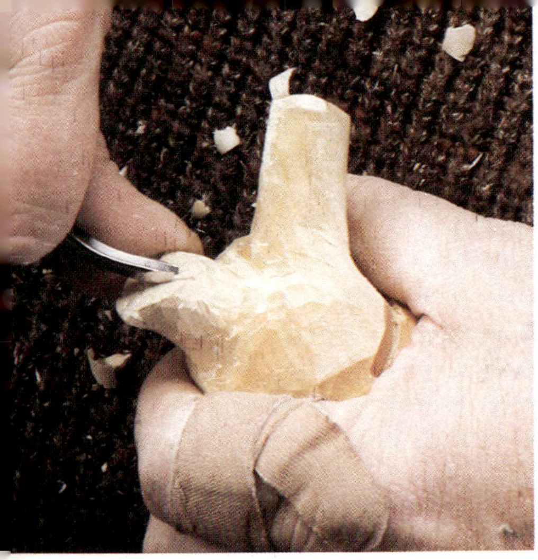

or a veiner. One tool works about as well as the other in this situation.

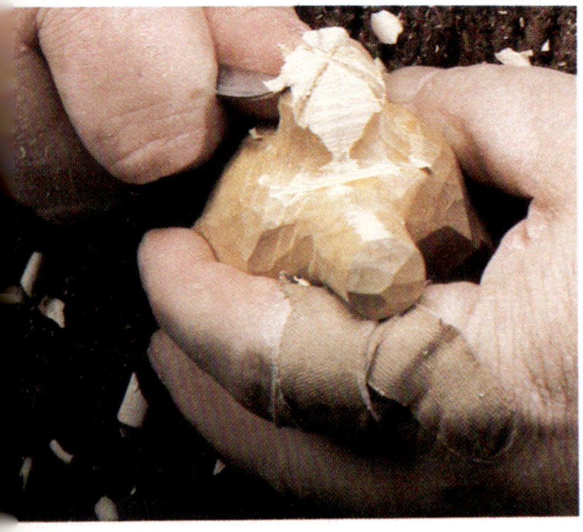

Round the muzzle...

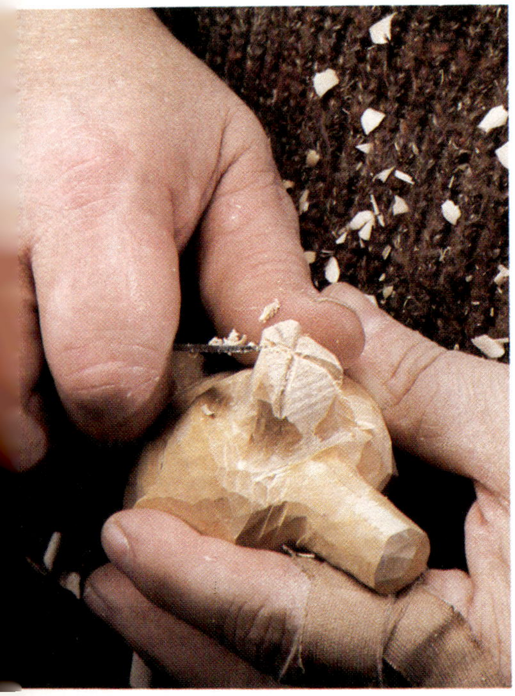

and bring the notch around the side of the nose to bring it out.

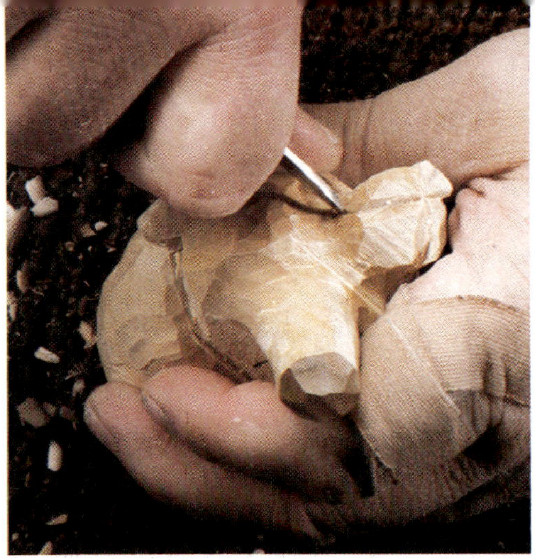

With the knife, bring the mouth around the side....

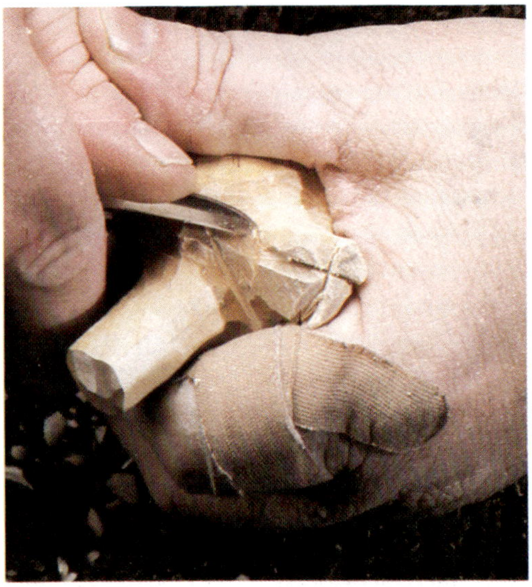

and end it with a little snarling grin.

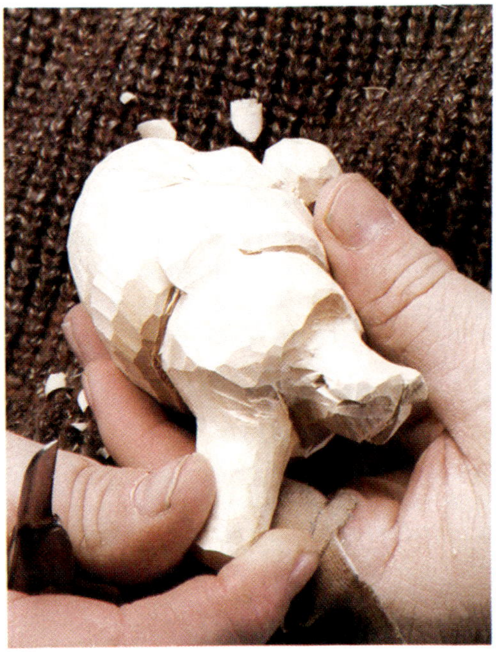

The result.

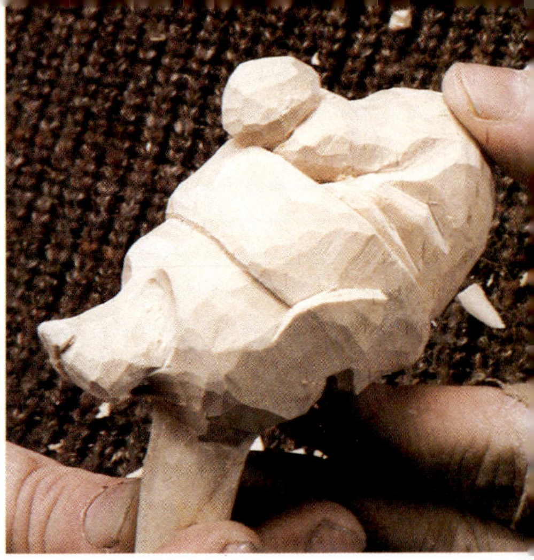

The head so far.

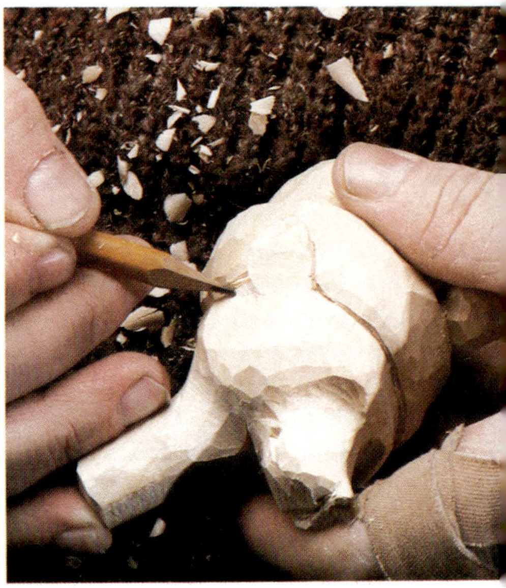

Start the ears by checking the general shape. I need to remove this little bit to make them ride better on the head.

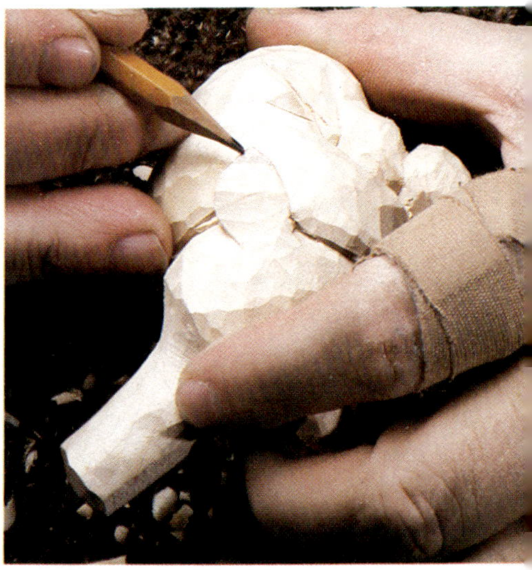

The ears are also too fox-like and need to be more rounded at the tips.

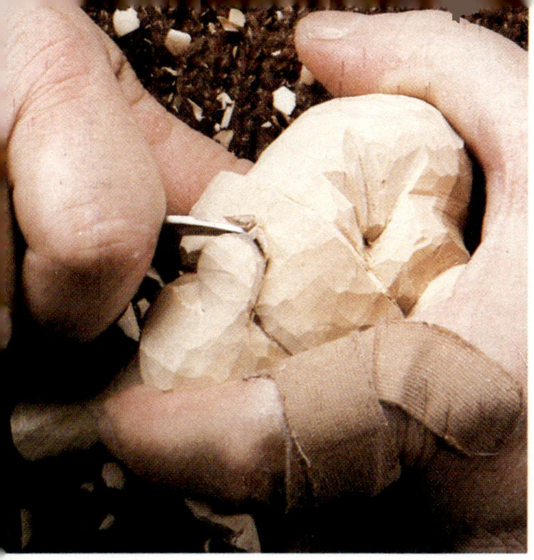

After marking it, simply nip it off with the knife.

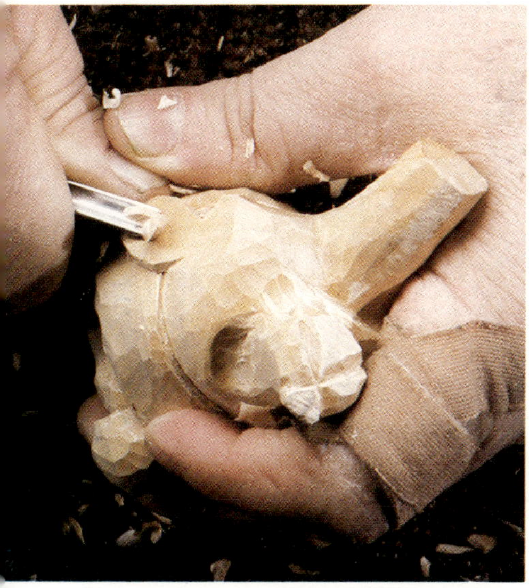

Use the #9 gouge to hollow out the inside of the ear. Start at the tip and cut toward the bottom so you cut with the grain.

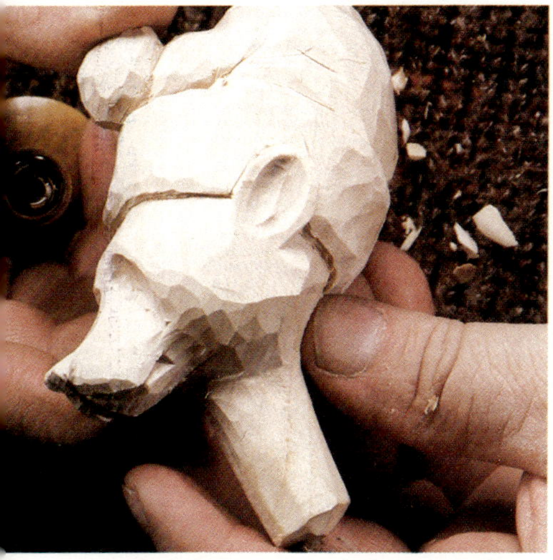

The finished ear. The ridge in the middle adds realism and is easily created between the two gouge cuts.

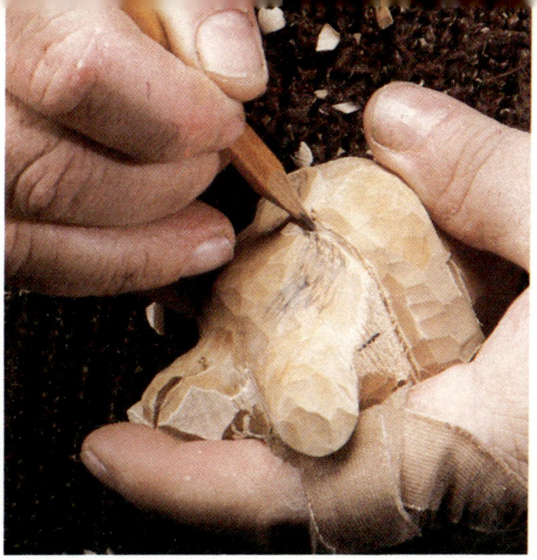

We need to create a little bit of cheek whiskers. We do it by carving away this area and blending it into the neck.

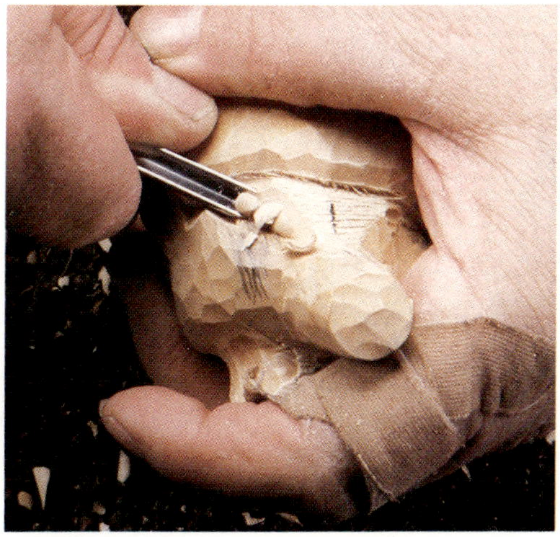

Go behind the cheek with a gouge, rounding the back of the head as you go. When using a chisel like this, there is always the risk of it slipping and going into your hand. I would suggest that you use a protective glove.

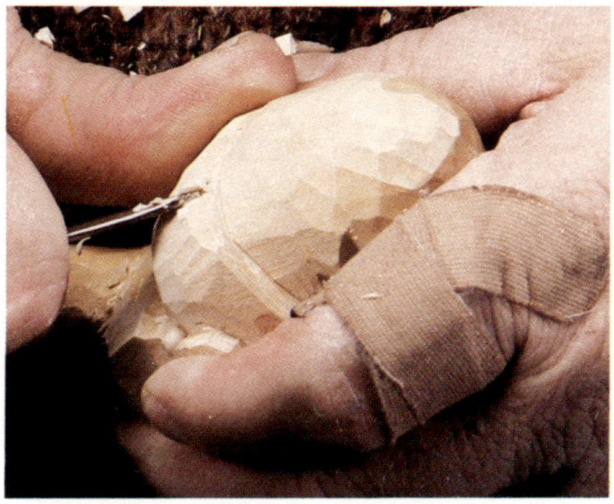

Go over the piece refining the problems you see. I need to round the top edge of the fur trim on the cap.

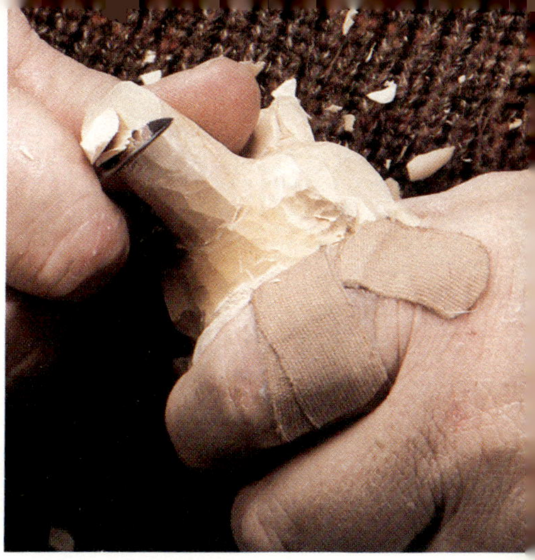

Fit the head into the body, shortening and trimming the neck as necessary.

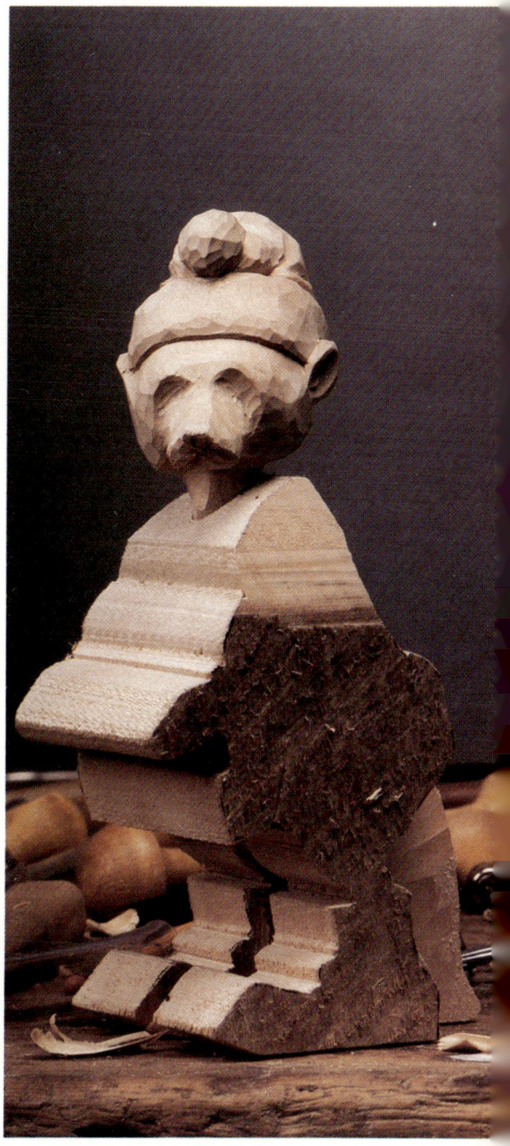

This seems pretty good.

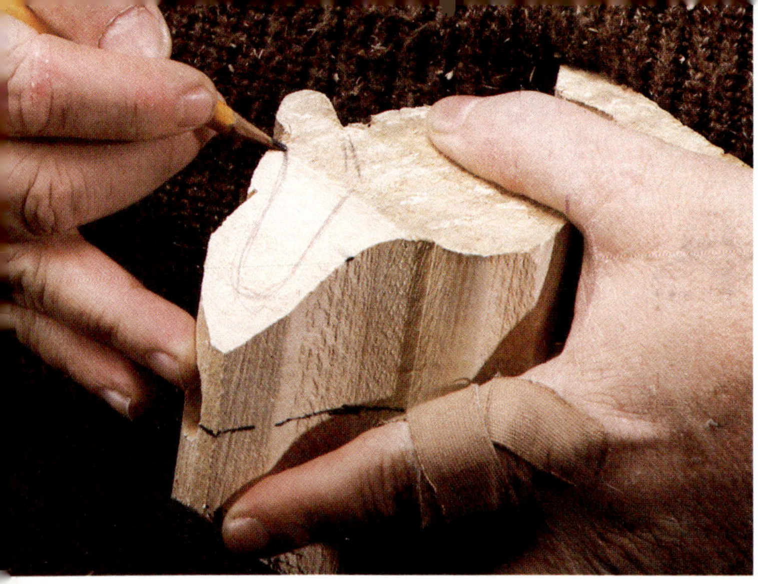

Moving to the body, draw in the arms...

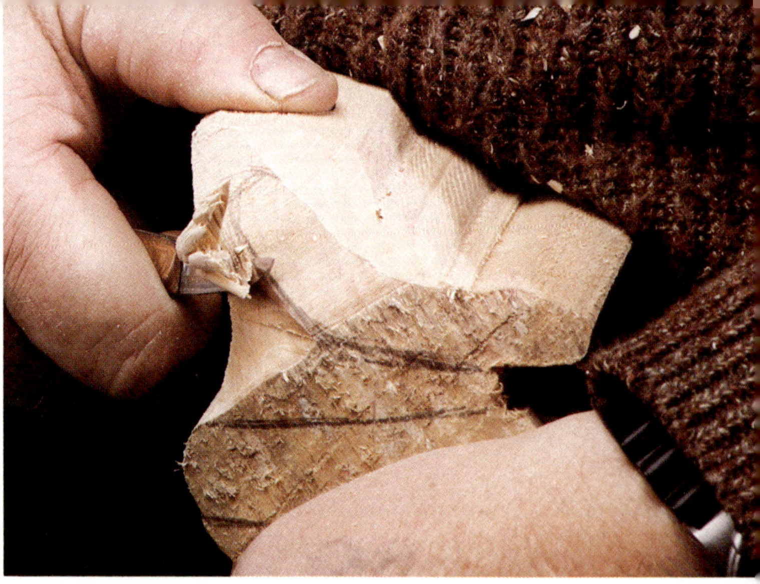

Do the same thing on the back behind the arms.

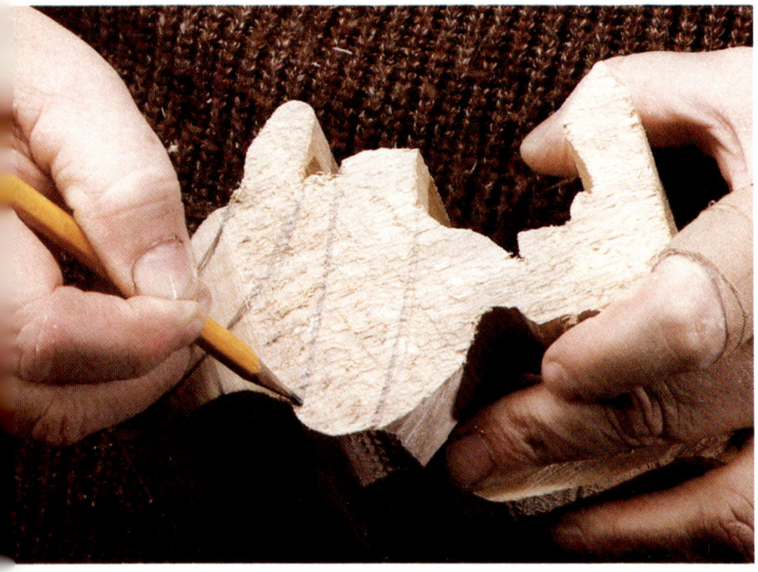

and the lines of the fur trim.

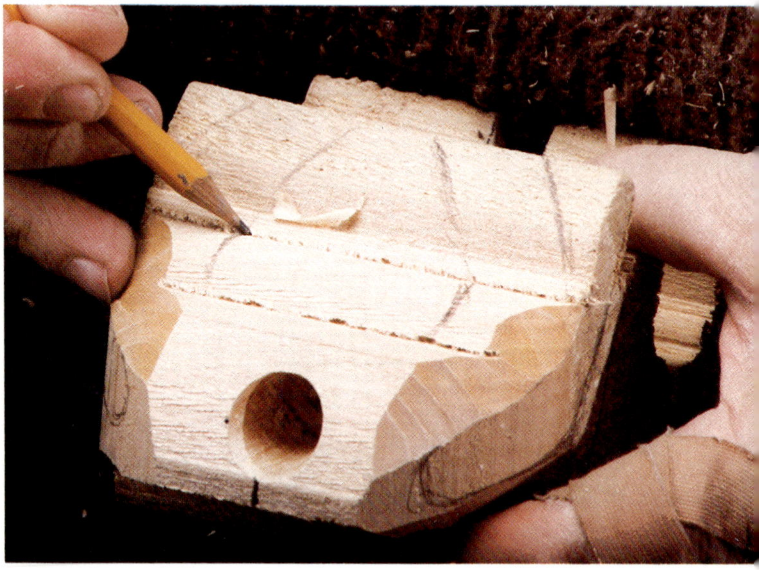

Draw in the top view of the arms...

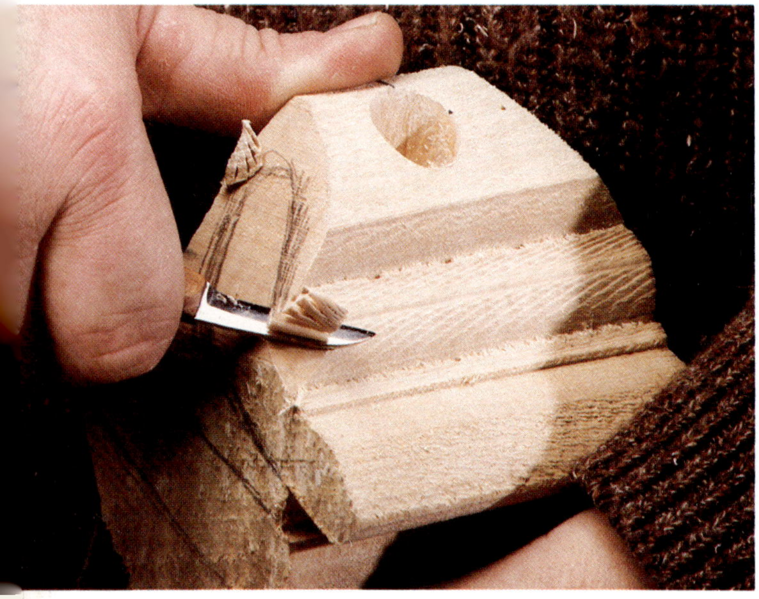

Knock off the front edges down to the line of the arms.

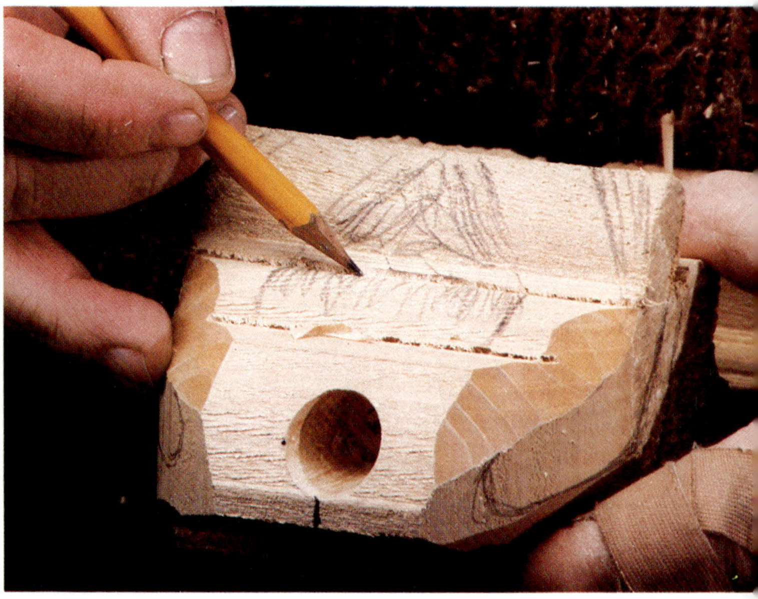

and mark the area to be removed.

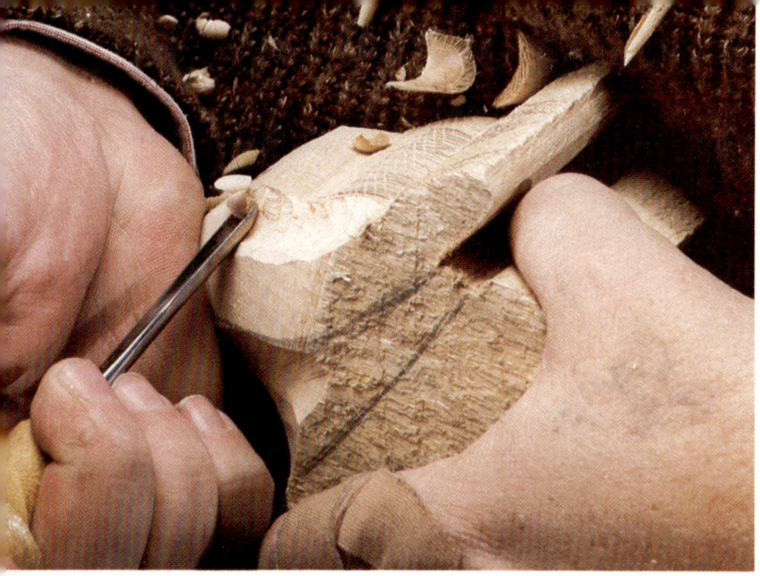

With a controlled, rolling wrist action, remove the wood in the front of the arms. For speed, I use my left hand to hold the piece. Over the years of making my living carving, speed has been very important. But everything I do with my left hand can be done with a vise, and done more safely.

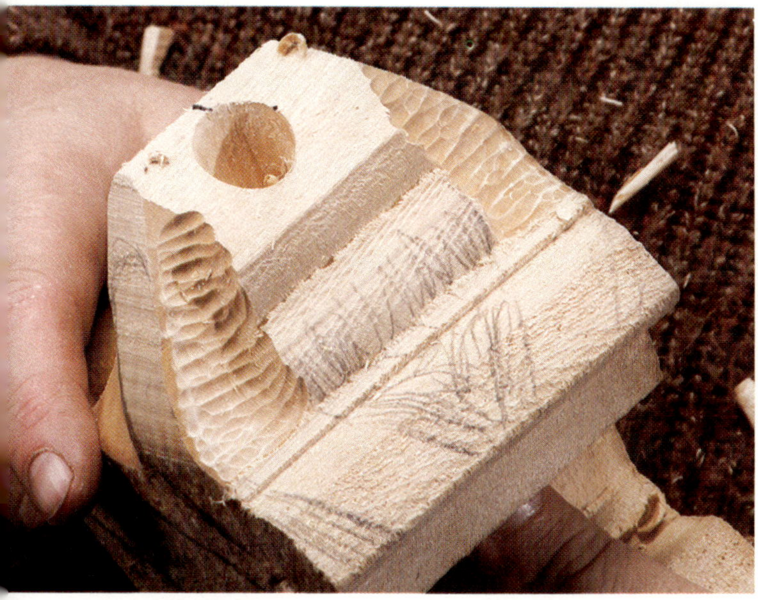

The front of the arms cleaned to the chest.

The same thing is done under the arms, but a little differently.

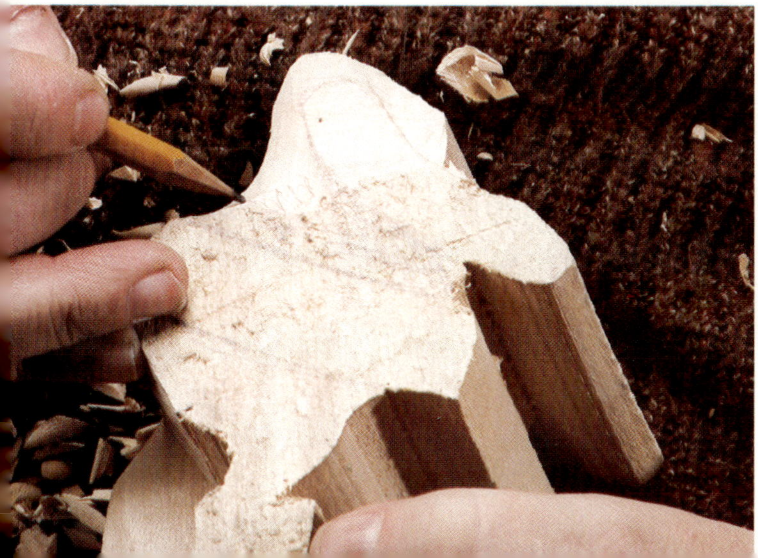

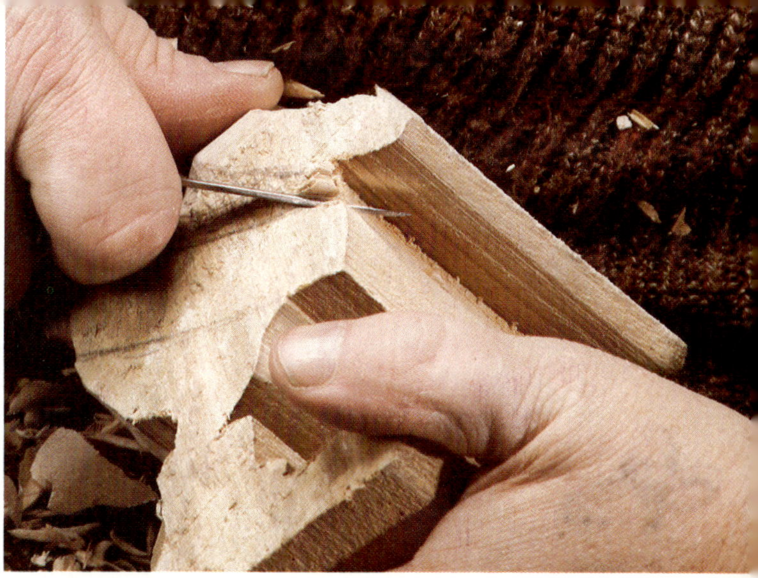

Using a knife, remove the area between the arm and the fur trim. As always, start on the corners.

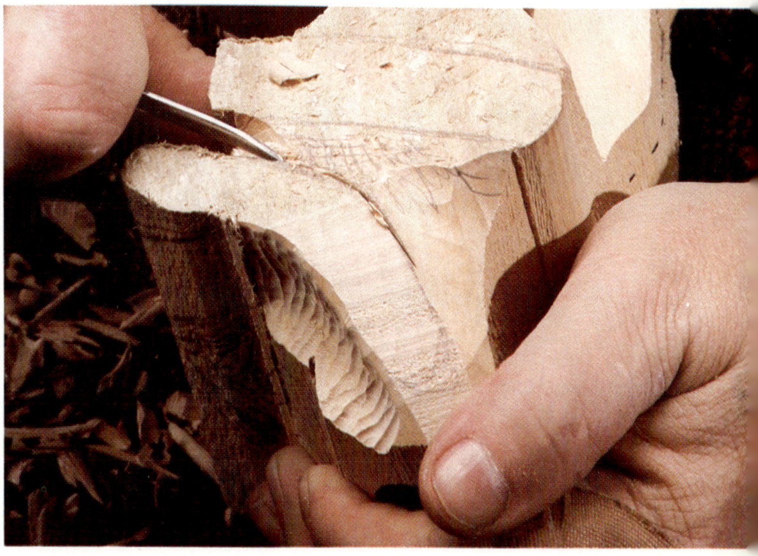

Bring a stop on the bottom arm line and the top line of the fur trim.

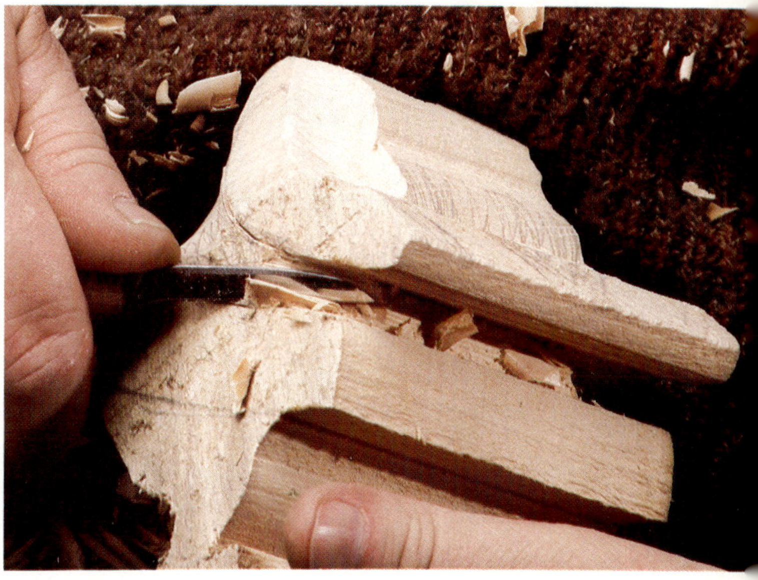

Work your way around the side...

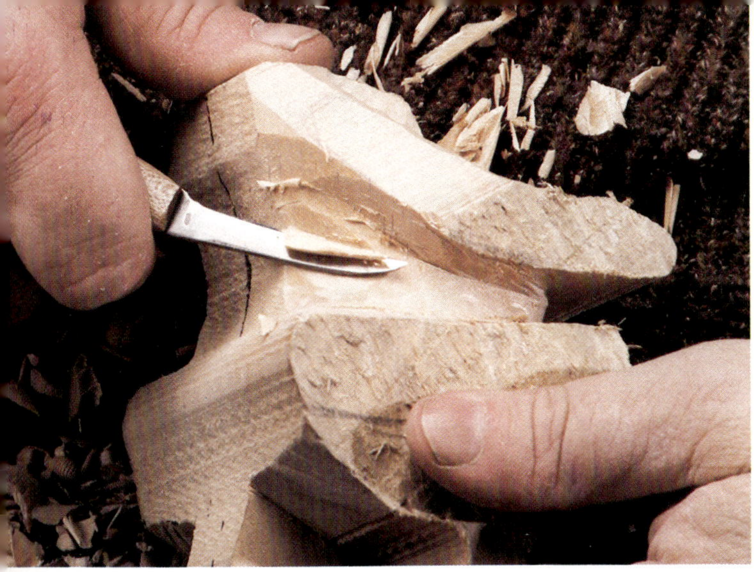

and the back.

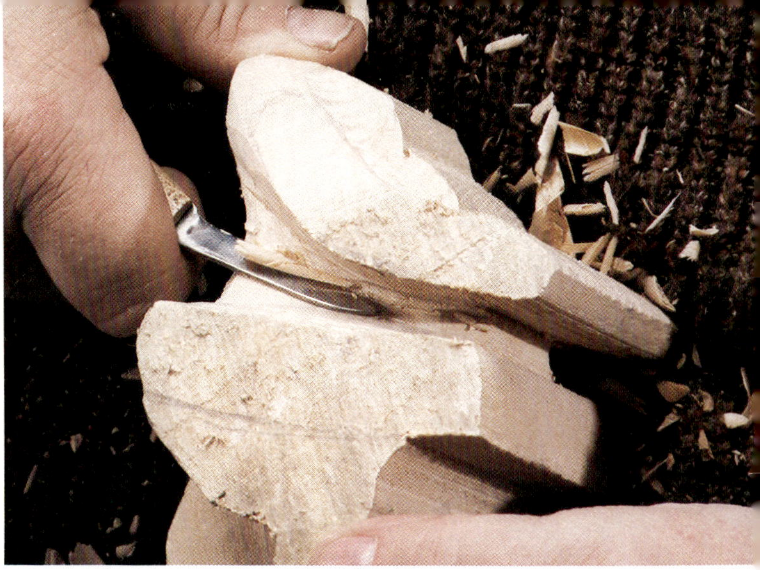

Use a long thin knife to give him a diet.

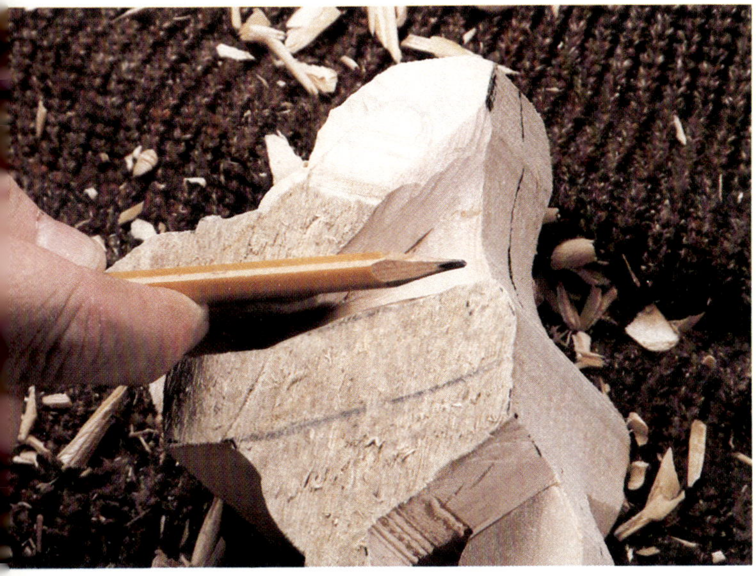

The midriff of our Santimal is not quite round. Using a pencil as a depth gauge, measure one way...

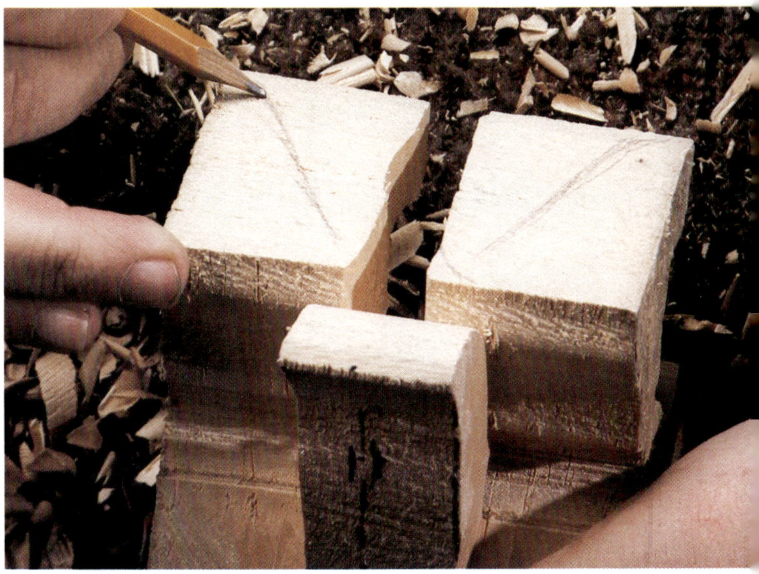

Mark the orientation of the feet on the sole.

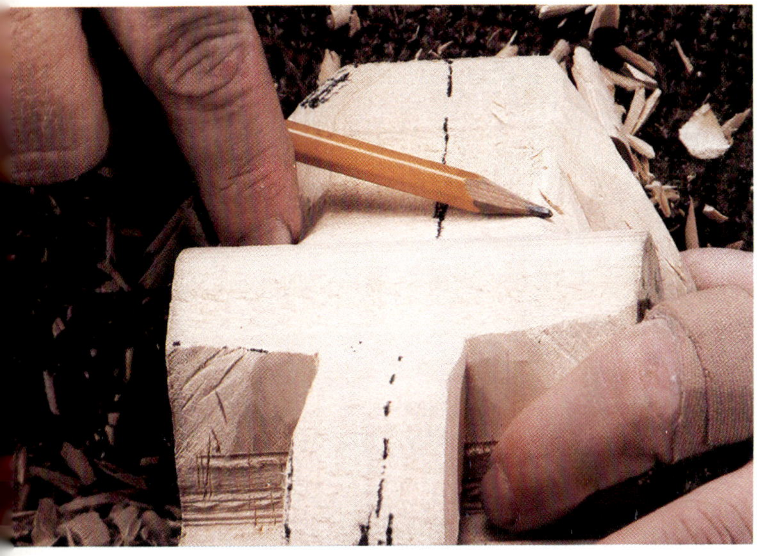

then the other. We need to make him about ¼" narrower from side to side.

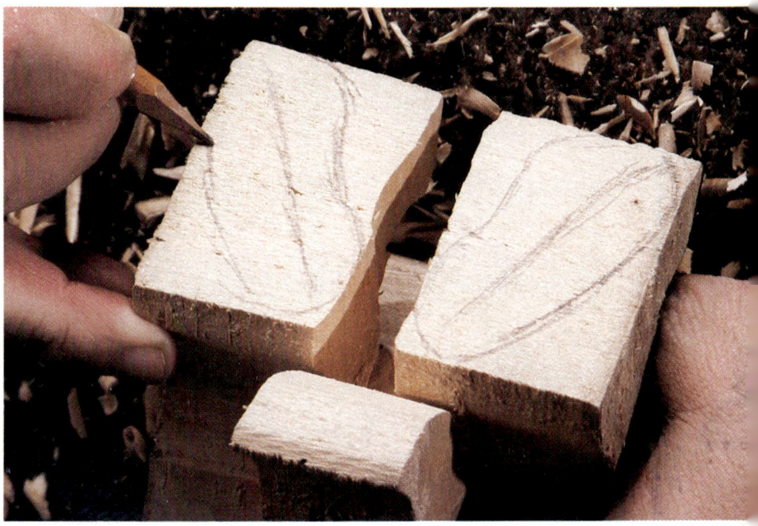

Draw the outline of the feet. With a character carving you never put the feet straight. Either make them point dramatically out or pigeon-toed to increase the comicality of the carving.

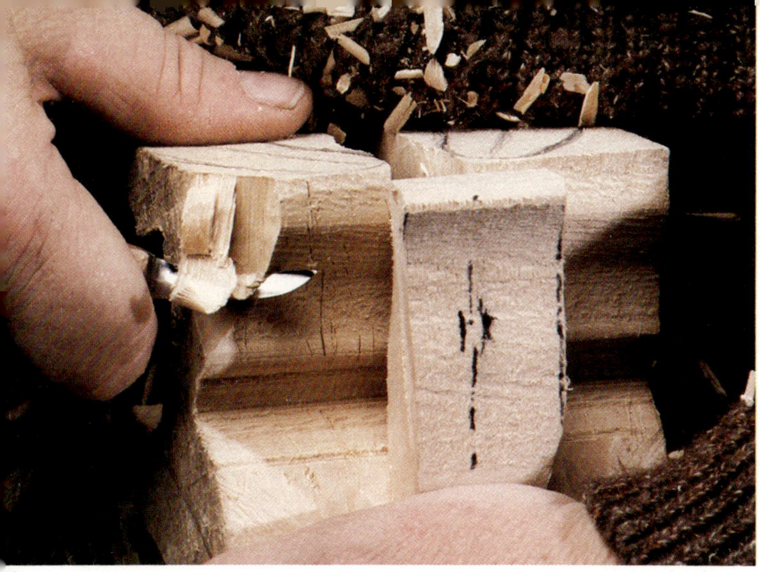

Starting on the corner pop off the excess wood around the feet.

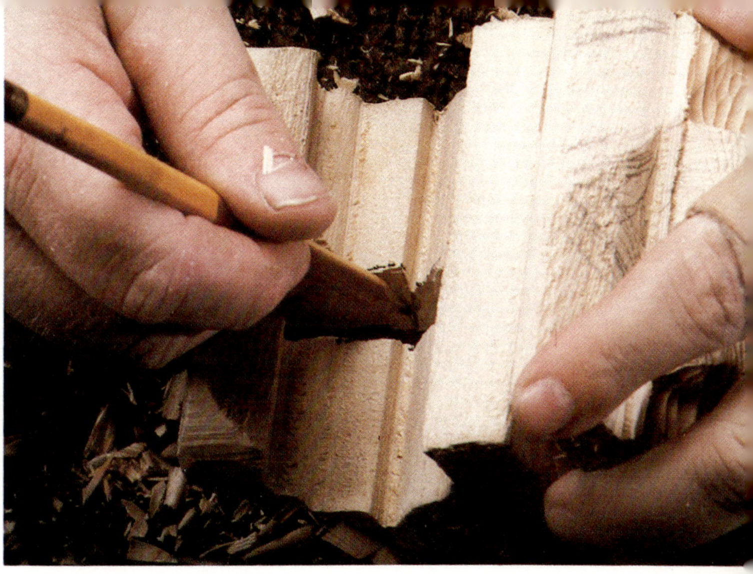

and inside.

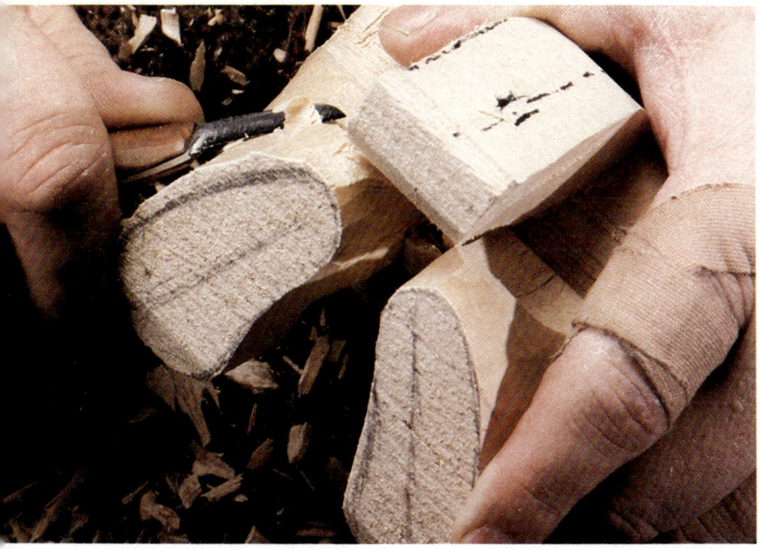

Continue trimming until the foot is shaped to the outline of the sole.

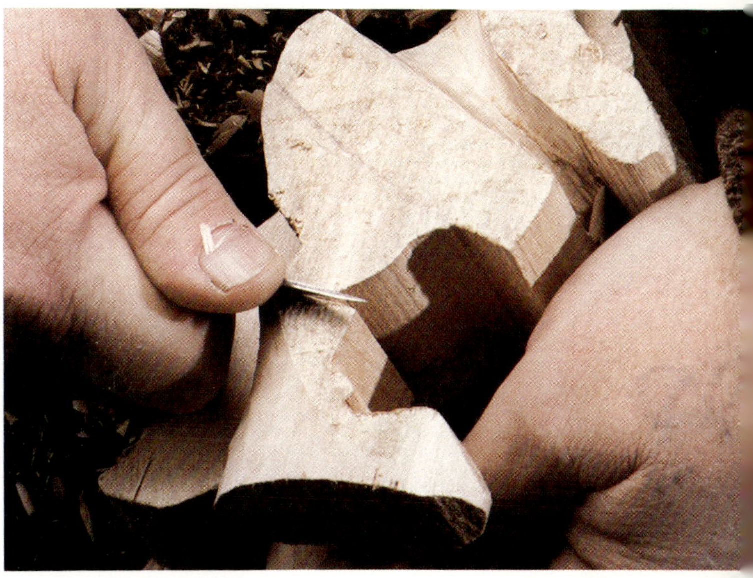

Cut a stop along the line...

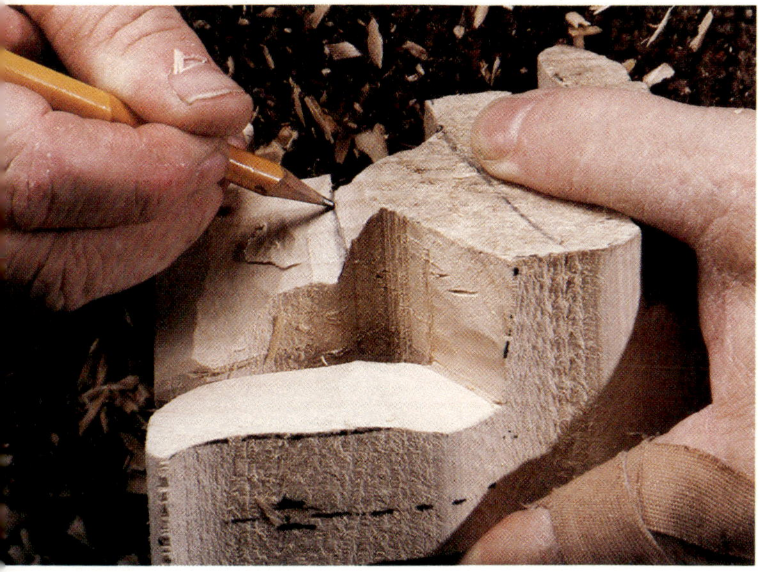

Draw in the top of the boot line, both outside...

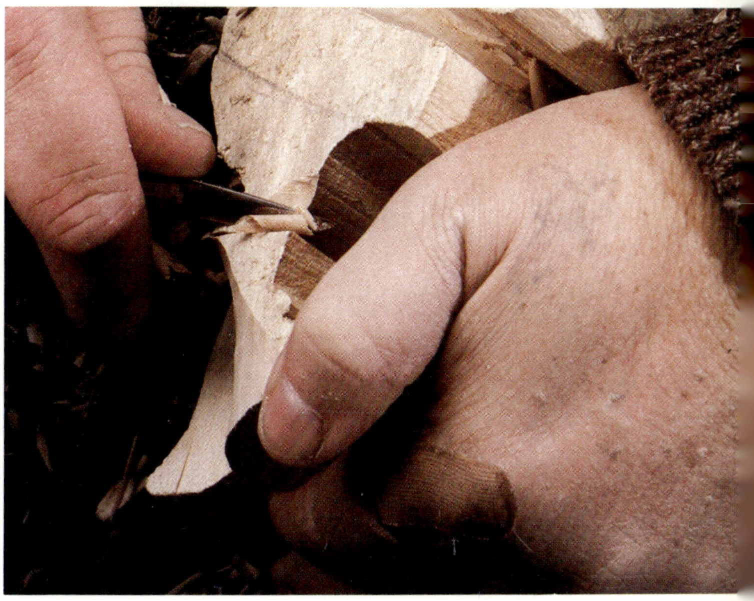

and trim down to it from leg. Go all the way around.

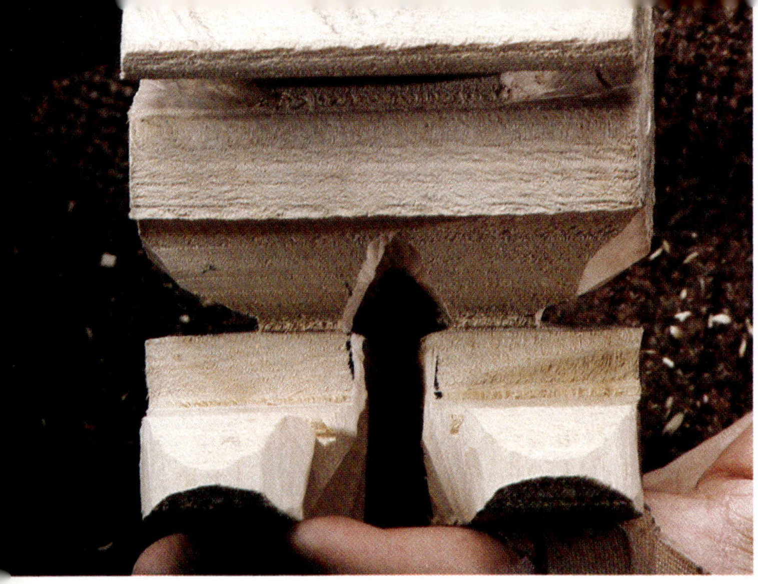

Continue until the leg is the size you want it. You can then bring the boot down to size. I usually do these extreme parts first because if you just start working down, the tendency is to get a flat looking piece.

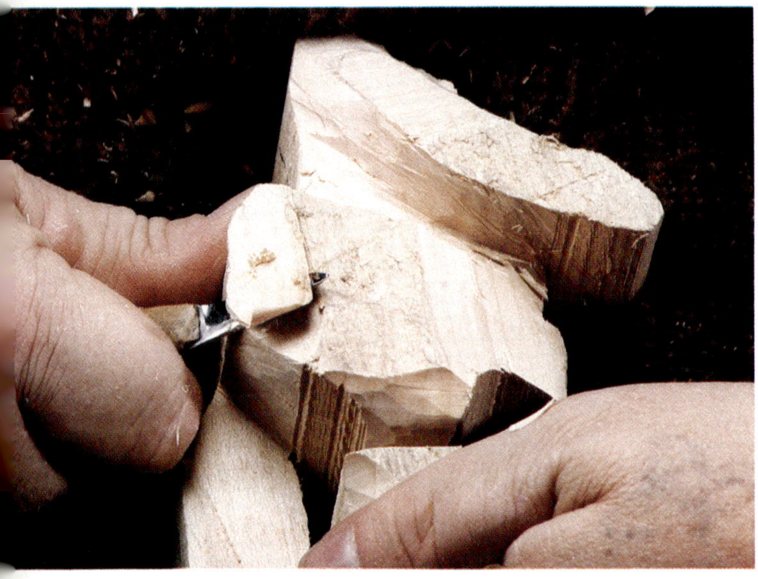

Pop off all the corners of the body, all the way around.

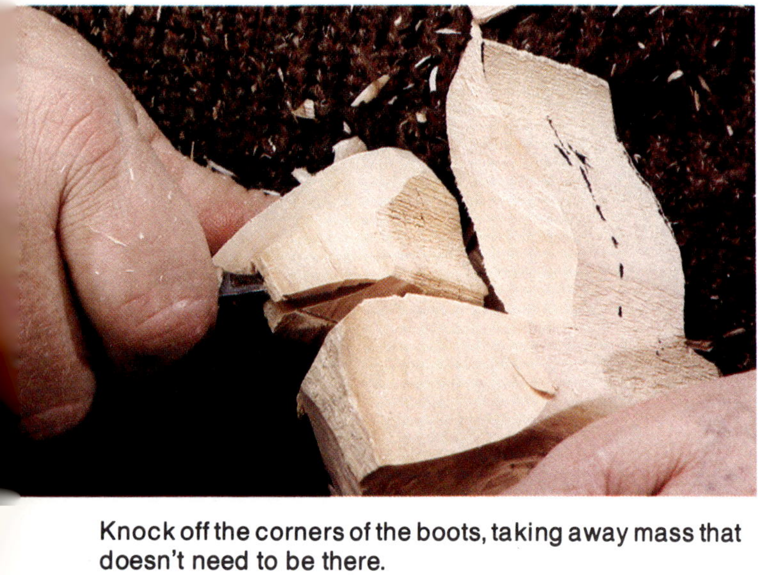

Knock off the corners of the boots, taking away mass that doesn't need to be there.

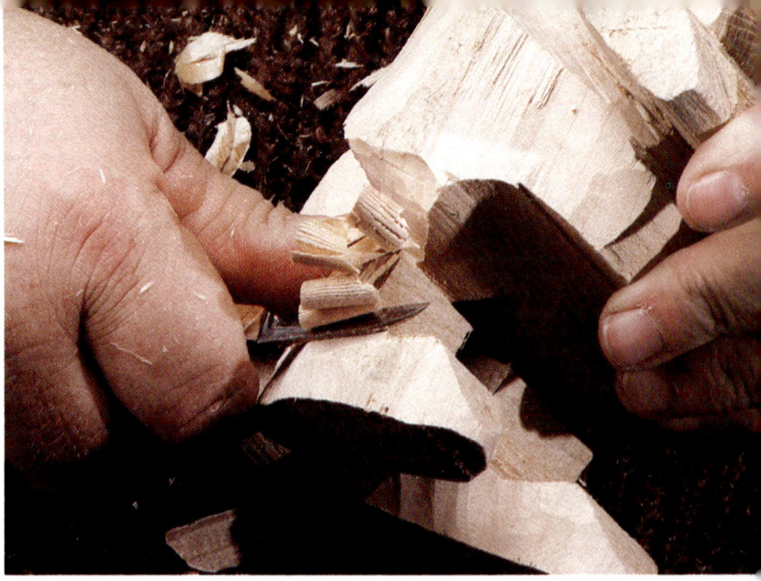

Concentrating on the boot, take away the front corner, bringing the side around the front.

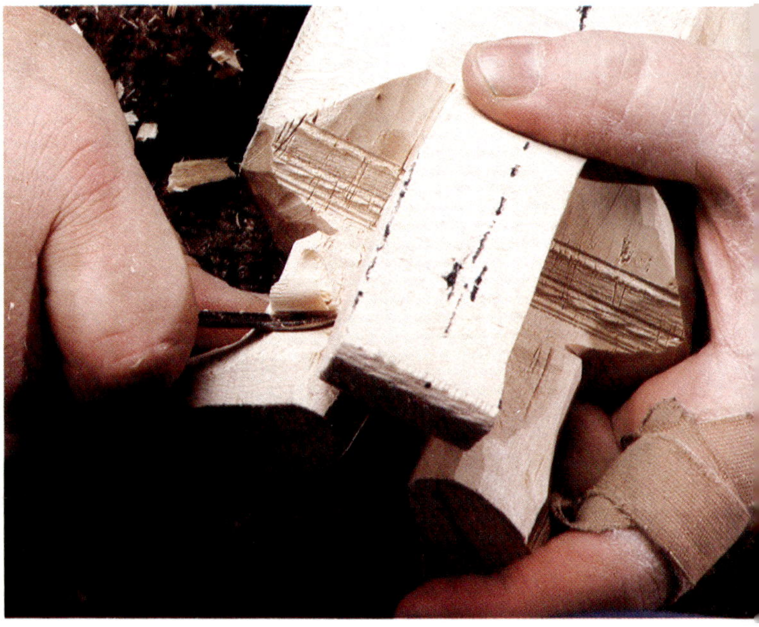

At the back of the heel I run into a problem with the tail being in the way.

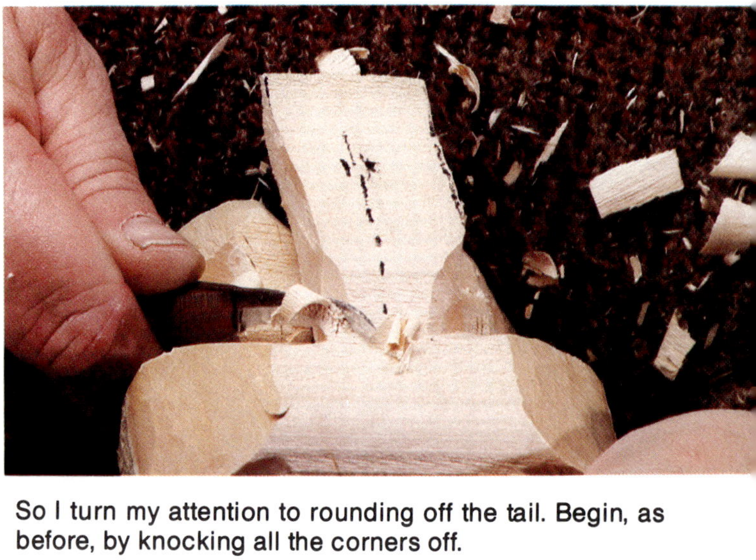

So I turn my attention to rounding off the tail. Begin, as before, by knocking all the corners off.

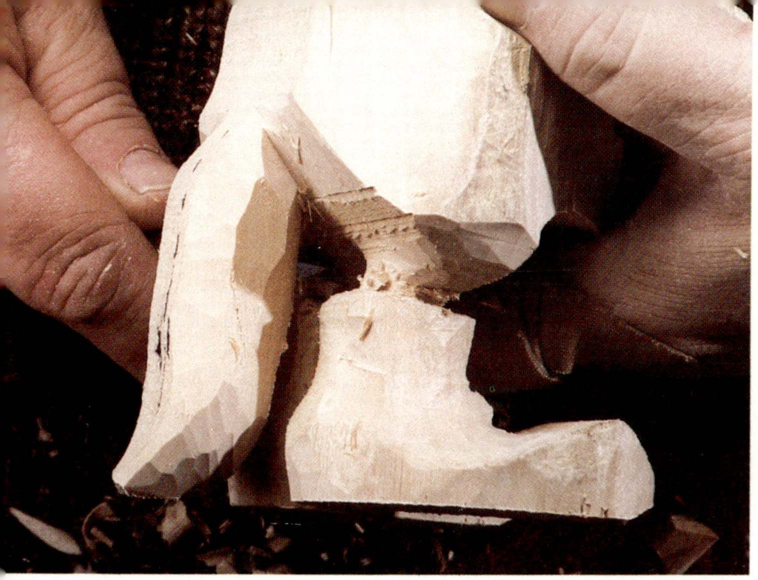

By roughly blocking out the tail, I can now get to the legs. That is kind of a rule of thumb. If you can't get to a place, wait awhile. As the carving continues, the access might get better.

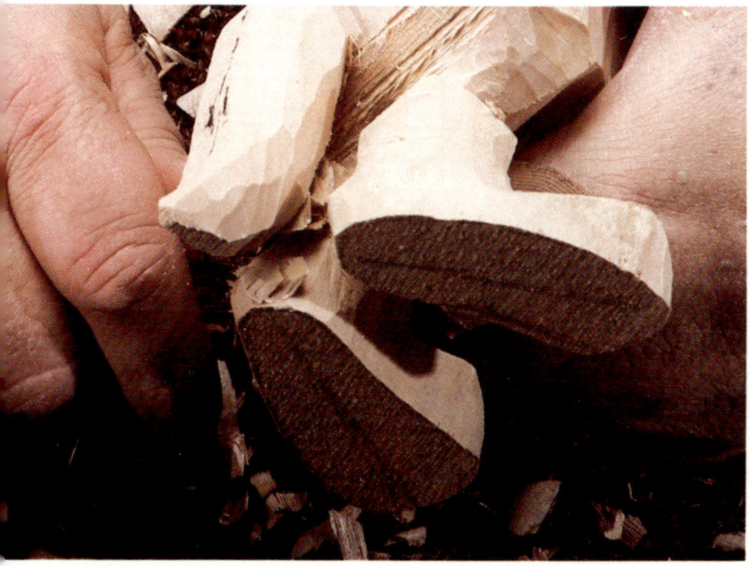

Now that I can reach it, I will round the boot some more.

The roughed out figure.

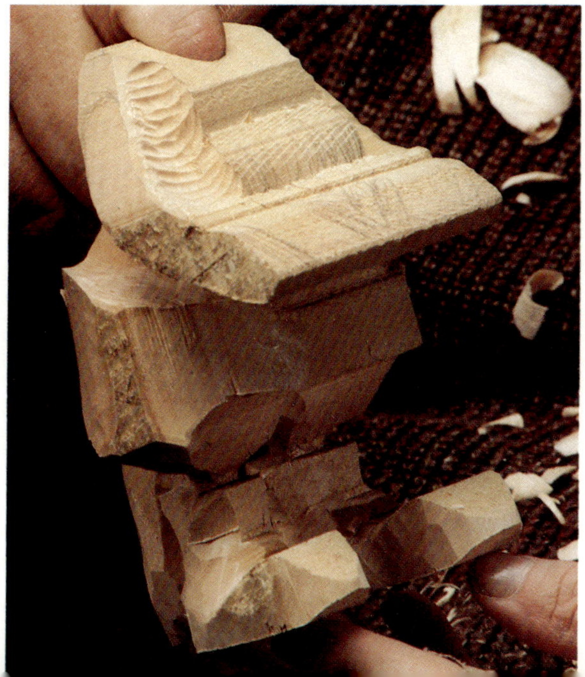

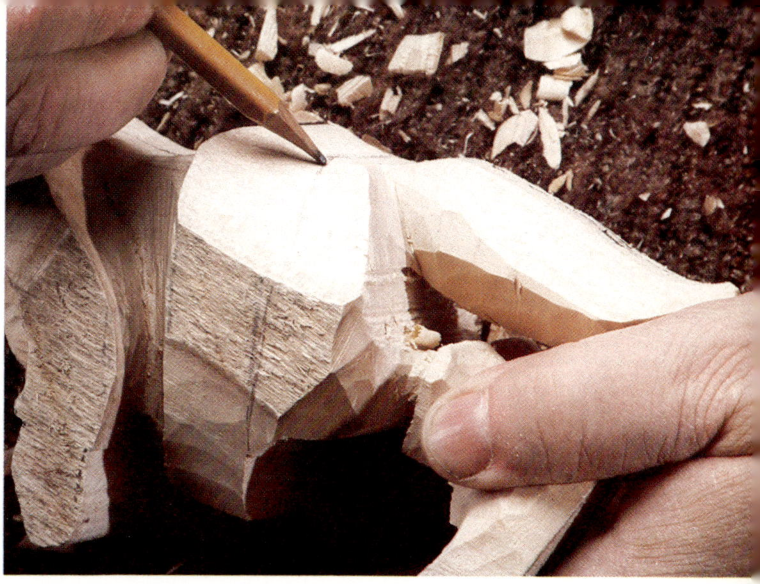

Remark the line of the coat.

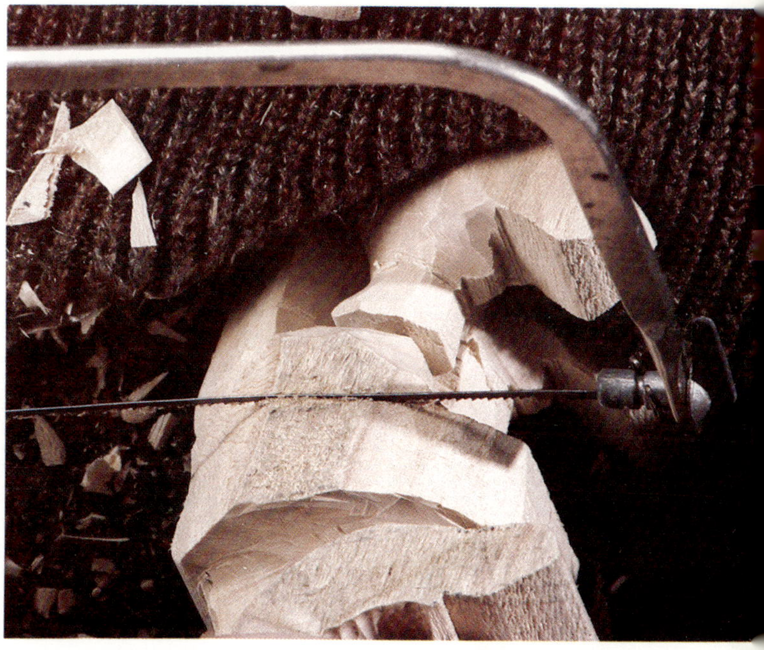

The stops along the bottom of the coat need to go quite deep, so I will make them with a coping saw.

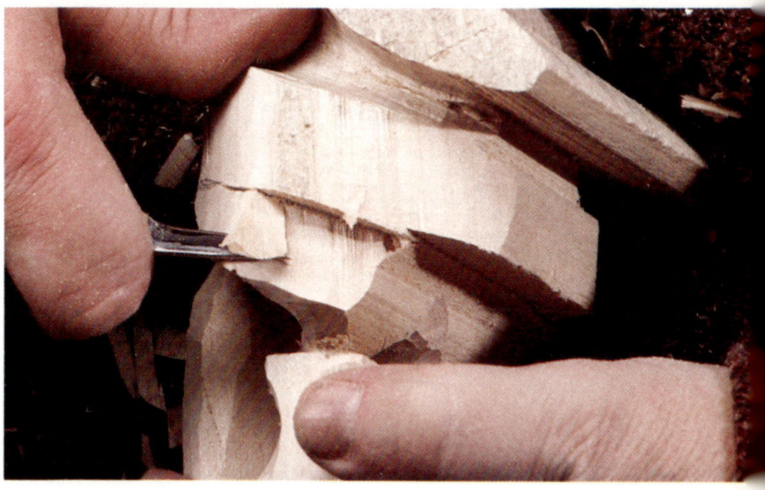

Cut back to the stop from the pants. With the deep stop and cutting with the grain, this is a pretty easy task.

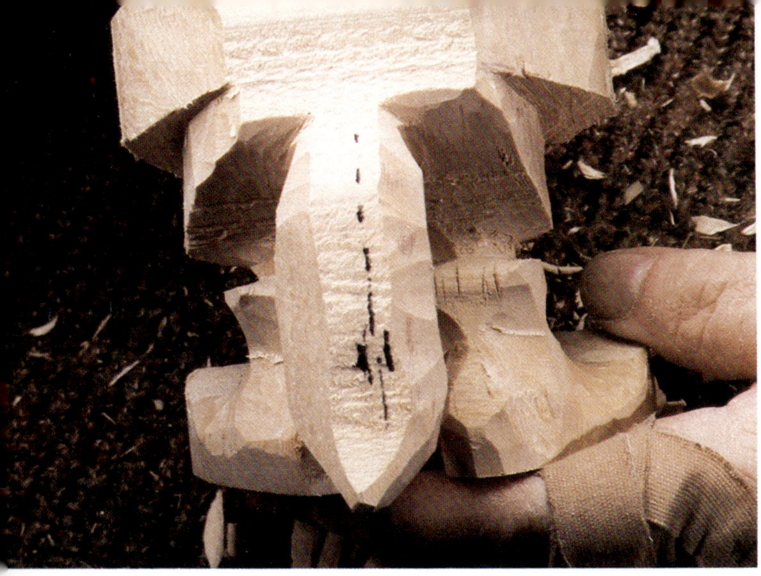

The pants roughed out under the coat.

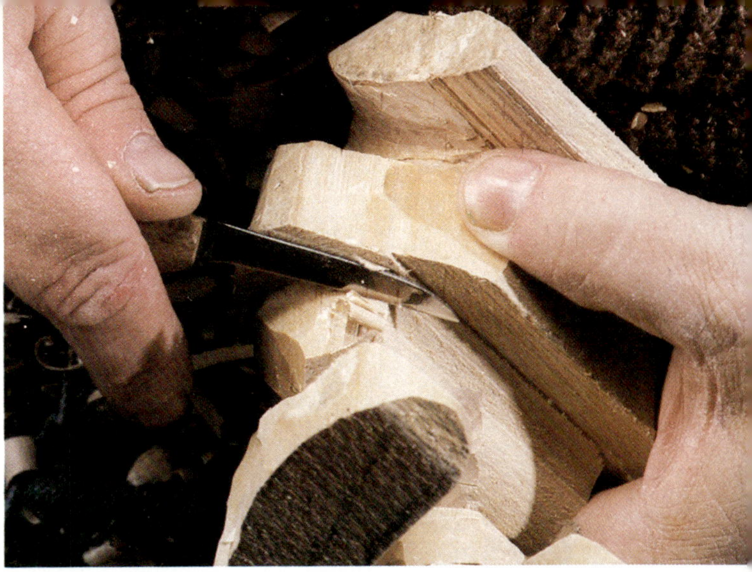

Round the pants, starting at the corners.

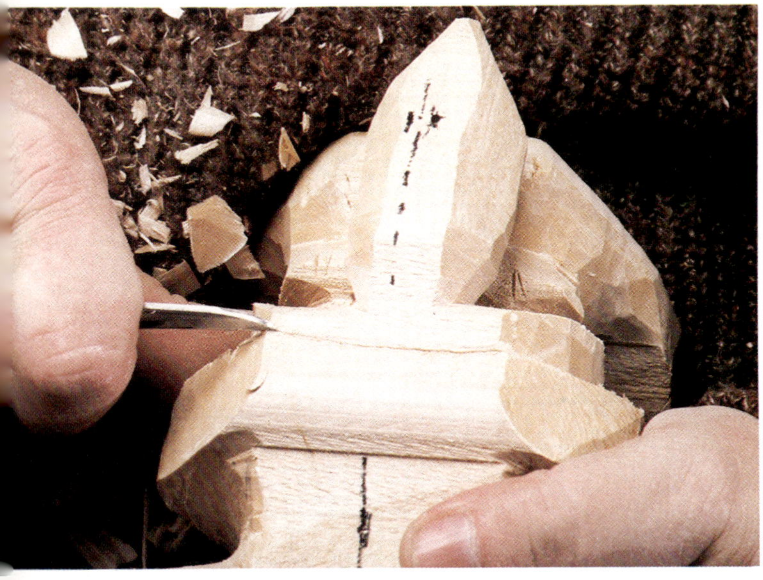

Cut a stop across the bottom edge of the fur at the back.

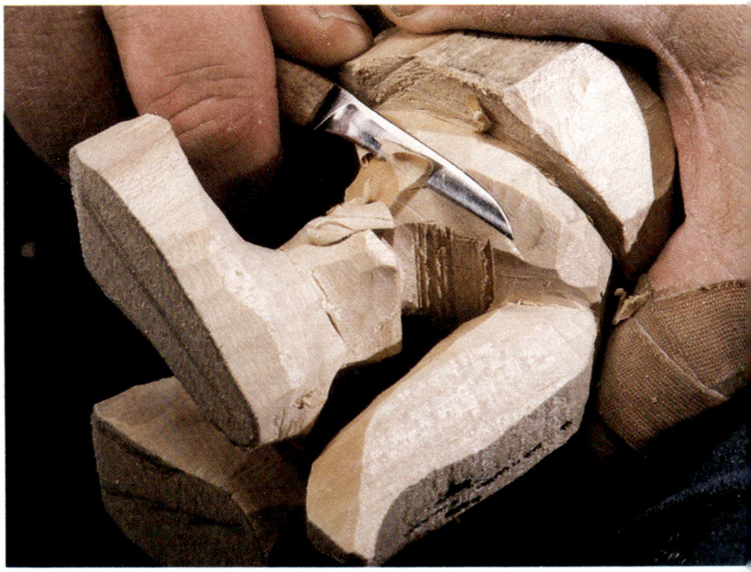

Continue to round and shape the pants.

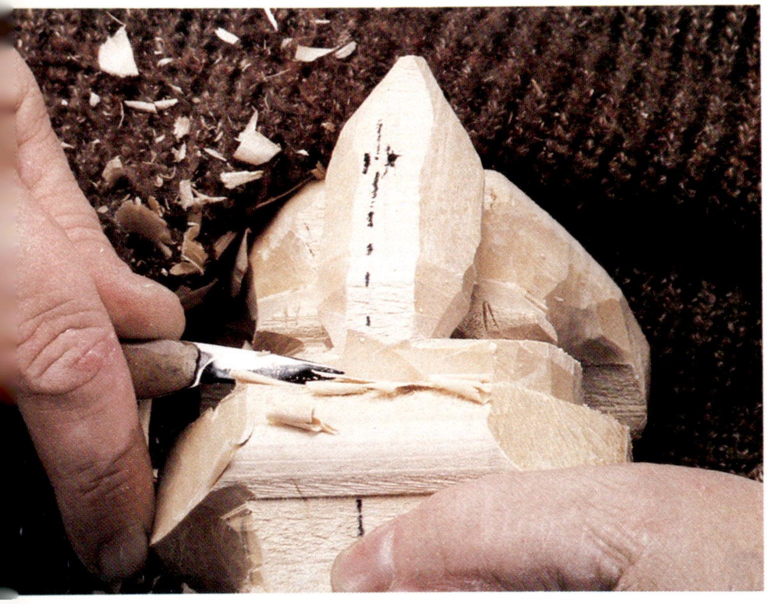

Carve back to it from the pants.

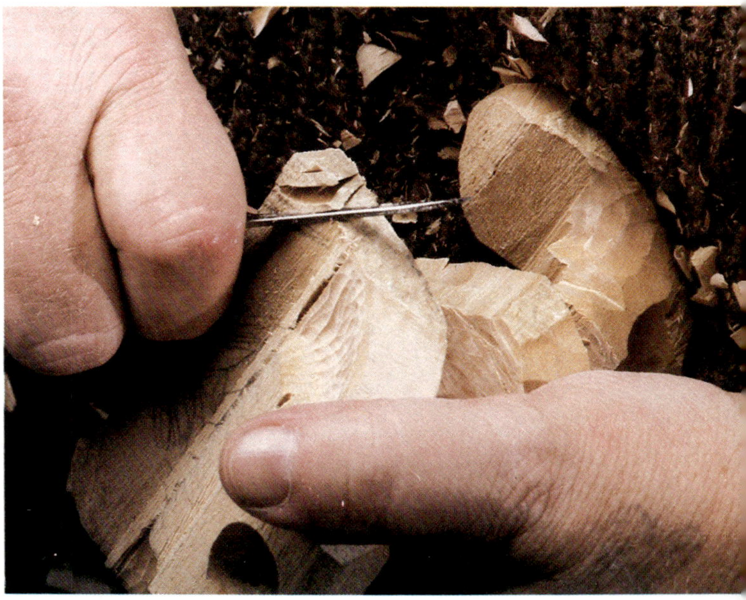

Knock off the excess from the front of the arms.

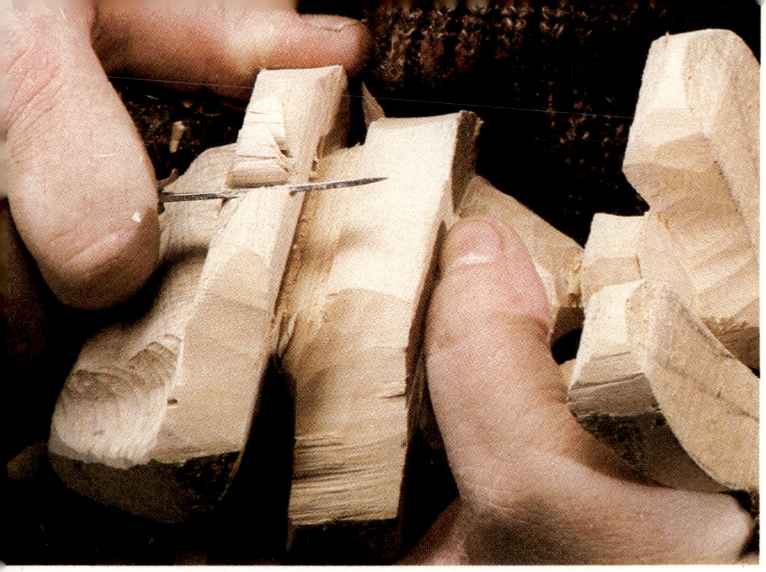

To remove the area between the arms, chip it away with the knife. With the arms out like this, the carving is open to a number of variations: human hands, animal paws, mittened hands, hands holding objects, and many others.

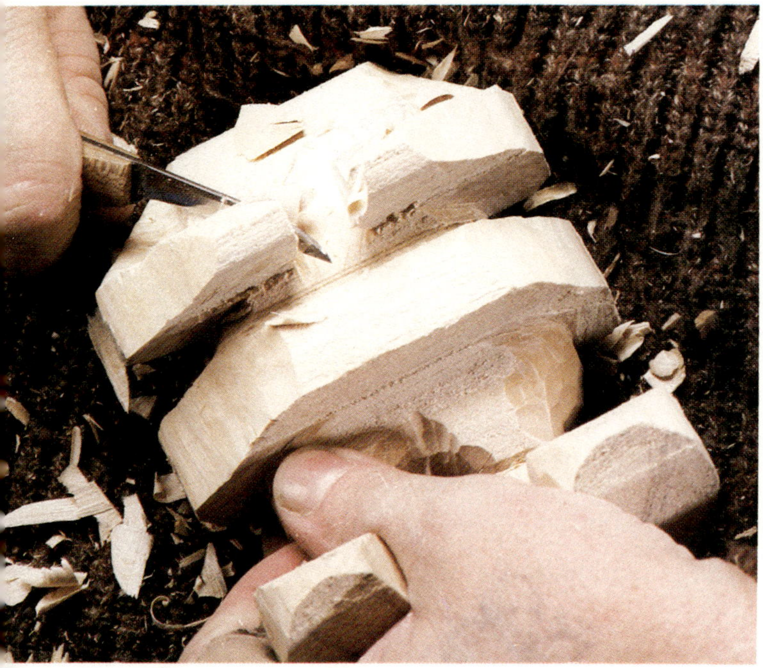

Continue carving back to the chest.

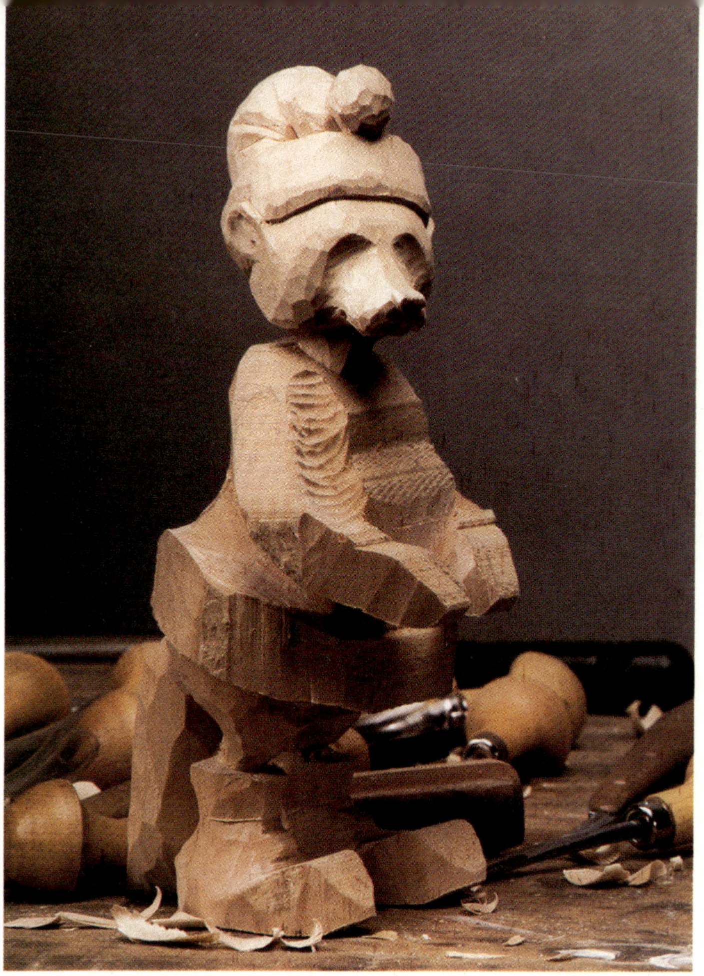

The raccoon Santimal so far.

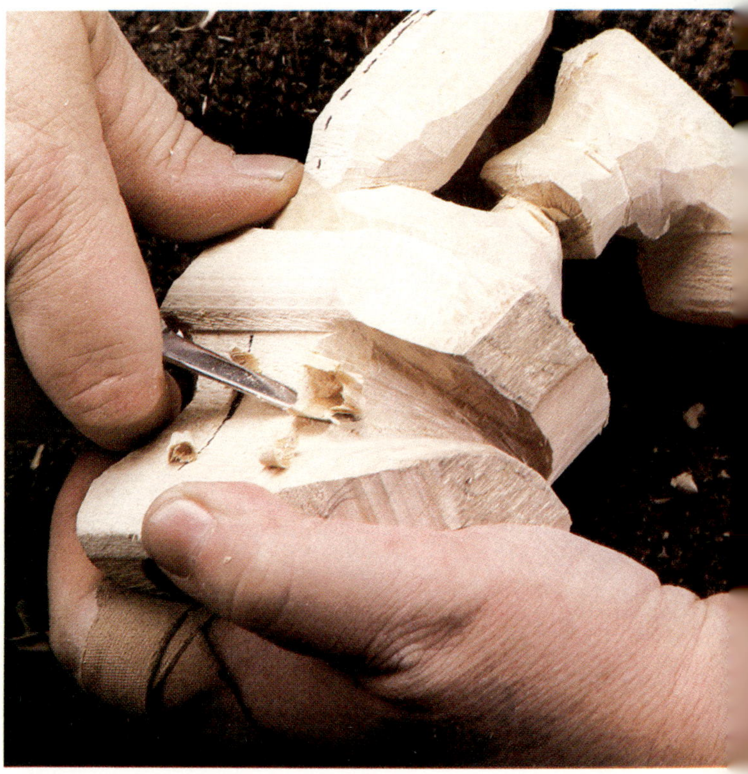

Before carving the wood trim I need to round off the back, which seems squarish right now.

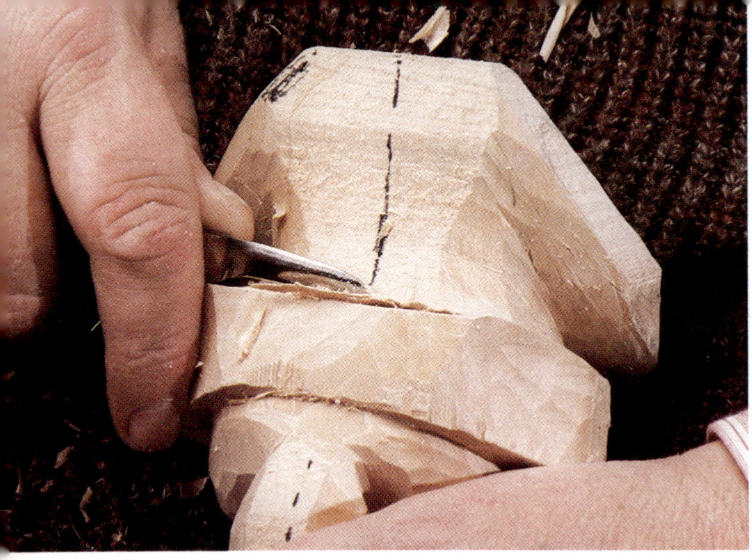

I start working on the trim at the place where it is thinnest. This time it is around the back, so I start shaping it there to make it look believable. After that is in good shape I adjust the rest of the trim to match. I try to define the top edge first, then carry it around.

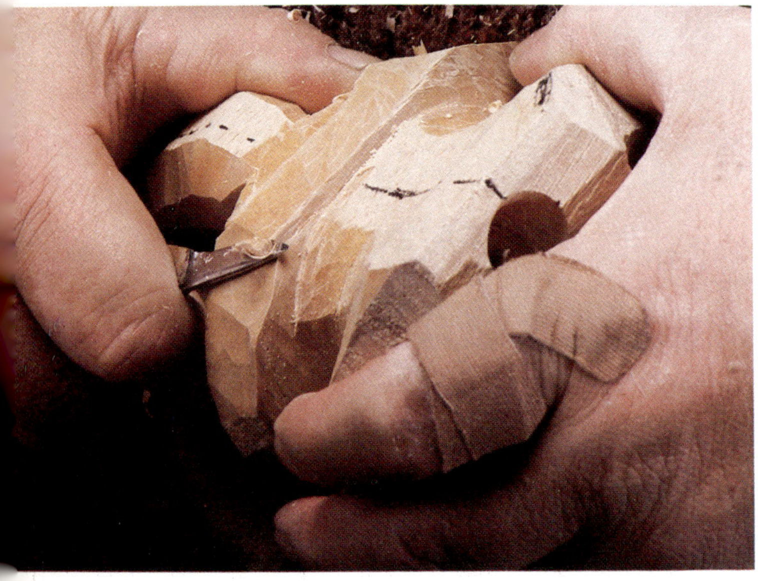

After establishing the thickness I want in the back, I carve the rest of the trim.

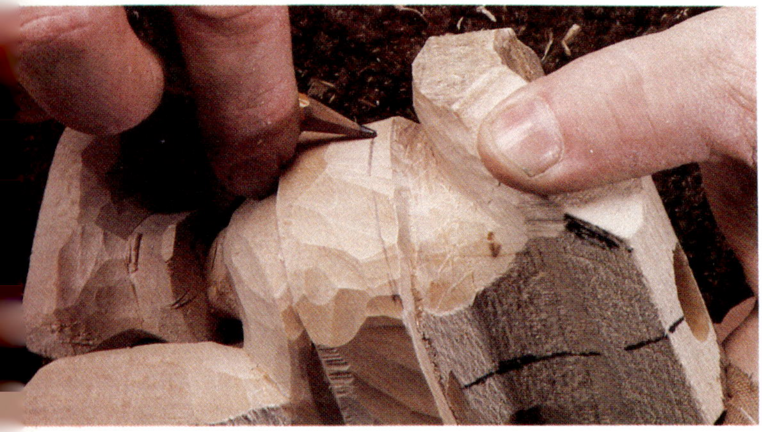

When the thickness is set, I use a pencil and my finger to mark the width of the trim all around.

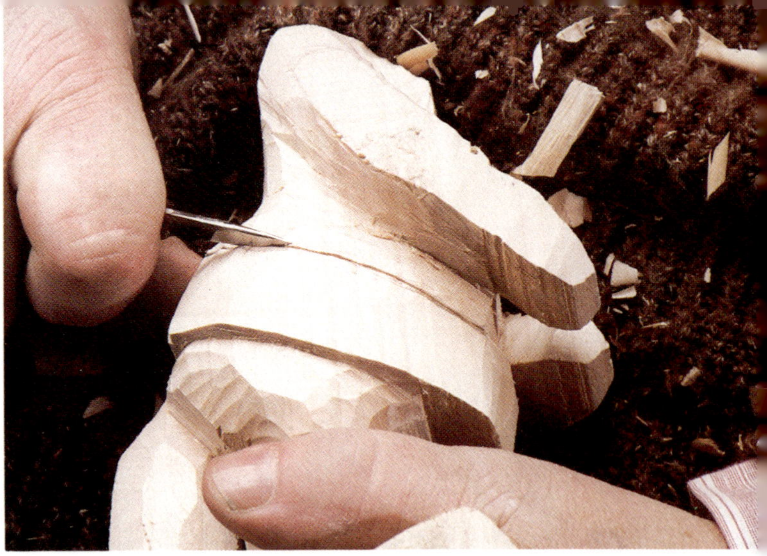

Cut a stop around the line...

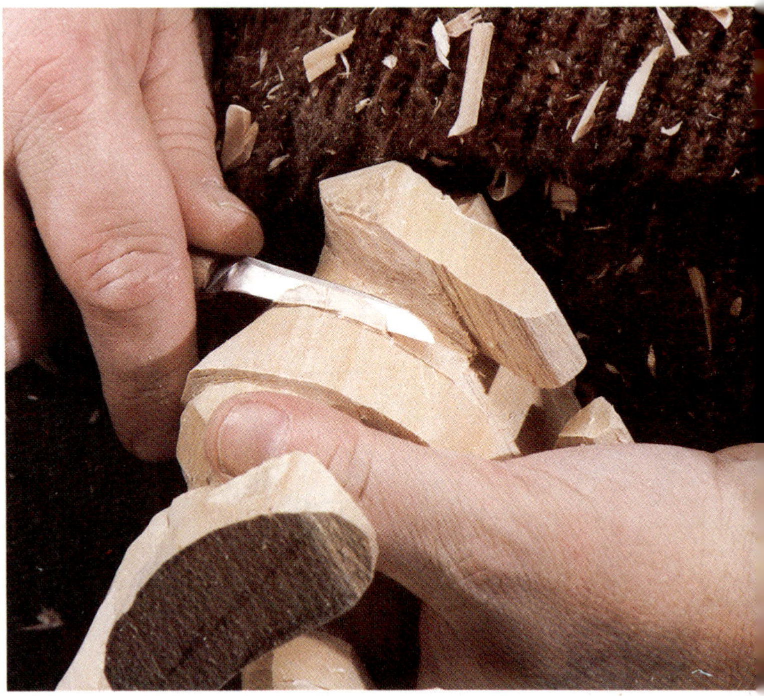

and trim back to it from the coat.

We are about to clean up the carving, so it is a good time to sharpen the knives. This will help us get good clean cuts on the fine chips we will be taking. If the knife won't shave your arm or slides on your fingernail, it is too dull.

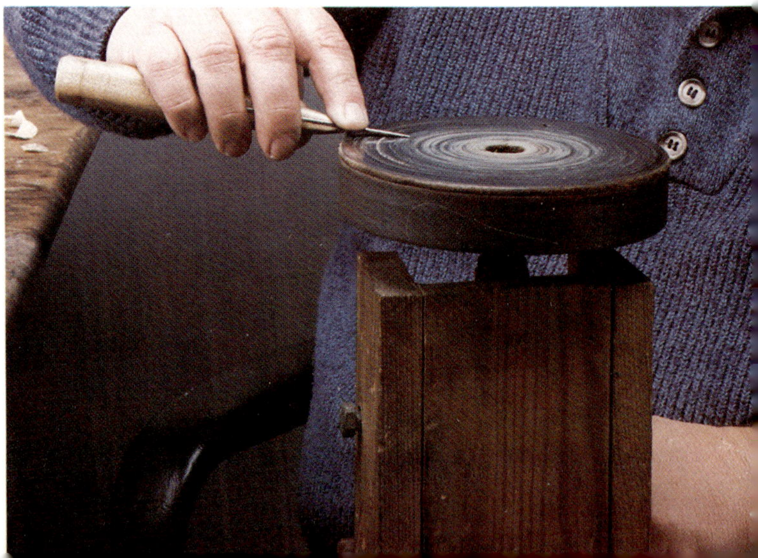

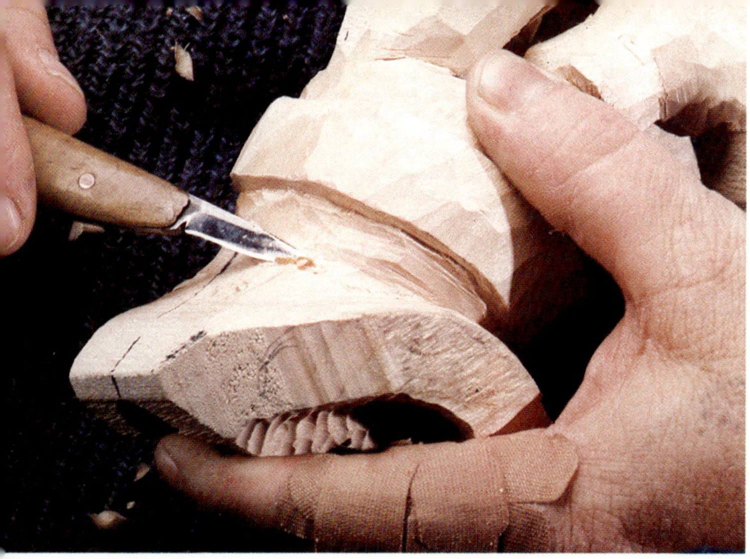

While we use the knife for most of the clean-up work, there are place like here, in the small of the back. The cut is across end grain, and no matter which direction you use the knife it will not cut cleanly.

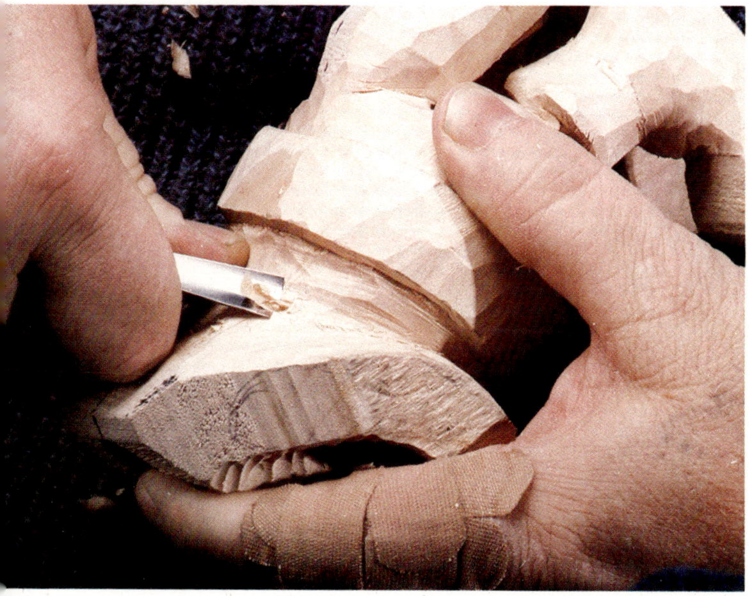

In these areas it is best to use a gouge and move from side to side in a motion I call "shaling."

This clean-up takes away pencil and saw marks. It is best to do this kind of work as you go instead of waiting until the piece is finished and going back to do it.

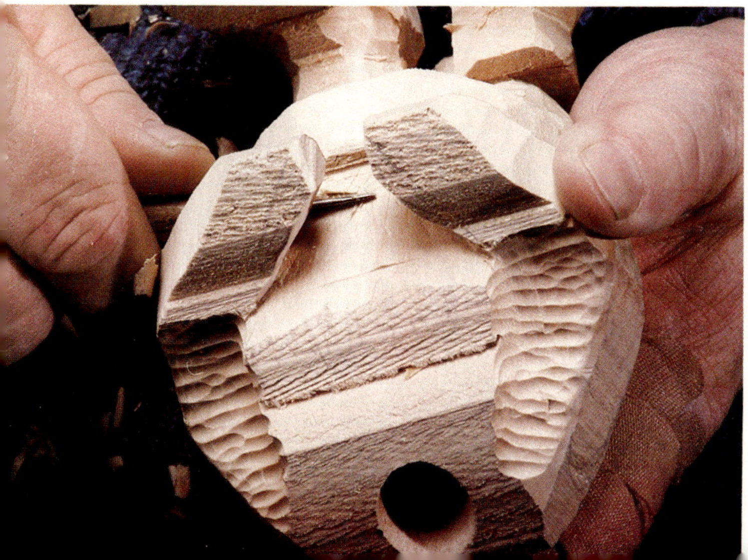

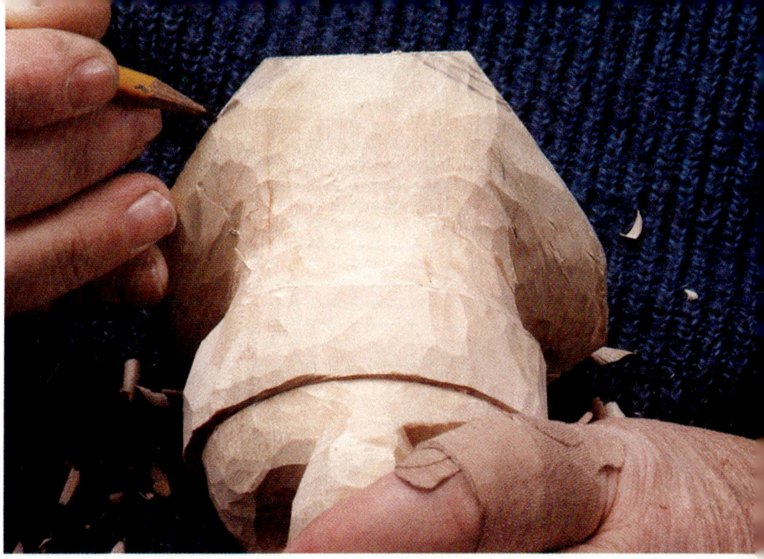

I want the shoulder about here, to leave room for the fur collar. The darkened area needs to be removed.

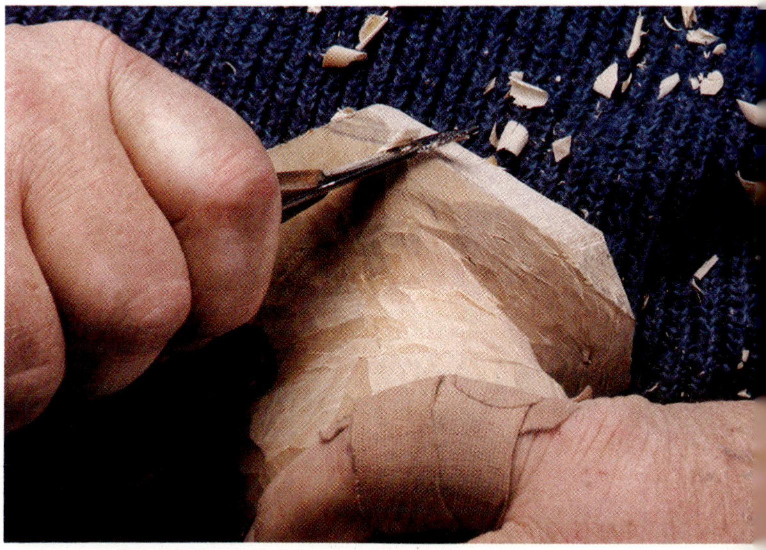

The knife works well in this situation.

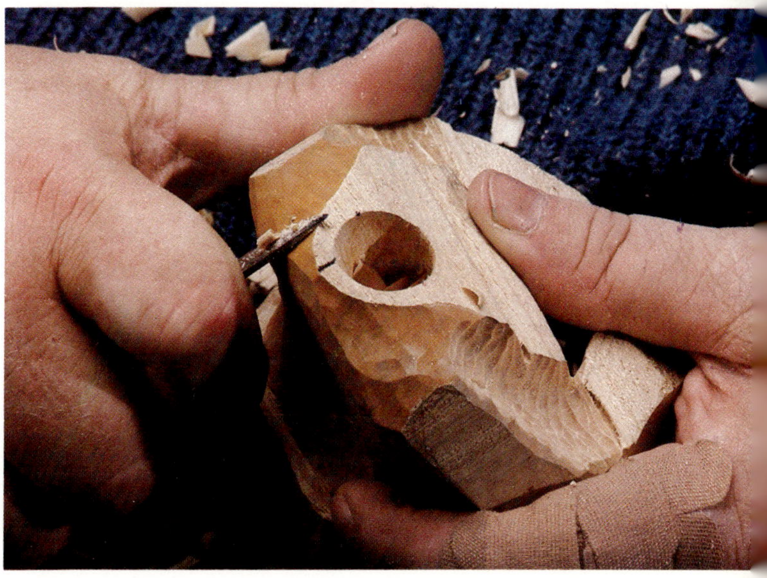

Leave this edge around the neck to be rounded over later. This will make the fur collar lie more realistically.

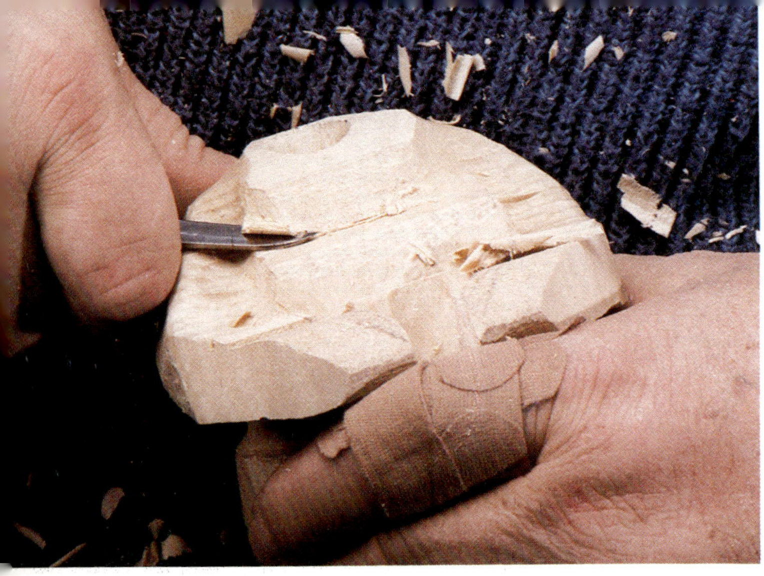

Moving to the front I carve from the chest to leave a bulge around the neck for the collar.

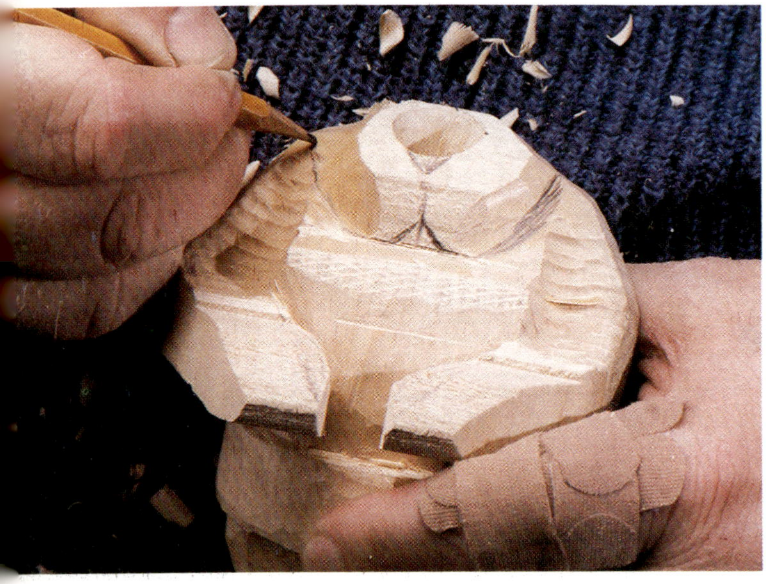

Mark the collar in the front...

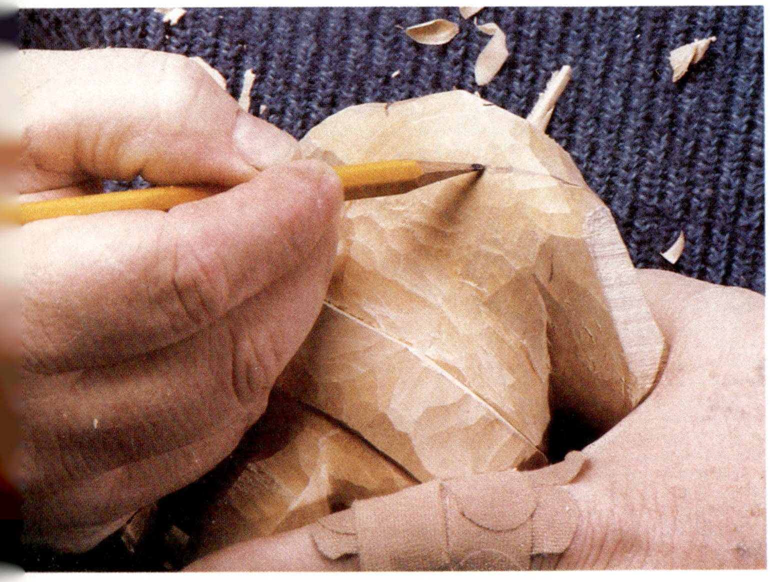

and the back.

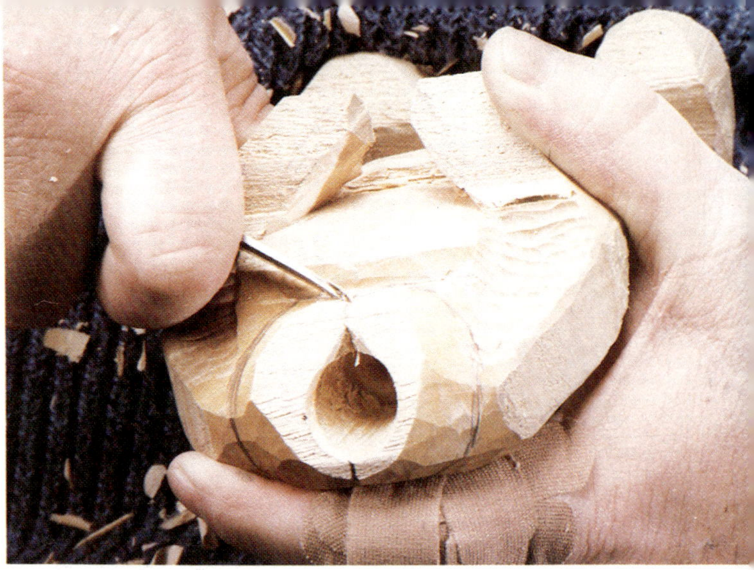

Begin shaping the collar by cutting the little nitch in the front at the neck and at the opening.

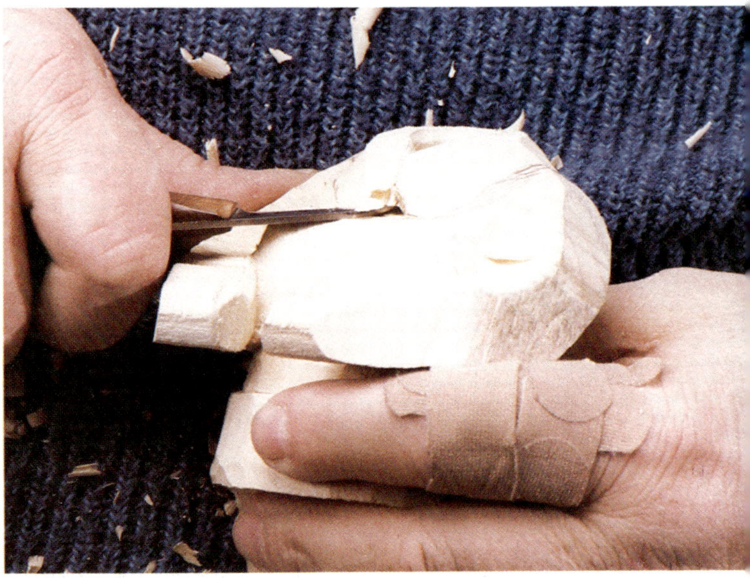

Create this nitch at the opening by cutting in along the collar line on both sides and then across the bottom. This makes a triangle that just pops out.

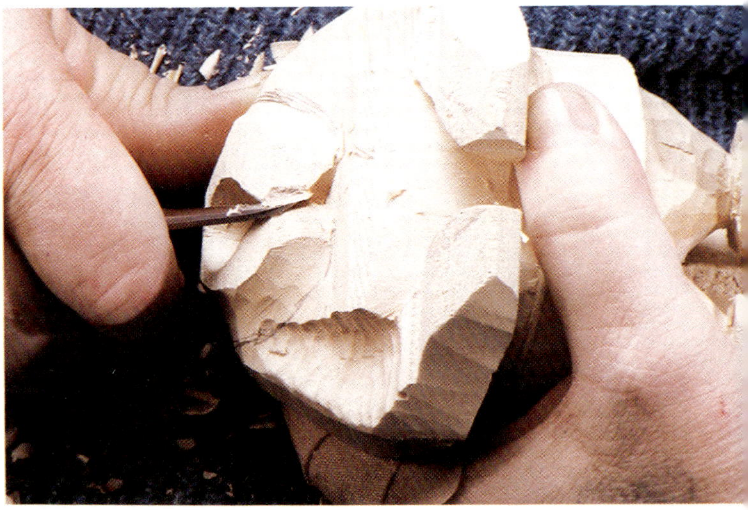

Cut a V-groove on the line between the two sides of the collar.

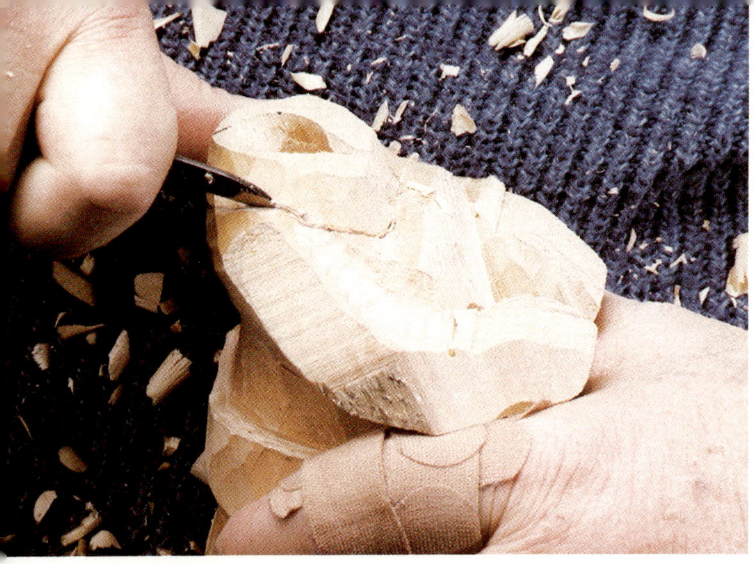

Cut a stop all around the collar.

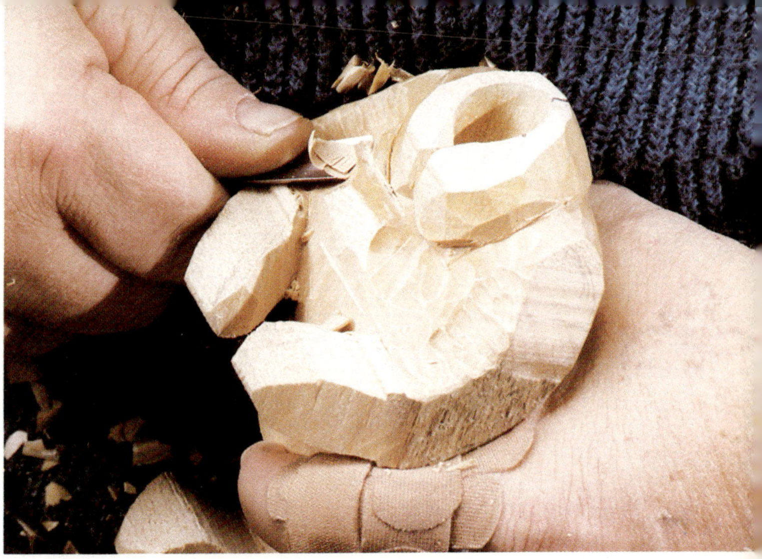

On the front it is easiest to use a gouge, and it also gives a cleaner cut. Gouge up to the collar stop line.

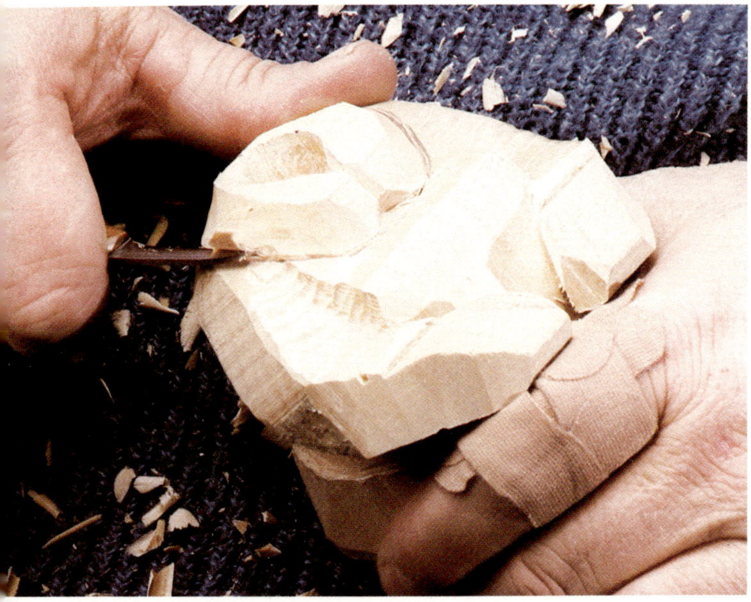

Cut back to the stop from the shoulder, back and chest, going all around the collar.

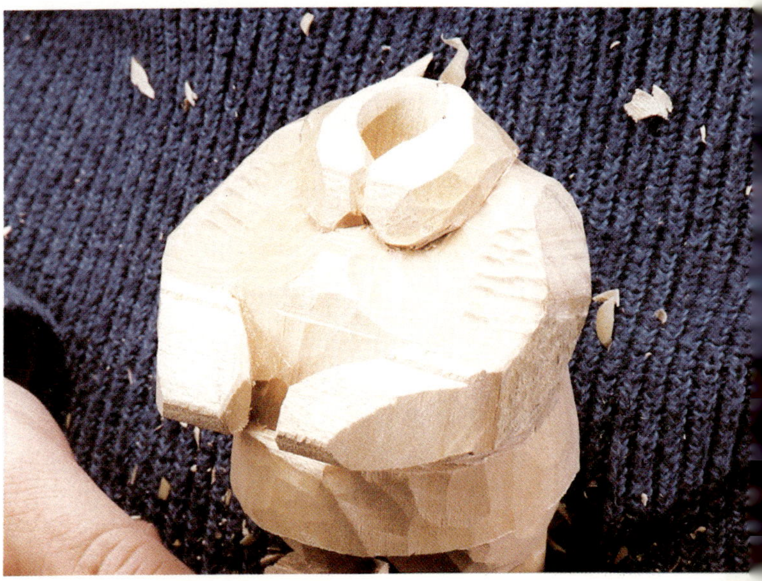

The collar is taking shape.

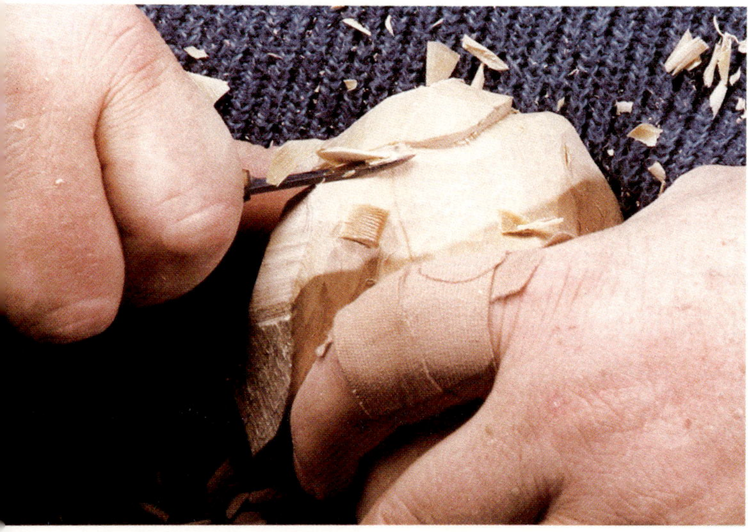

You want this collar to look thick like fur, not flat like cloth, so make the defining line quite distinct.

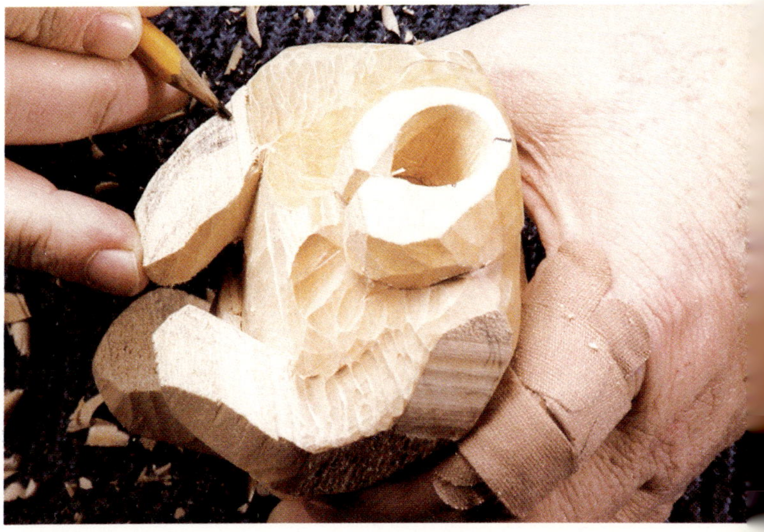

Now we move to the arms. The saw mark defines the top of the mitten or paw, so I start there and draw in the rough shape.

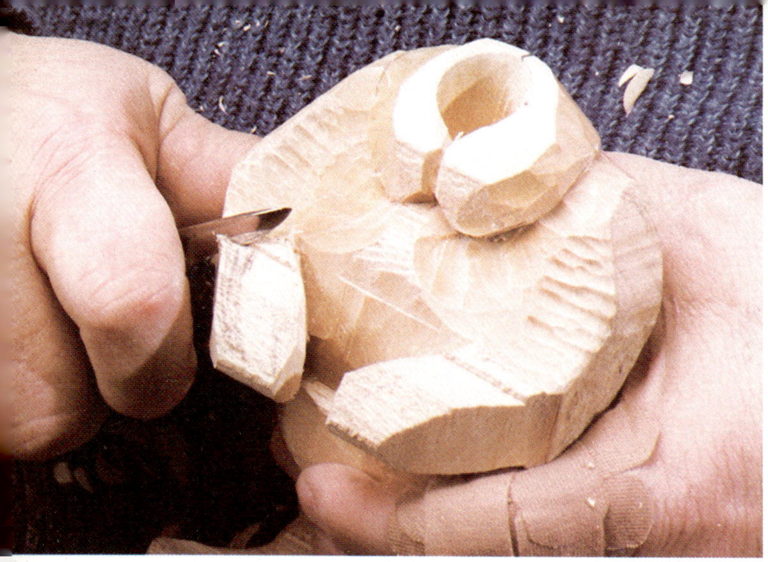

Make a stop on the corner...

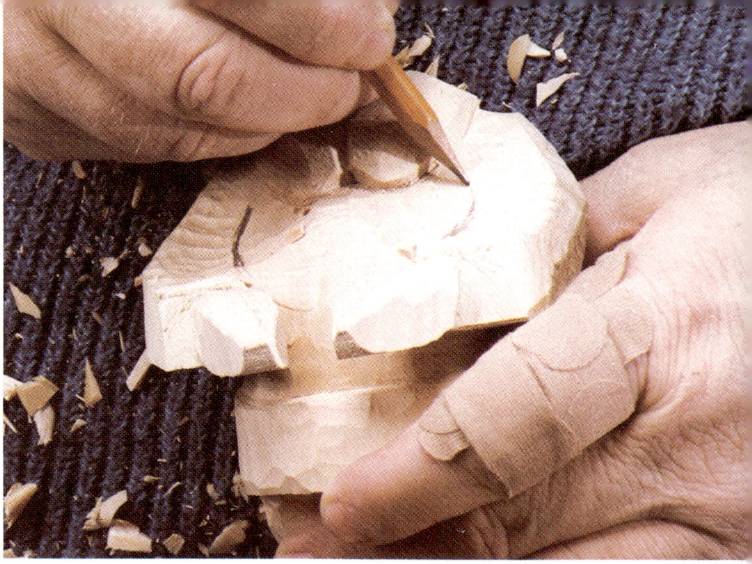

Draw in the inner line of the arm.

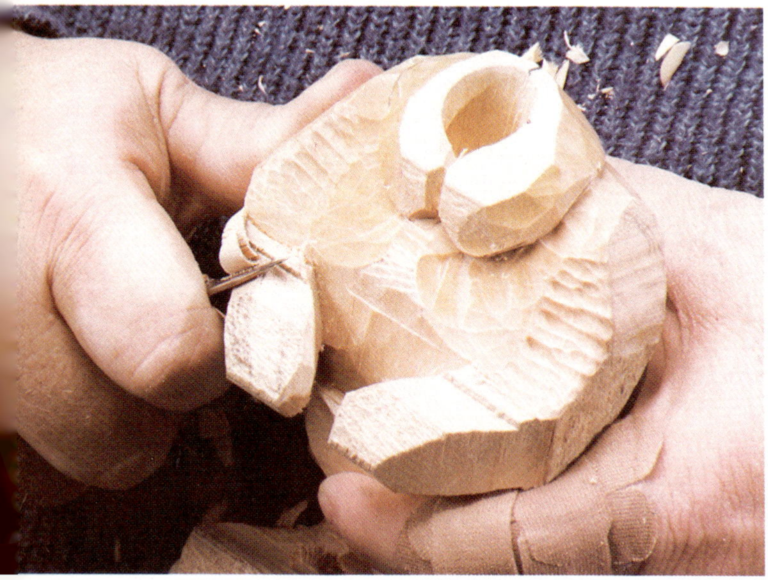

and come back to it from the hand.

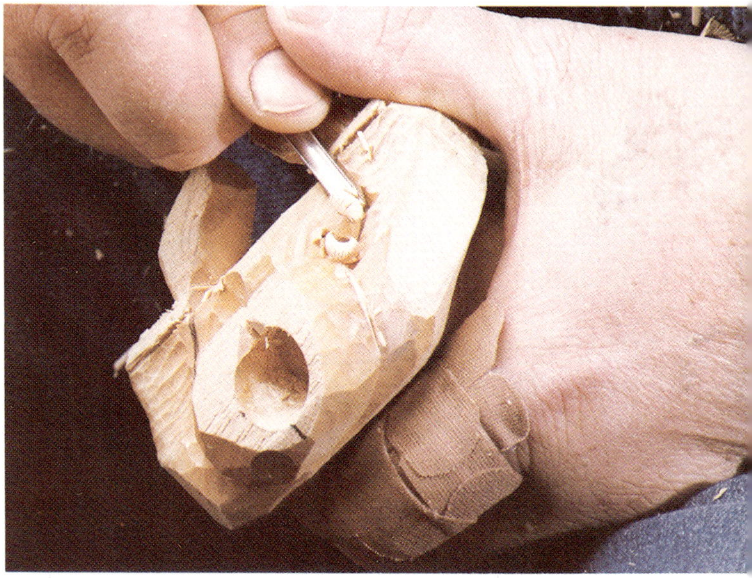

Follow the line with a gouge to remove the wood. While this is a #9 Swiss-made gouge, I don't go by any set size. I just look at the job and choose the tool that looks right.

When I get to this point with the larger gouge, I switch to a smaller one. I this case it is a #11.

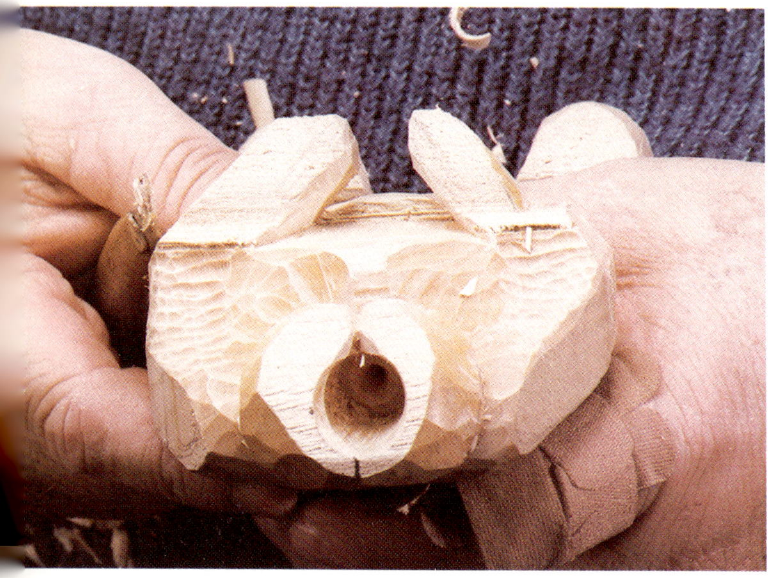

Continue removing wood until the hand is the shape you want.

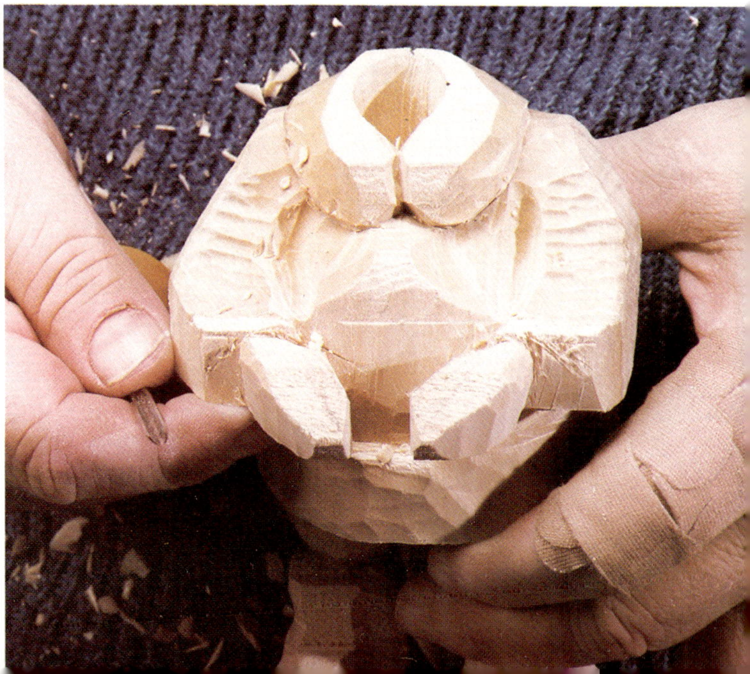

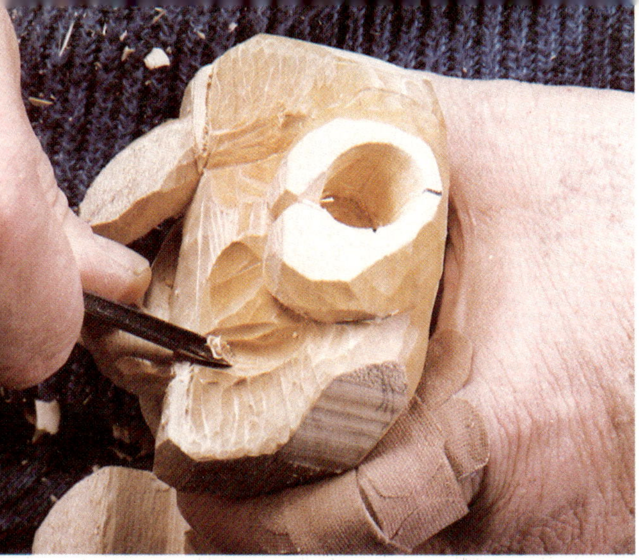

Follow the same line. The smaller gouge gets you deeper without going wider.

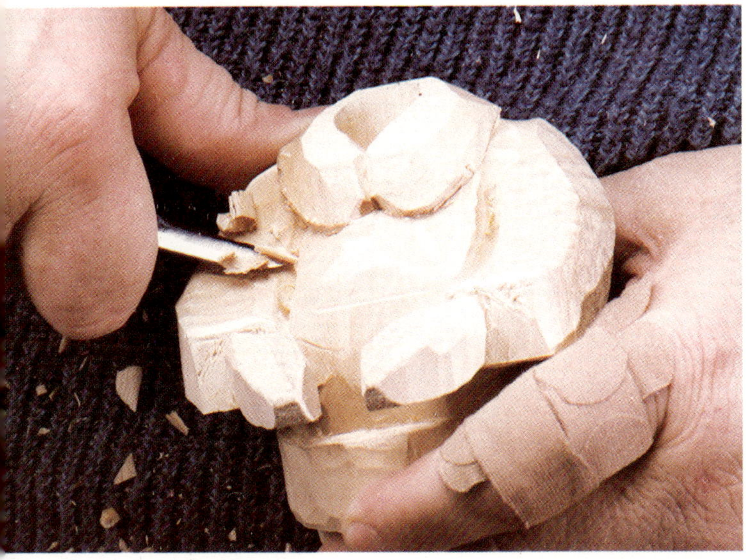

When I get deep enough, I switch to a knife to start rounding the sides.

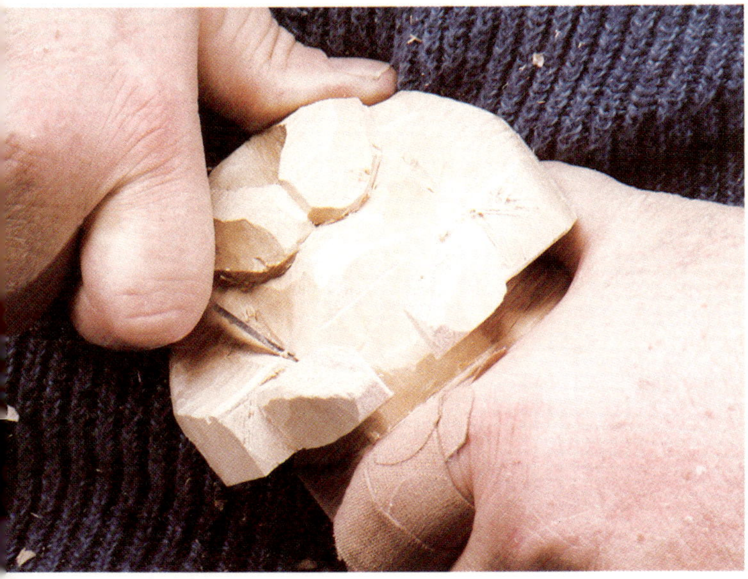

Cut some deep stops along the insides of the arms.

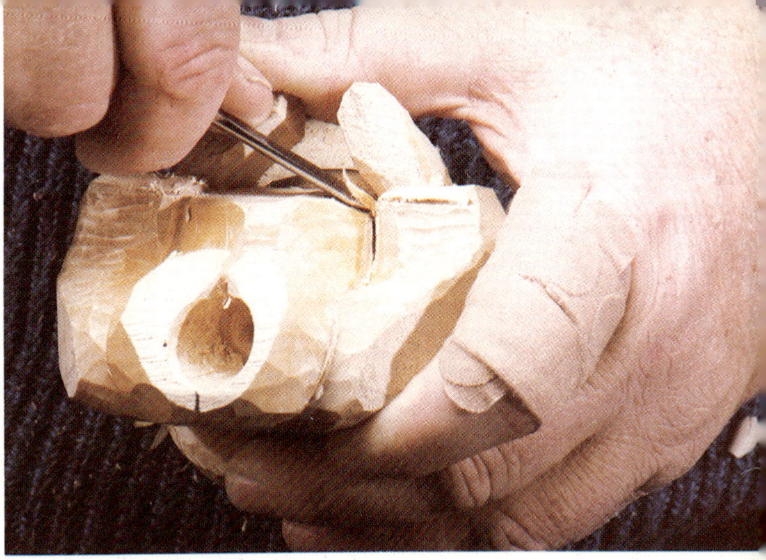

Using a gouge round the chest back to the stops. I have left the lump in the middle of the chest in case I want to create a scarf or something as I go.

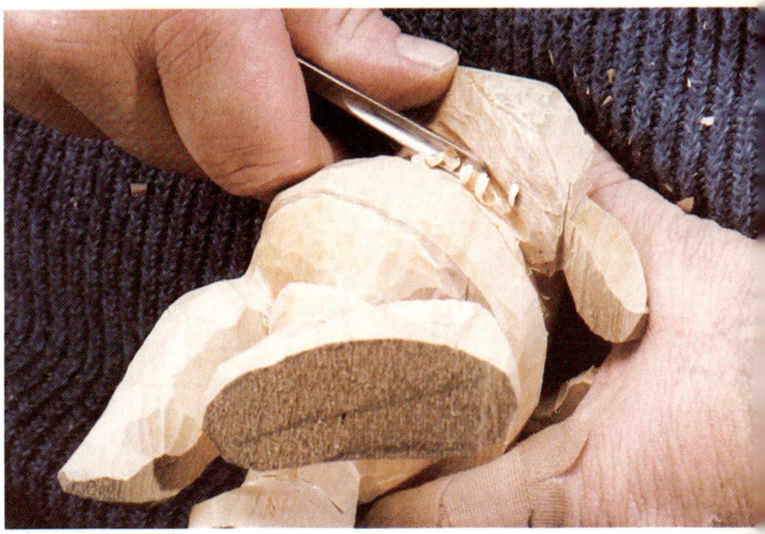

To define the line on the underside of the arm, gouge it as you did before, starting with the larger gouge...

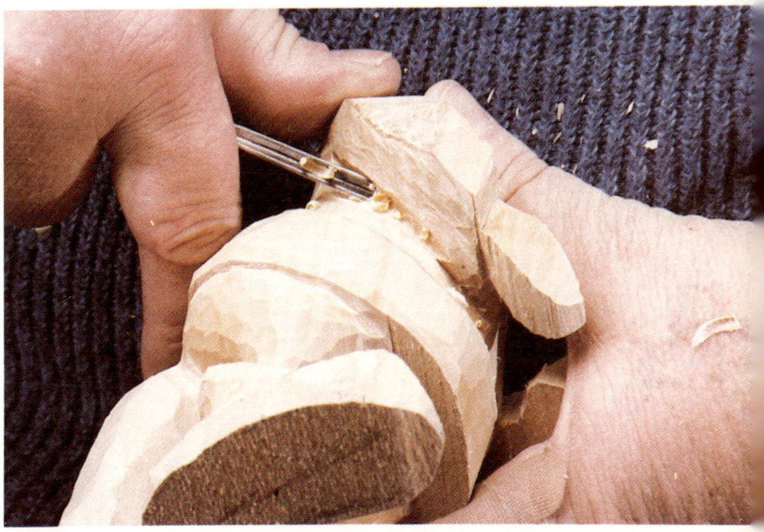

and finishing with the smaller. Note the position of the fingers and thumbs. They act as stops which keep me from cutting myself. The alternatives are injury or a vise.

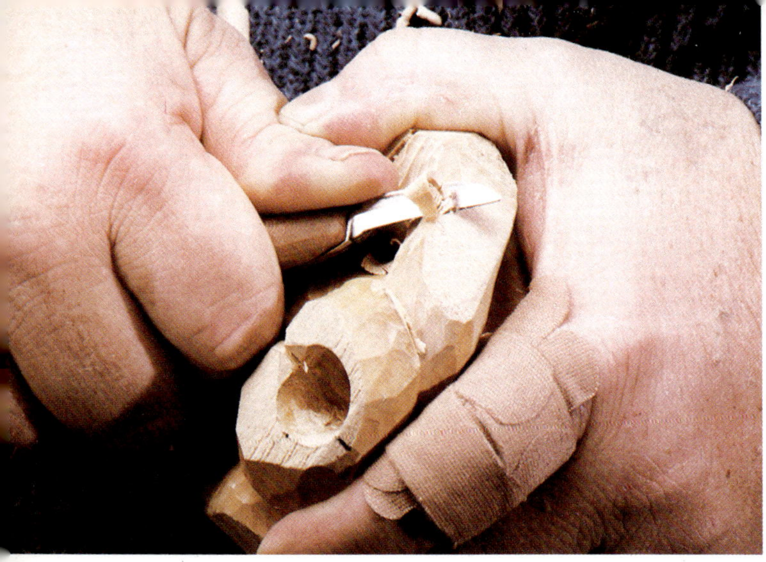

Use the knife to round off the arms. Begin by knocking off the corners.

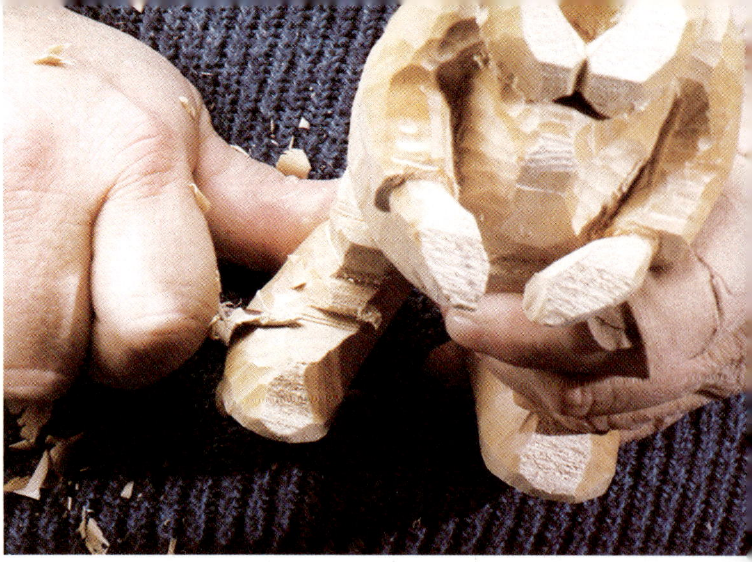

When the edges are removed, go back and round the boots off until they look like shoes.

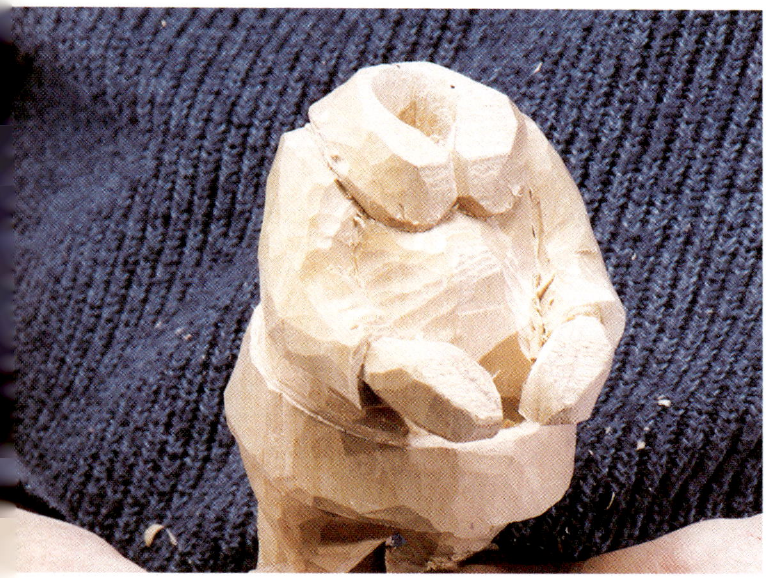

Continue to round until you get to this point.

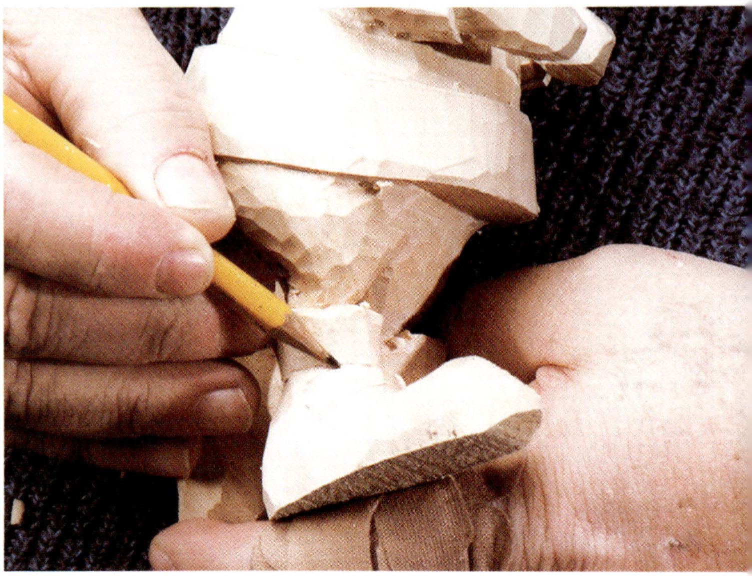

The boot can be plain, have a buckle, a strap, or other design. The bump on the front gives that flexibility. In this case I think I'll use a strap, which I mark with a pencil.

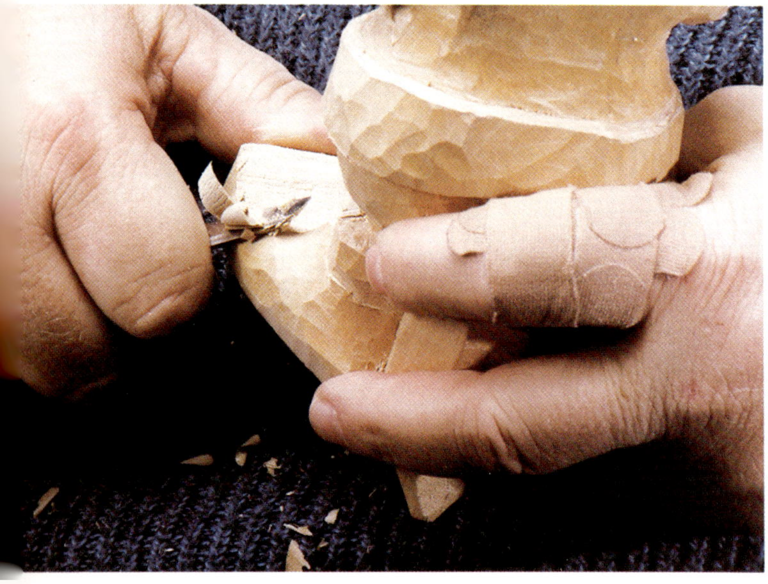

Move to the boots and knock the corners off.

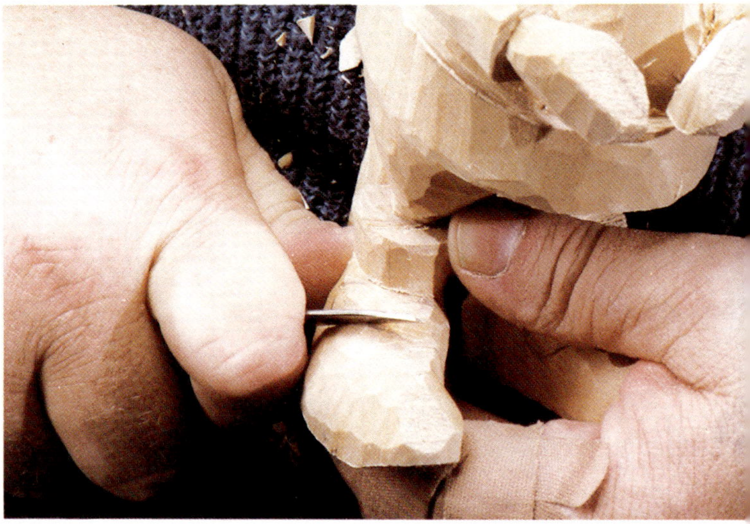

Make a straight stop into the lines you have drawn...

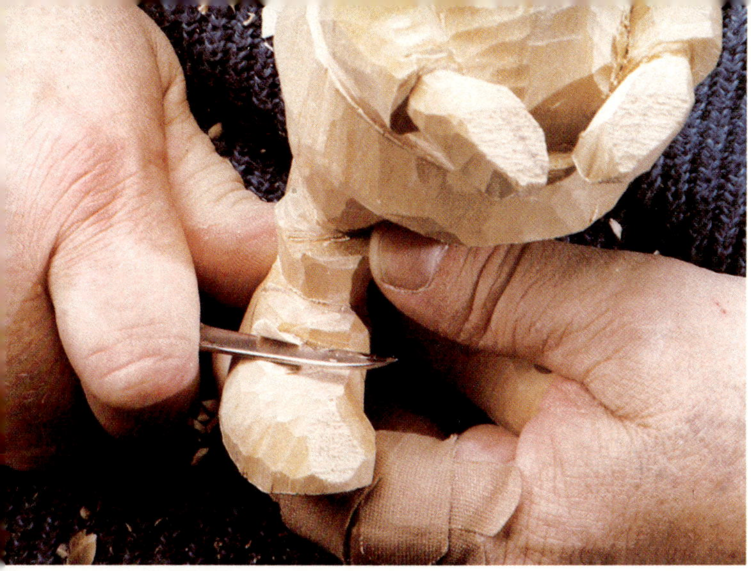

and cut back to it from the shoe.

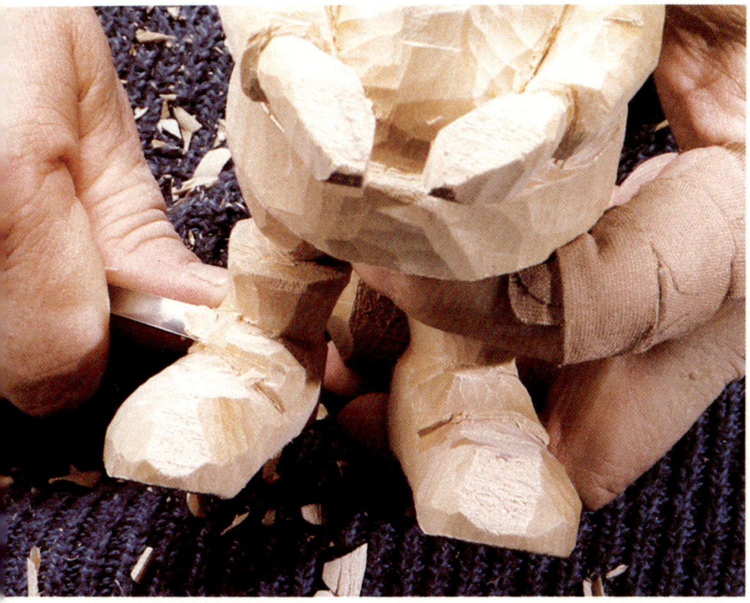

I use a flat gouge to cup the straps. This gives it the appearance of leather, instead of just a clump across the top of the boot.

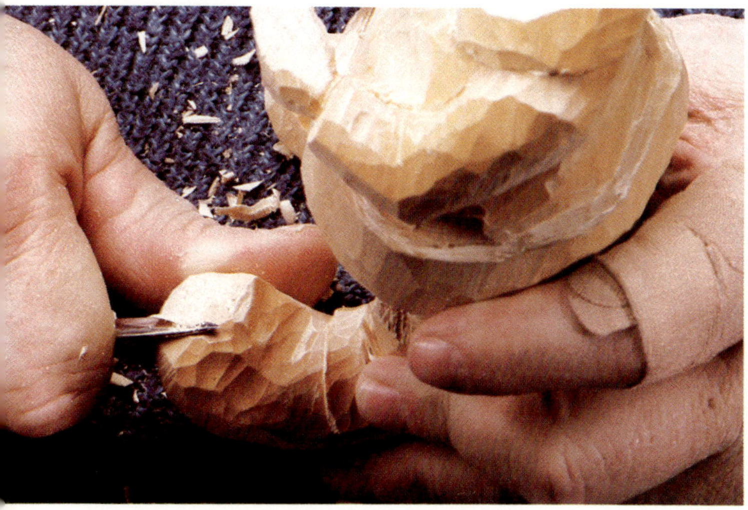

Use a knife to refine the boot, taking off bumps, blemishes, saw marks, and anything else that doesn't look natural.

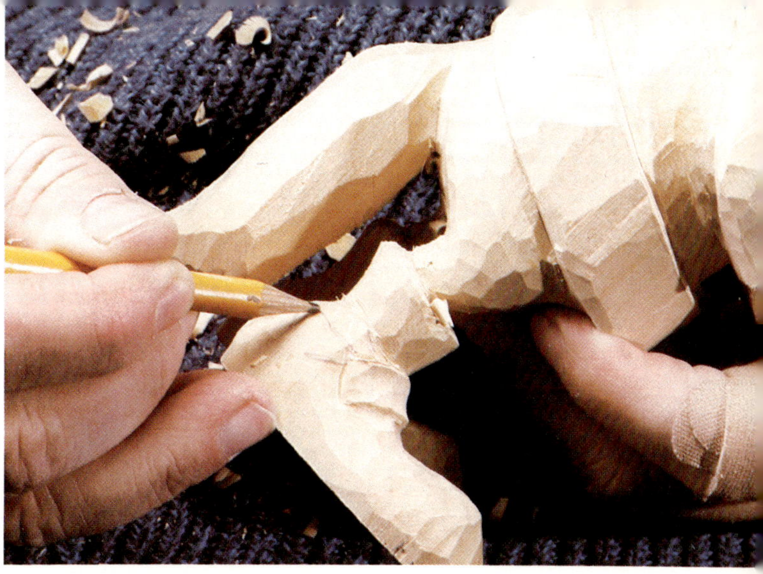

The boot needs some folds. I usually do one fold up and one down, with one in the middle. It looks something like <–> when I'm done.

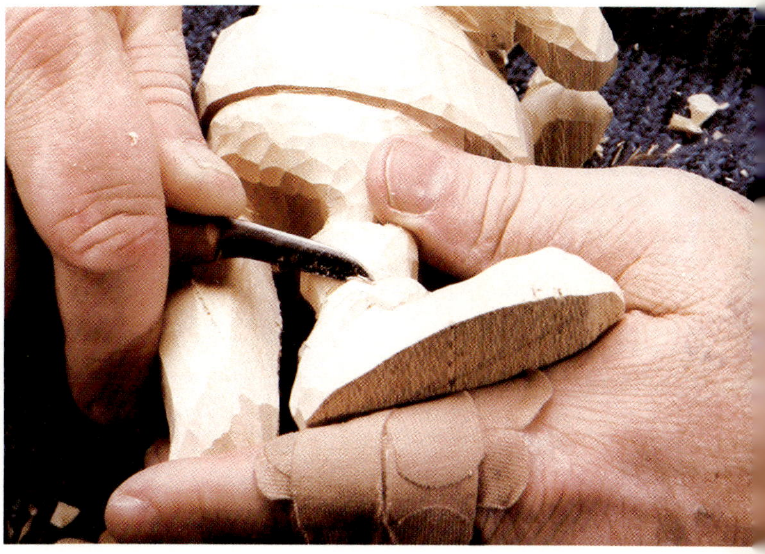

I make these wedge cuts with a knife, which I think works better than a v-tool. First a cut down...

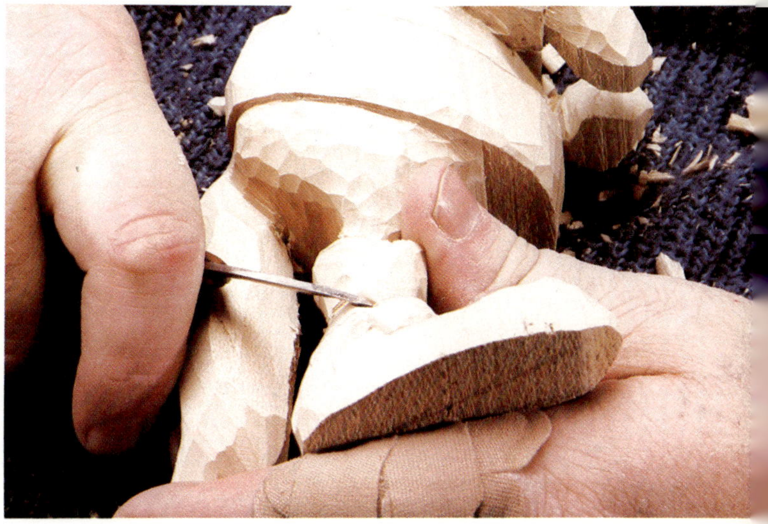

then up along the lines I've drawn. Do the same thing on the outside and inside of each boot.

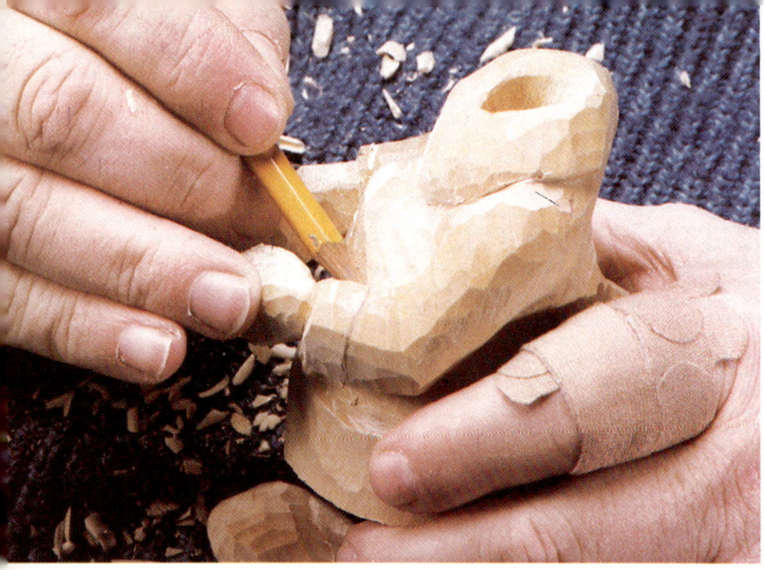

With a pencil, mark cuffs on the sleeves...

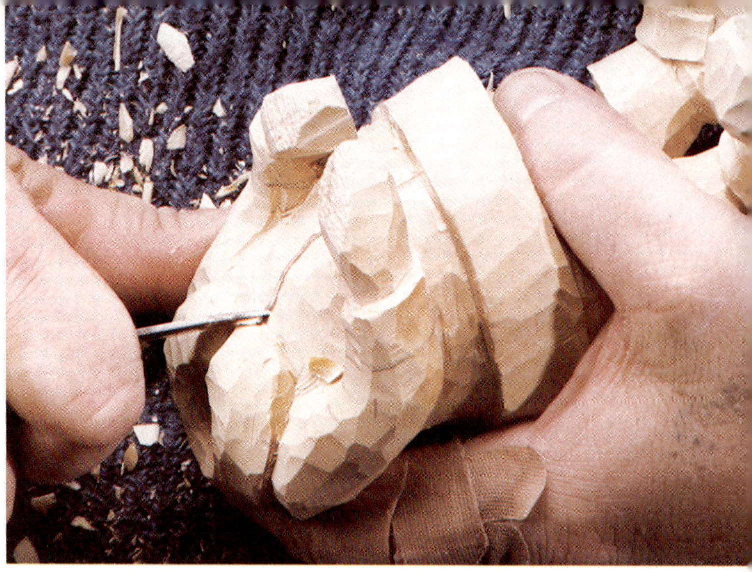

Follow the line in front with a stop.

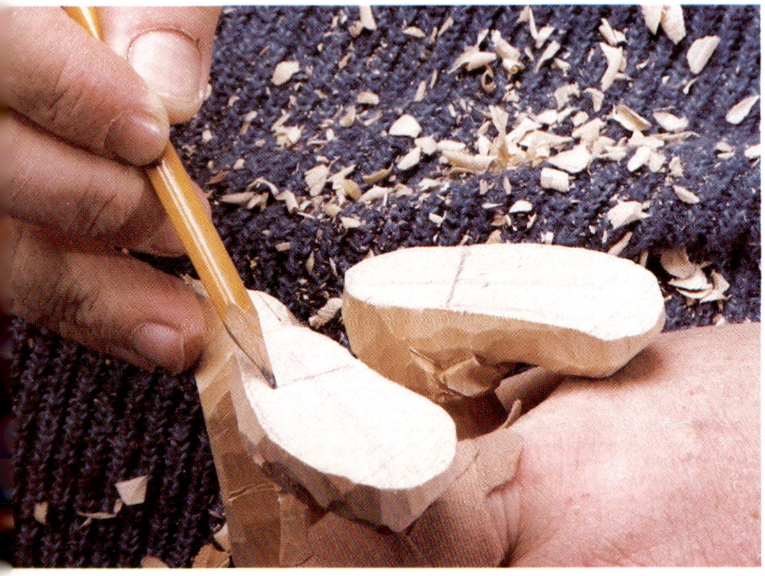

and the heels of the boots.

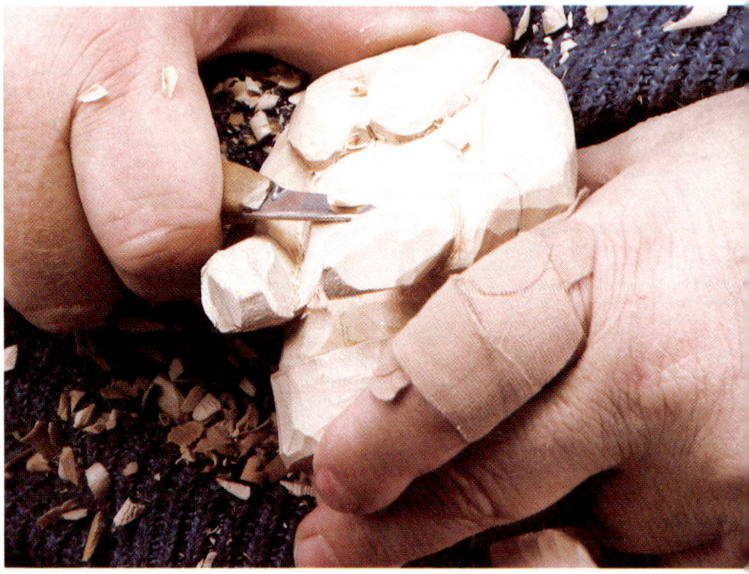

Cut back to the stop from the right side of the coat. Use a knife or a gouge where necessary.

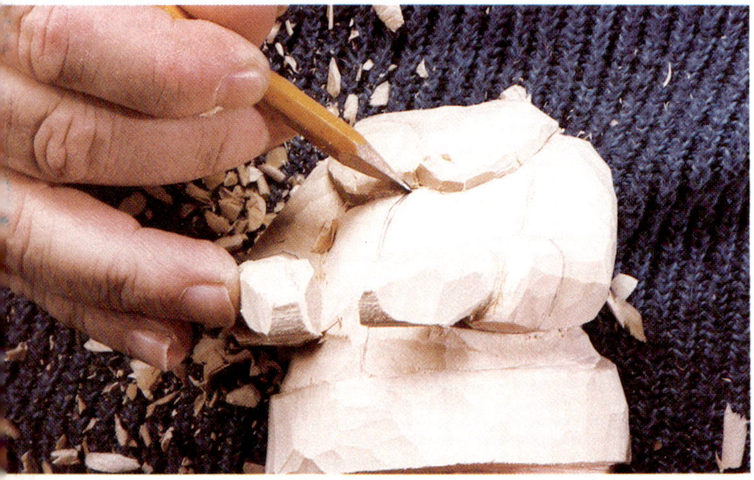

Earlier we left wood on the front of the coat for future use. After contemplating the situation for some time, I've decided that a scarf is not appropriate, so I am going to cut off the excess. Now I draw in the line for the front of the coat.

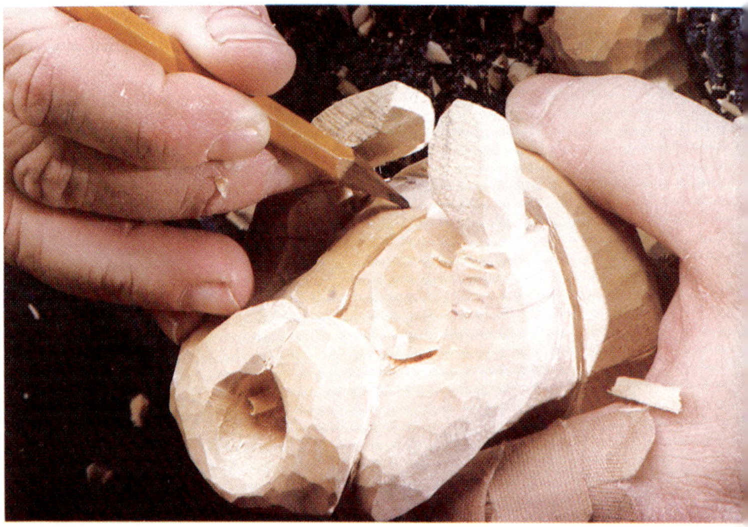

Draw in the buttons. I draw the top and bottom buttons first and then decide how many and what spacing the ones between have.

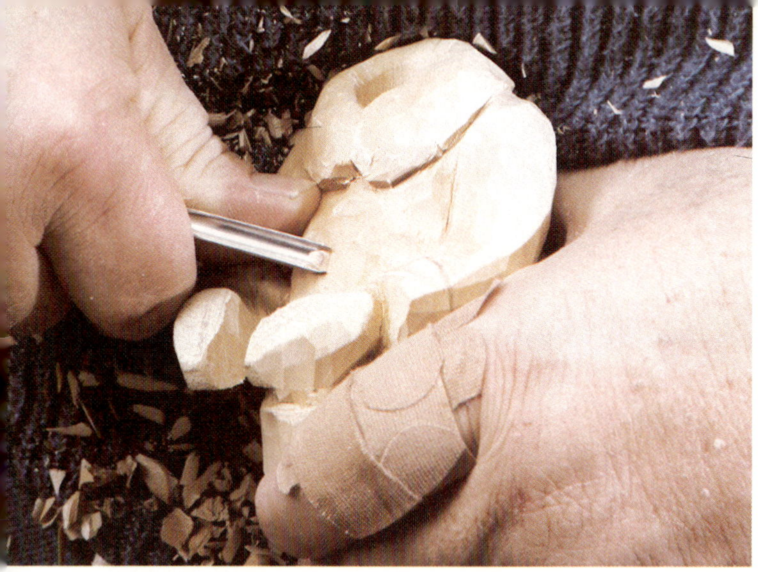

Make a depression for the buttons by going from the side with a gouge over each marked button.

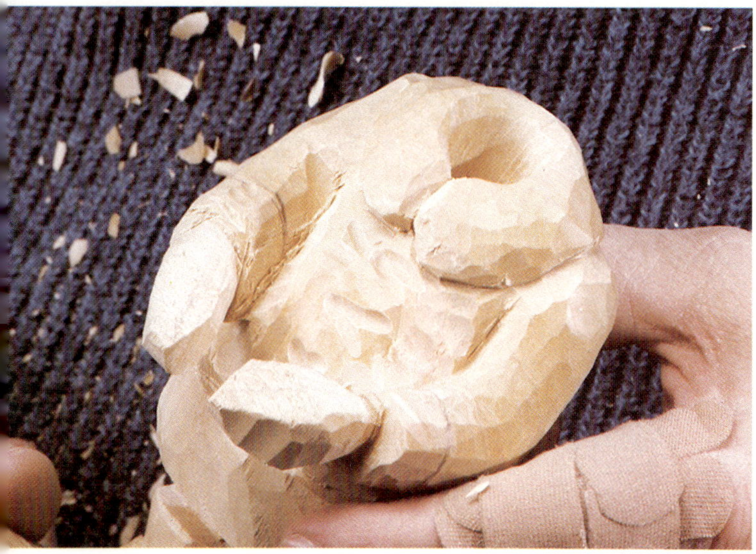

Bring two longer gouge marks out from each side of the button to create the look of the fabric being stretched by the Santimal's girth.

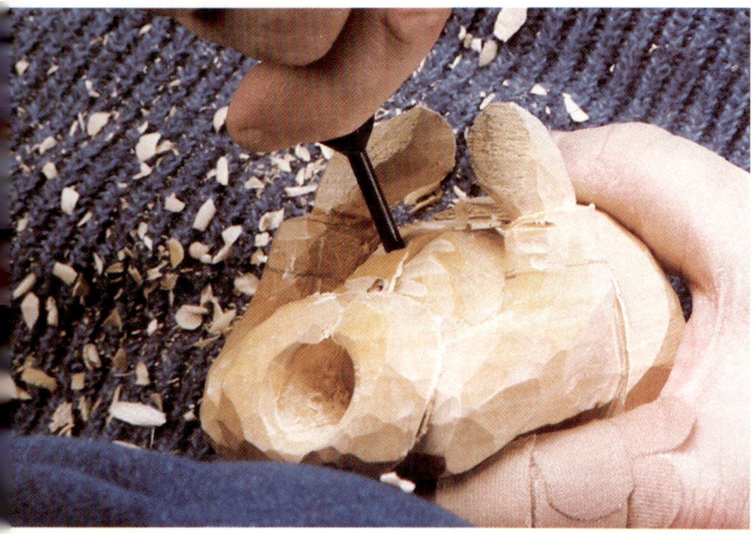

Buttons are made with eyepunches or nailsets. Choose the right size and push and twist it to form the buttons.

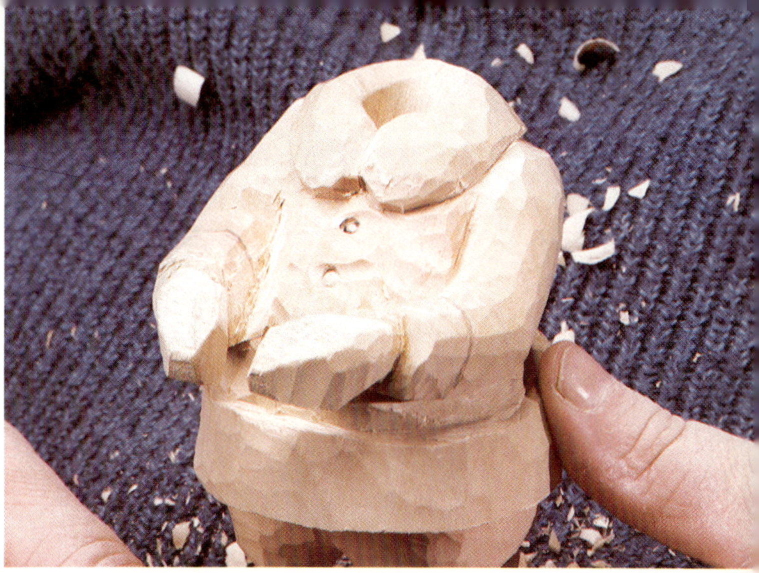

This is how the buttons should look.

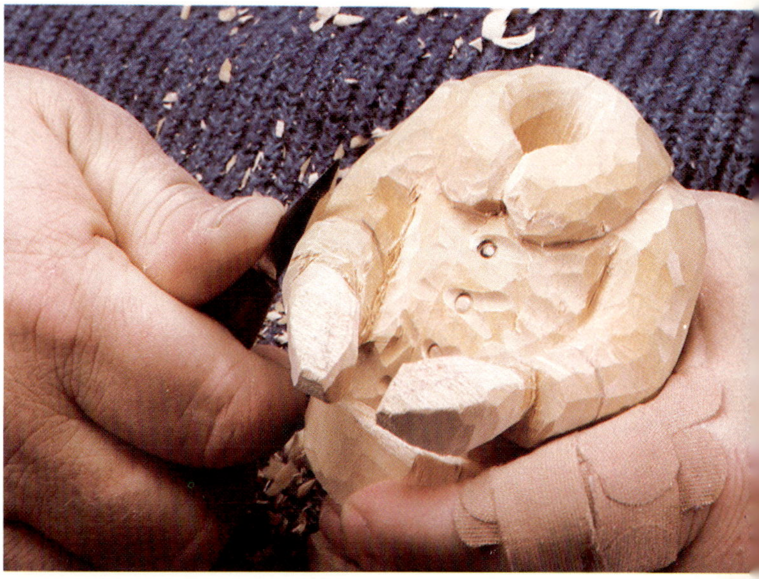

Make a stop at the cuff line...

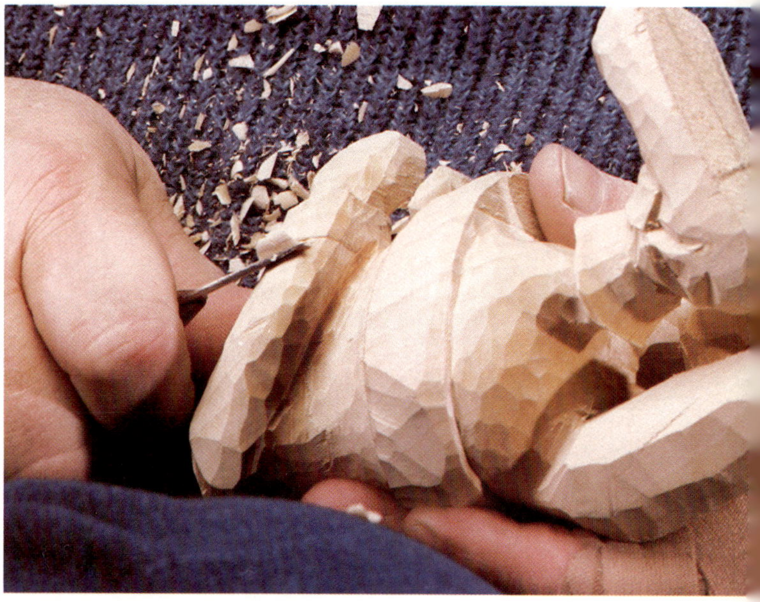

and cut back to it from the sleeve.

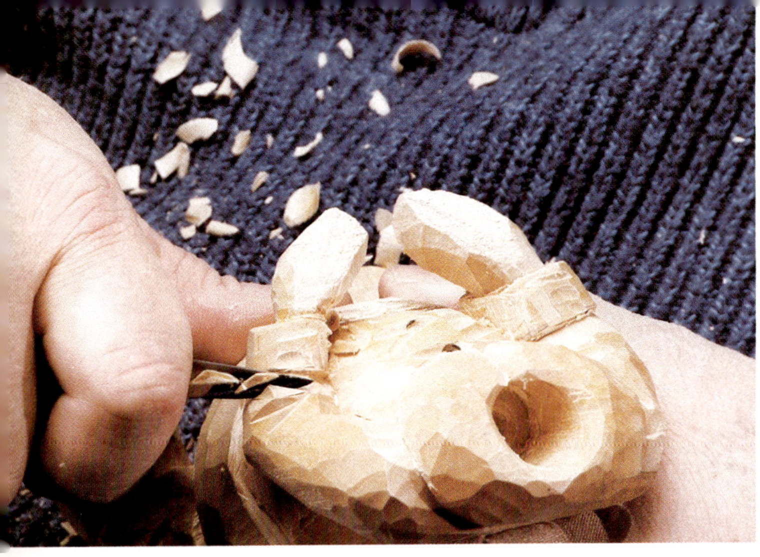

Add folds to the crook of the arm, using the same method you did on the boot.

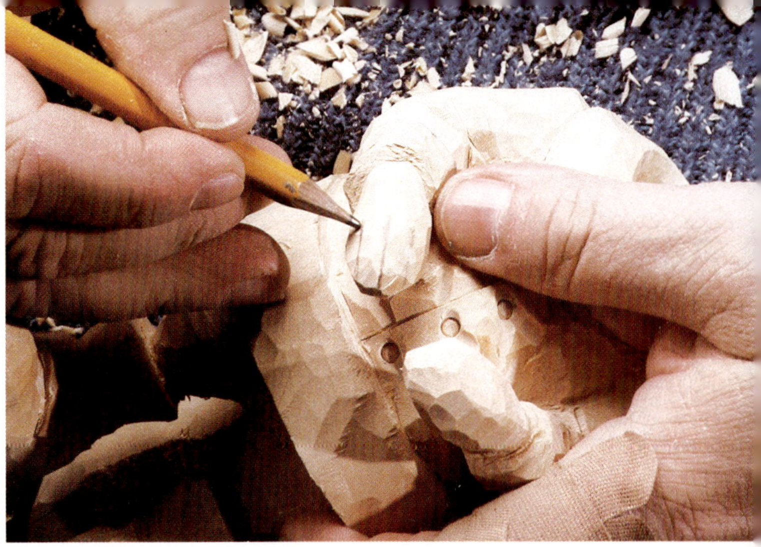

Mark the center finger line first and then one on either side. This gives you the four fingers you want.

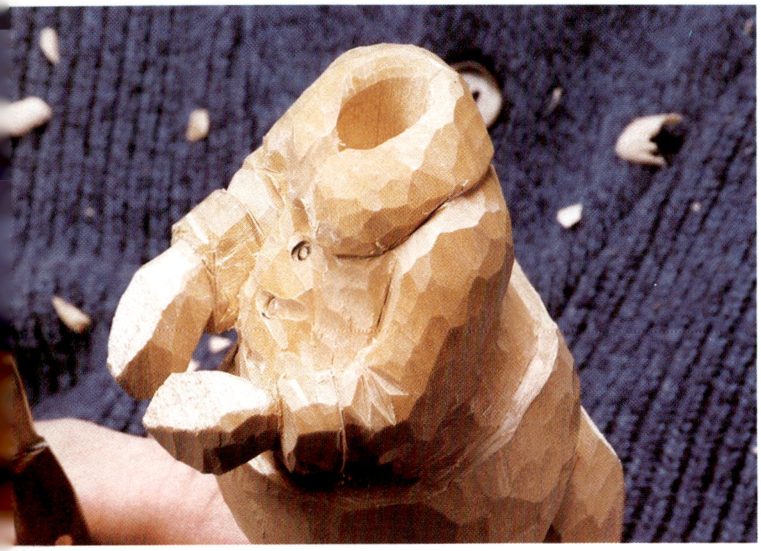

Progress so far.

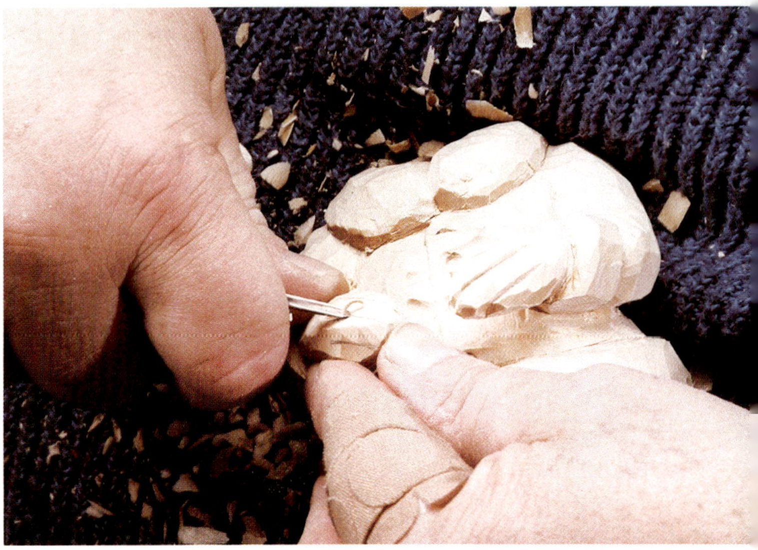

Holding the paw between your fingers for support, and using a sharp v-tool or veiner (whichever works best), run it along the lines to create the space between the fingers. On the tip of the fingers use a knife.

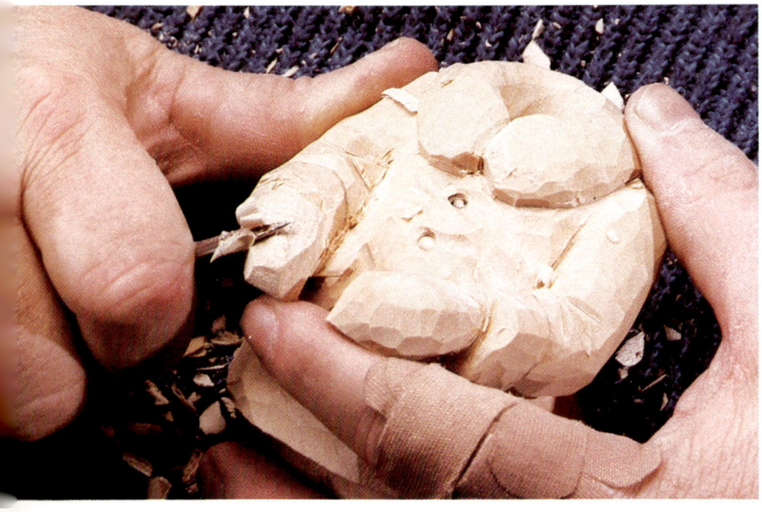

Moving to the hands, I've decided to make them animal paws, although I could just as well have had mittens or human-like hands. Begin by knocking off the corners and rounding off the paw. The hands are cross-grained so you must be careful or they will snap off.

Mark the notches for the heels on all sides. The notch does not need to go across the sole, and indeed it gives you a better gluing surface if it does not. Cut a stop in front of the heel and back to it from the sole.

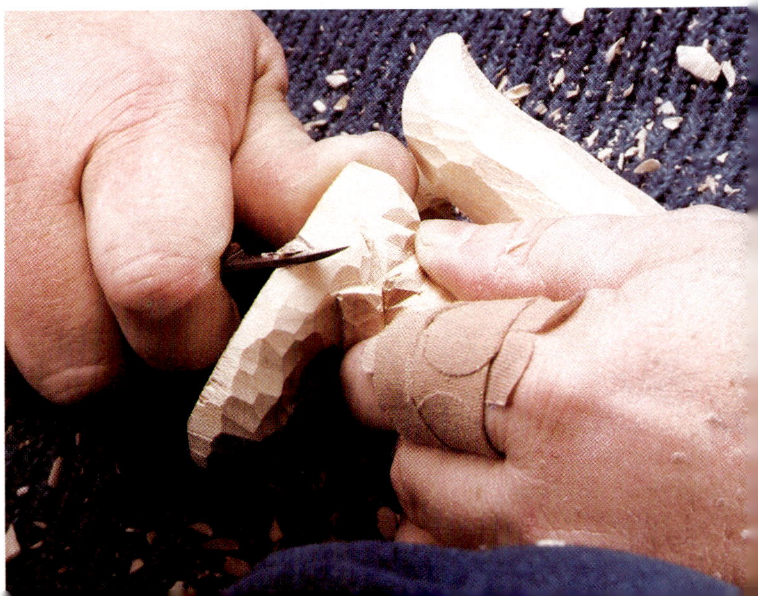

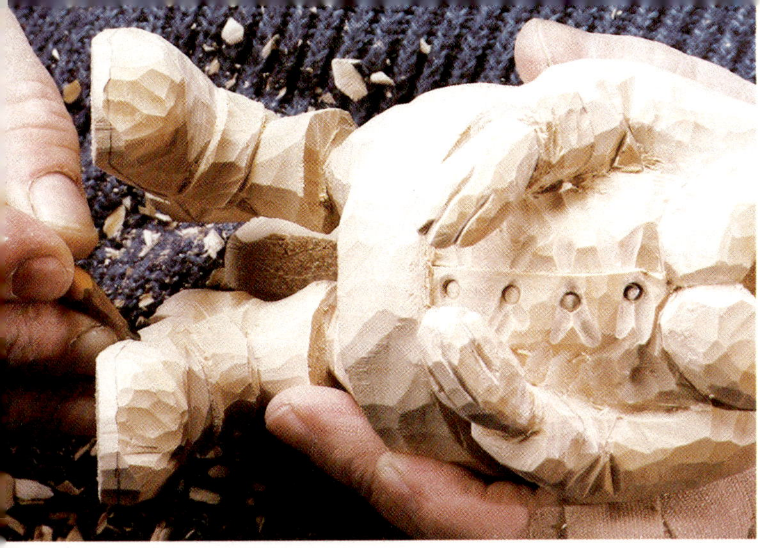

Draw in the line of the sole..

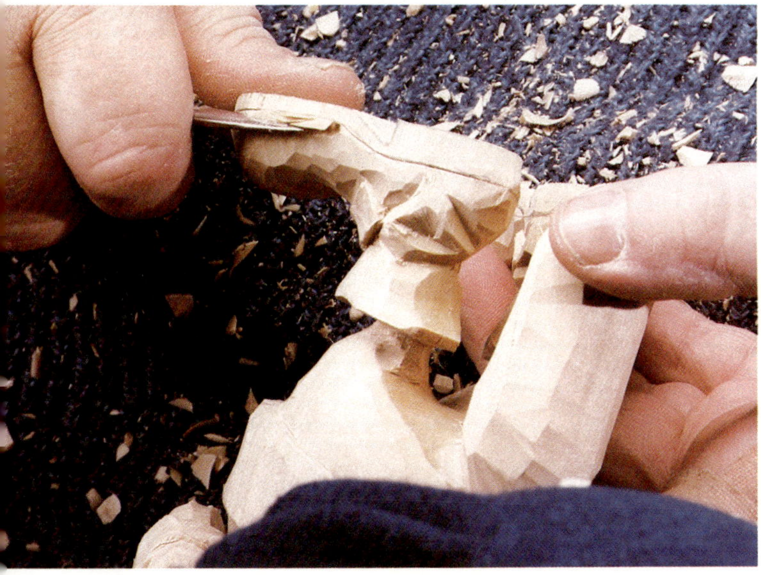

Make a straight-in stop all along that line using a turned down blade. Cut back to the line from the shoe using a turned up blade.

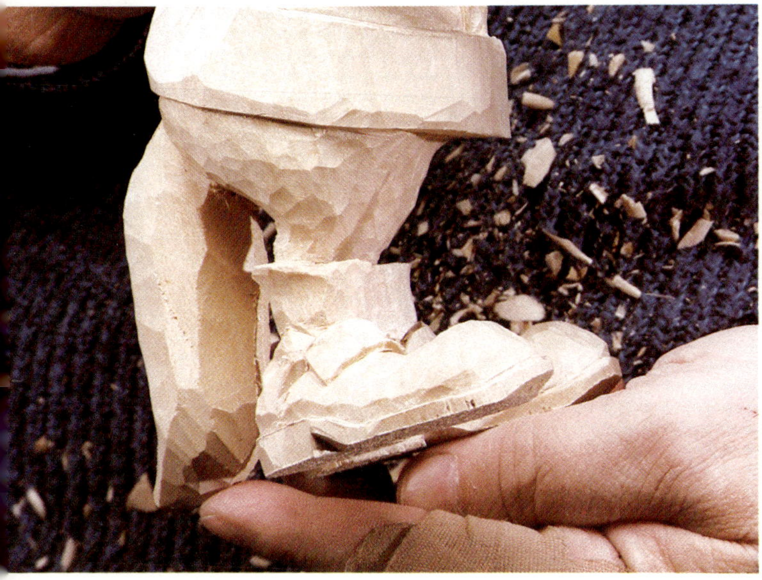

The finished feet.

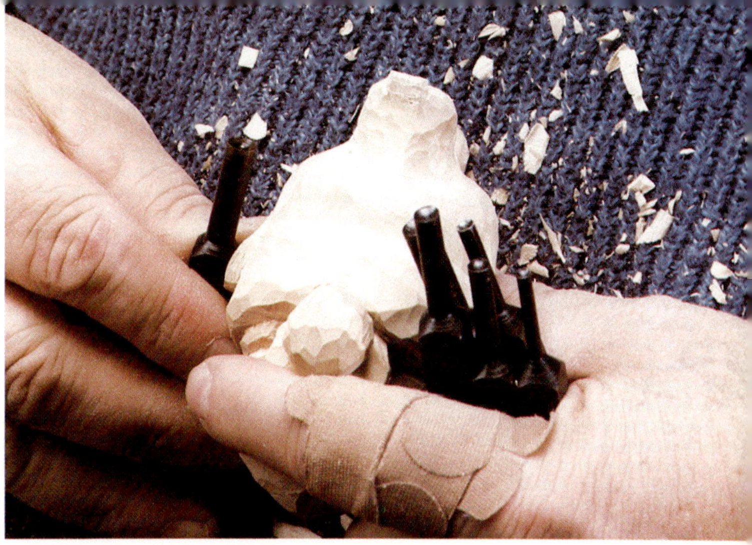

Moving back to the head, it is time to do the eyes. Choose the right size eyepunch for the eye.

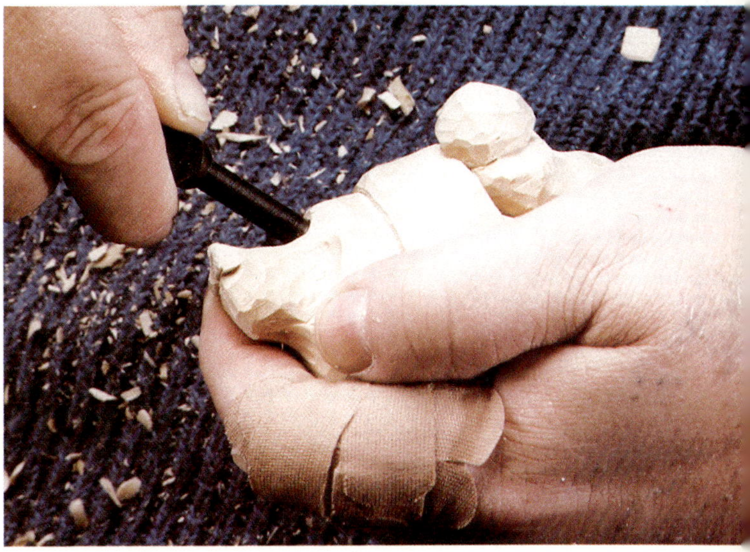

Starting with the right eye, position the eyepunch and push and turn. Then line up the left eye and do the same thing.

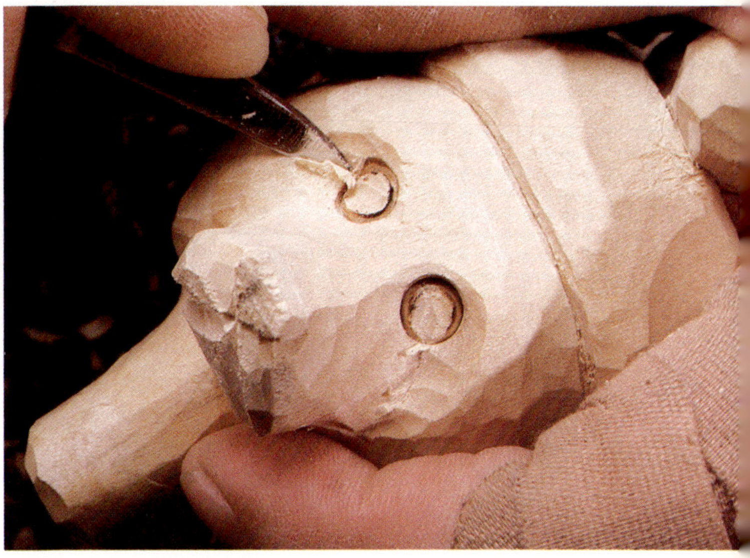

At the corners of the eye three cuts define its shape. First cut at an angle along the line of the upper eyelid.

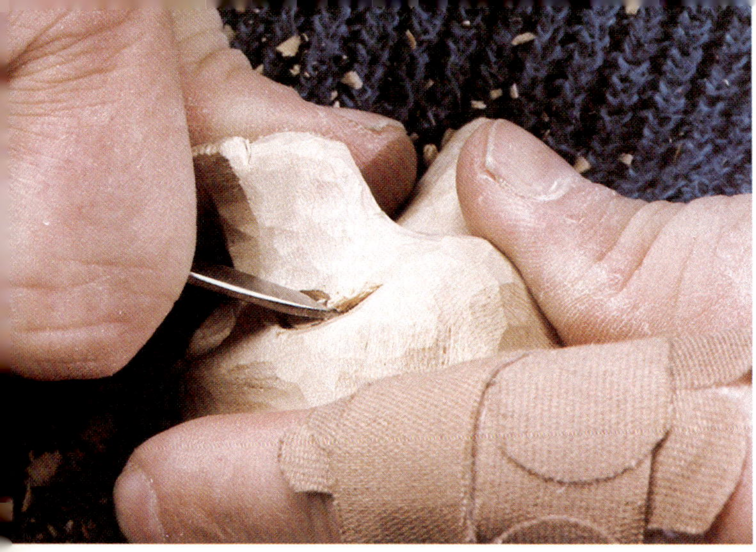

Next situate your blade so it is flat and follows the contour of the eye ball.

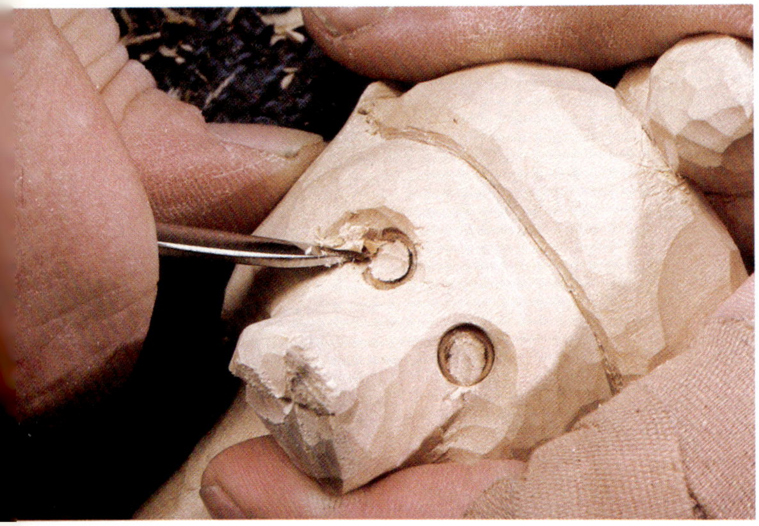

Finally cut in on the line of the bottom eyelid. A triangle of wood should pop out and the corner of the eye should be nicely defined. Repeat in miniature on the inside corners of the eyes.

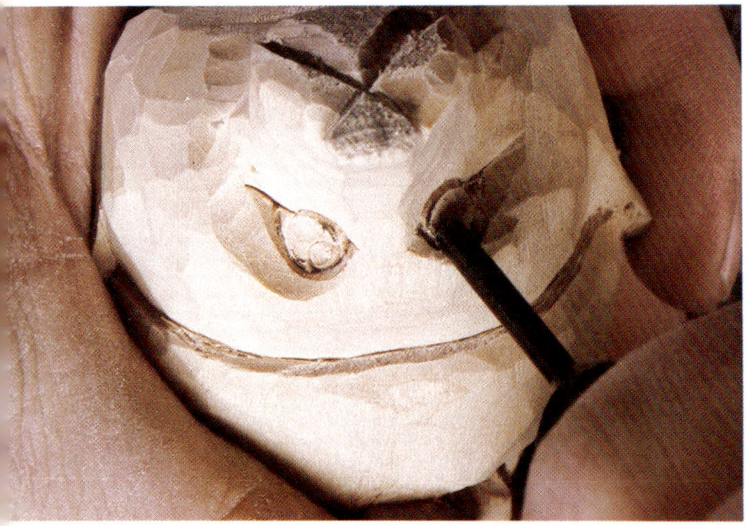

Use a smaller eyepunch to create the irises of the eyes. Having them near the top of the pupil usually gives a nice effect.

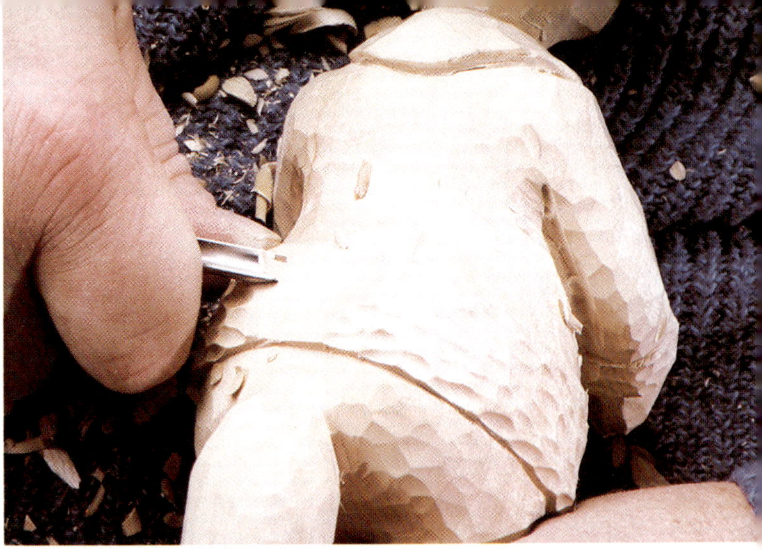

With the head in place go all over the figure, cleaning up the carving and correcting mistakes. On the fur trim at the neck, arms, and waist, we use the gouge to make little cupped cuts that give the look of fur.

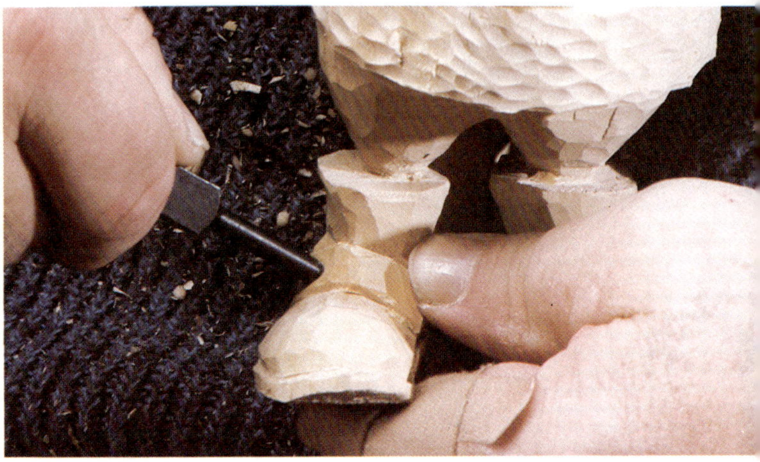

As a final touch, I think I'll add buttons to the strap of the boots. Again, use the eyepunch and the twist and push method.

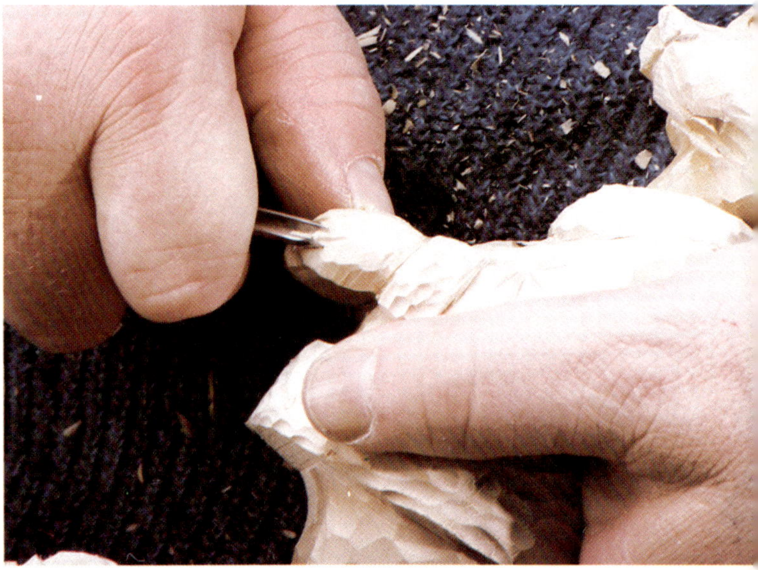

I also need to define the "fingers" more by using a gouge between the knuckles.

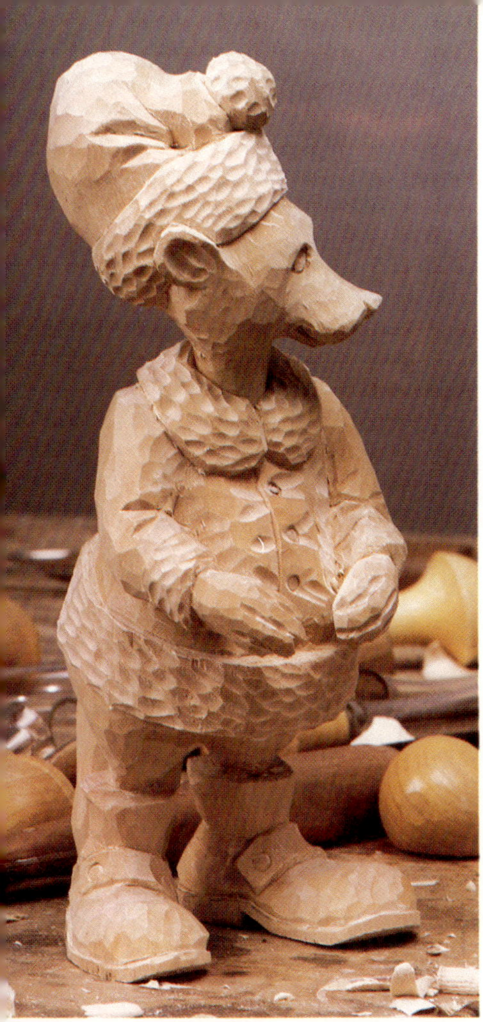
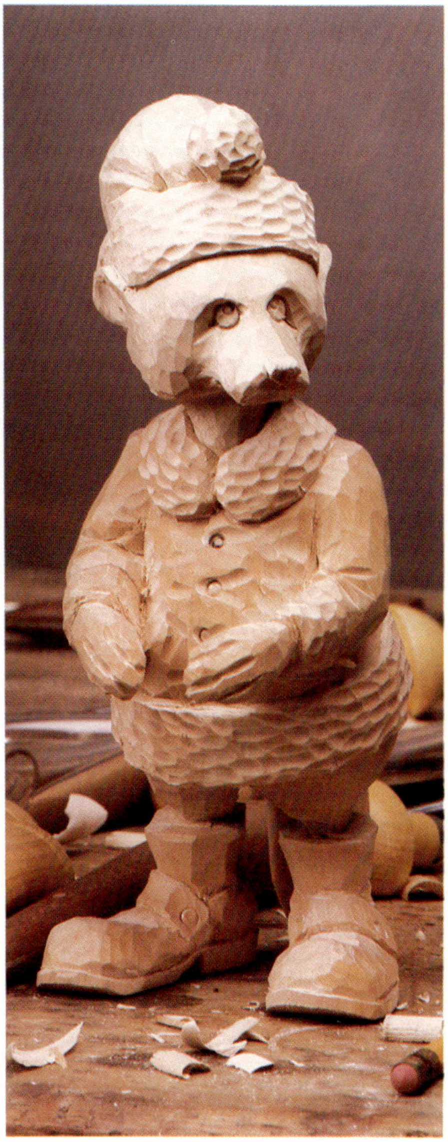
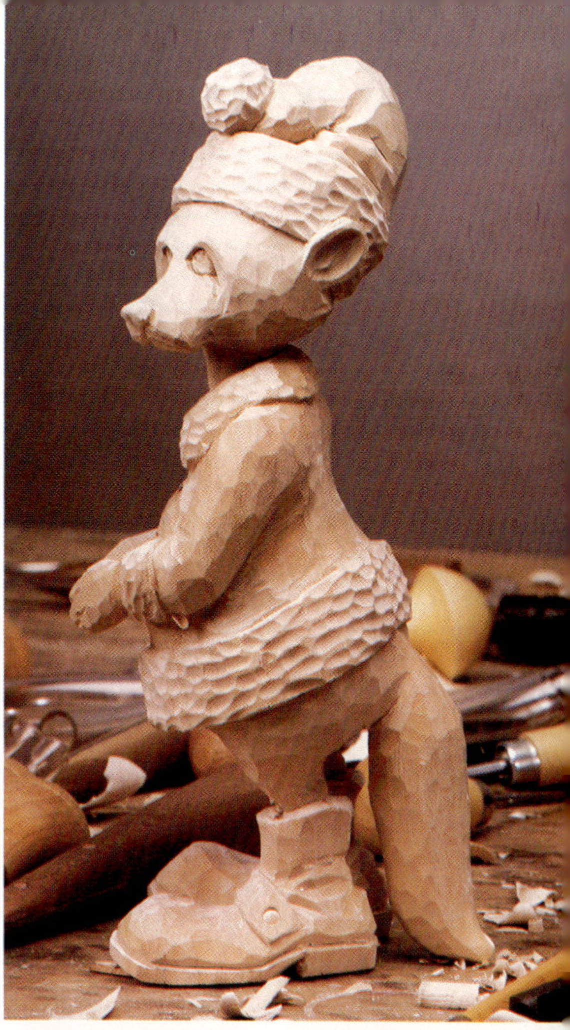
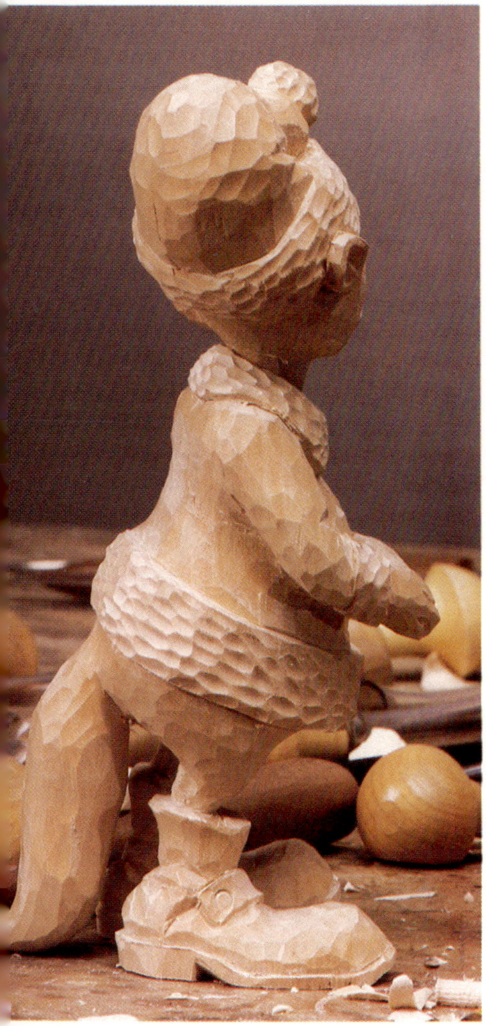
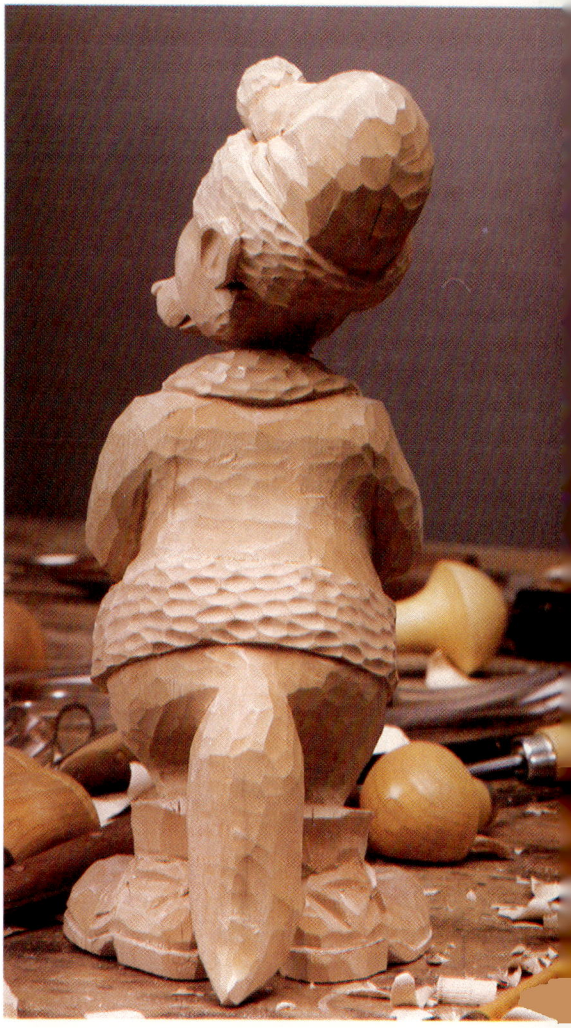

The finished carving

Painting the Raccoon

I use Winsor and Newton Alkyd tube paints for wood carving. These are thinned with pure turpentine to a consistency that is soaked into the carving, giving subtle colors. What I look for is a watery mixture, almost like a wash. In this way the turpentine will carry the pigment into the wood, giving the stained look I like. It has always been my theory that if you are going to cover the wood, why use wood in the first place. It should be noted that with white, the concentration of pigment should be a little stronger.

I mix my paints in glass juice bottles, putting in a bit of paint and adding turpentine. I don't use exact measurements. Instead I use trial and error, adding a bit of paint or a bit of turpentine until I get the thickness I want.

The juice bottles are handy for holding your paints. They are reclosable, easy to shake, and have the added advantage of leaving a concentrated amount of color on the inside of the lid and the sides of the bottle which can be used when more intense color is needed.

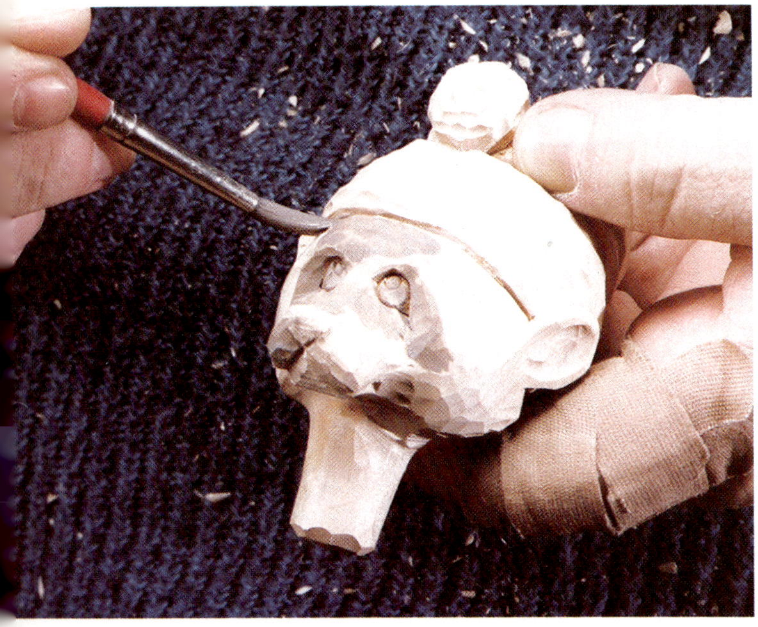

I begin the painting with an undercoat on the raccoon's fur...the face, hands, legs and tail. The gray paint is the slag from my rinse bottle with the turpentine poured off. This is good recycling and saves you from mixing black and white.

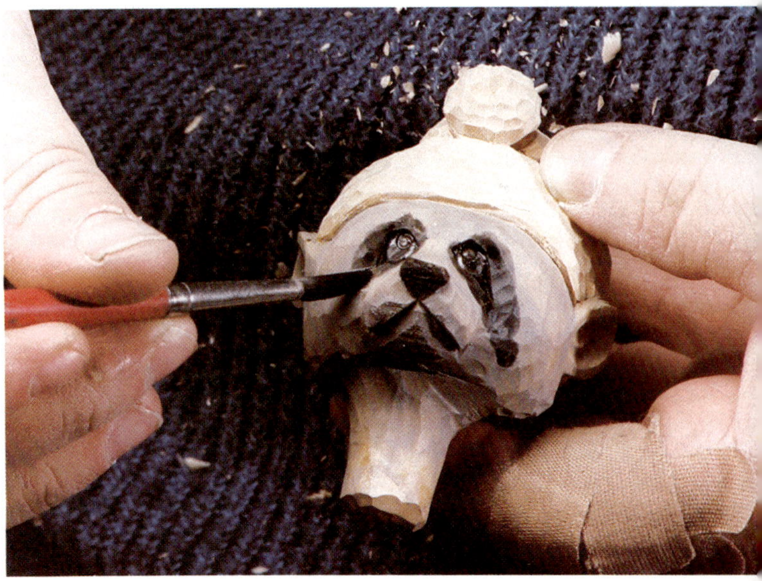

As you are painting be sure to keep your hands clean. Next we move to black to the nose and the eyes. The nose is the only area of the face that I did not undercoat with gray. This is to get a deeper black.

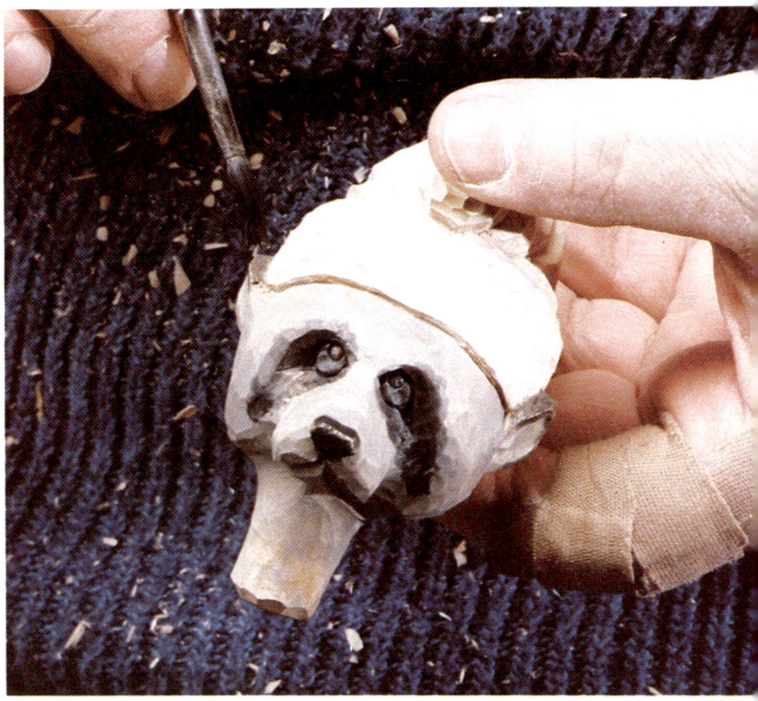

Silhouette the ears with a touch of black. As the paint dries you can add another coat, which helps you get a shading effect.

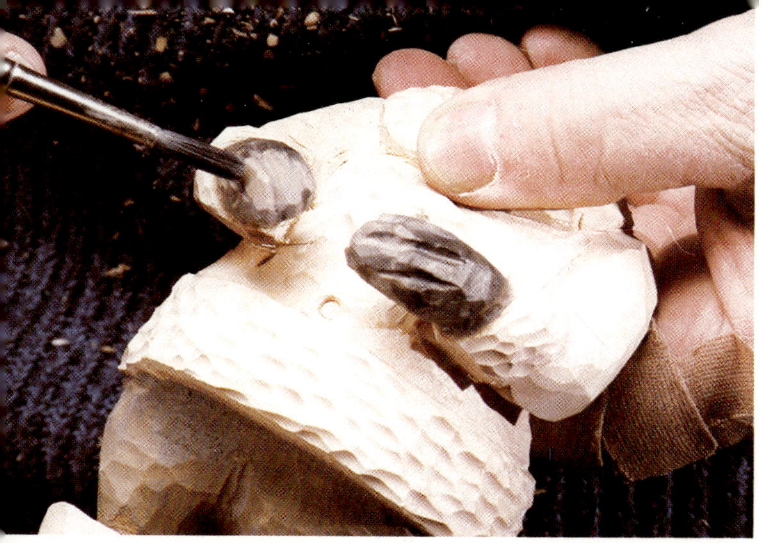

Using a dry brush, go over the hands, letting the gray show through more.

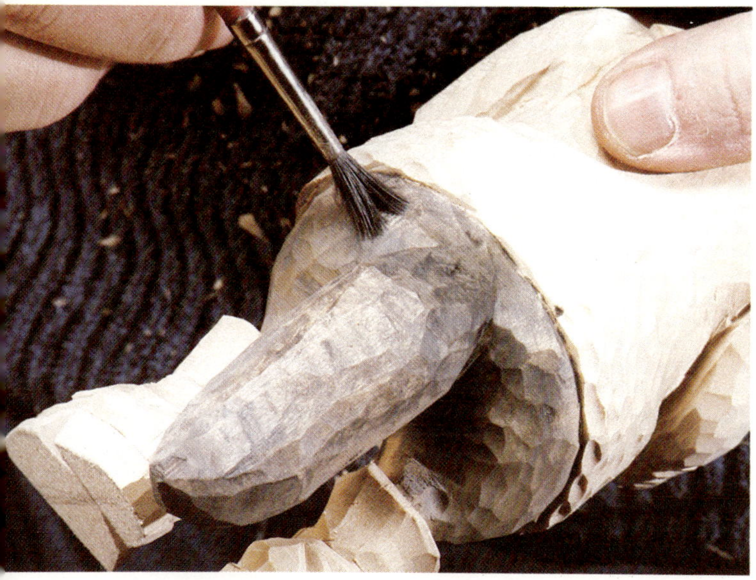

Do the same thing on the tail to highlight it before you add the black rings.

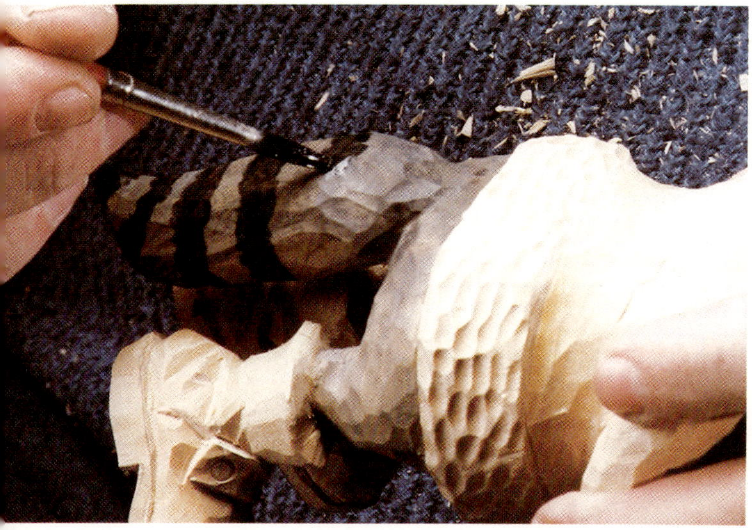

To do the rings, I need an intense black, so I pour the liquid off the top of the cap and use the residue. Start at the tip.

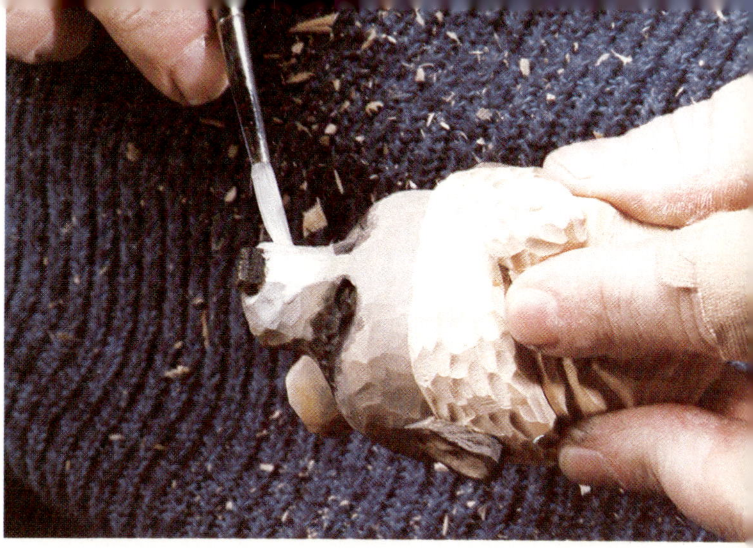

Add white to the muzzle to lighten it up. Apply it to the ridge, and dry brush it around so that it blends from almost white in the front to gray in the back.

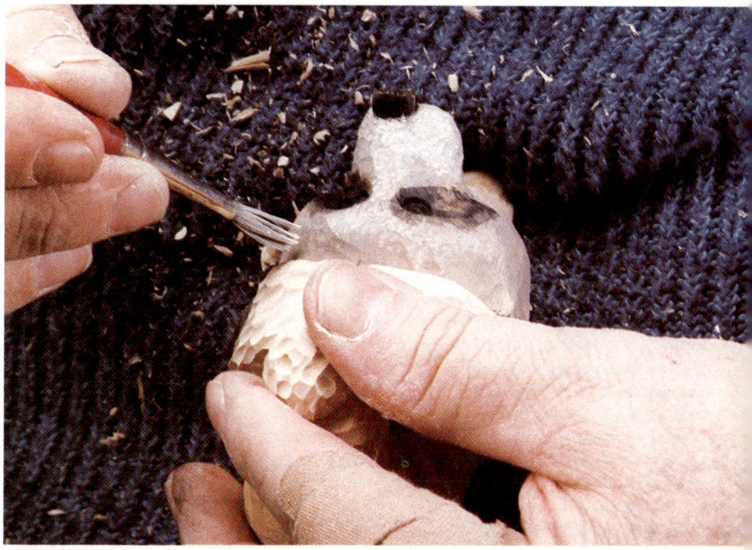

Carry the white up the forehead and in the ears.

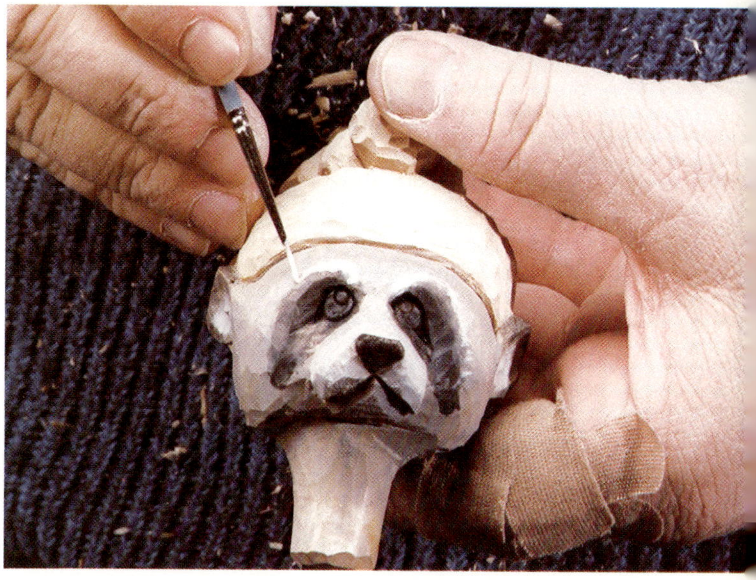

Use a finer brush to add some details to the face. Add intense white with small dabs in a line above the eye.

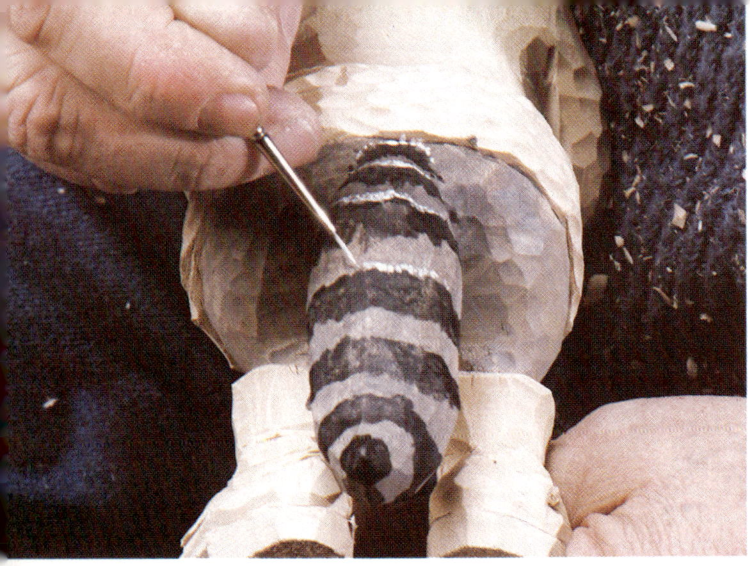

Continue the white highlights on the tail, using the same method.

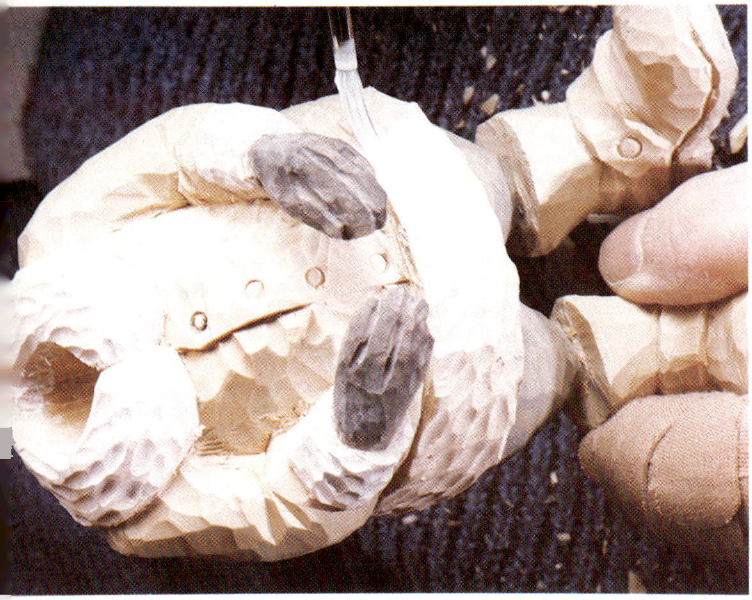

While the white is out, do the trim on the hat and coat.

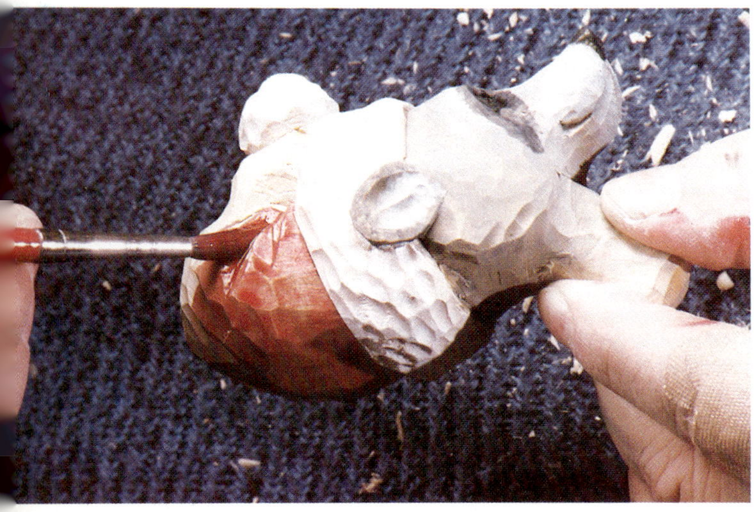

The red is Alizarin Crimson. Start around the edges where the red meets the white, and work your way in. Follow the same process on the cap and the coat.

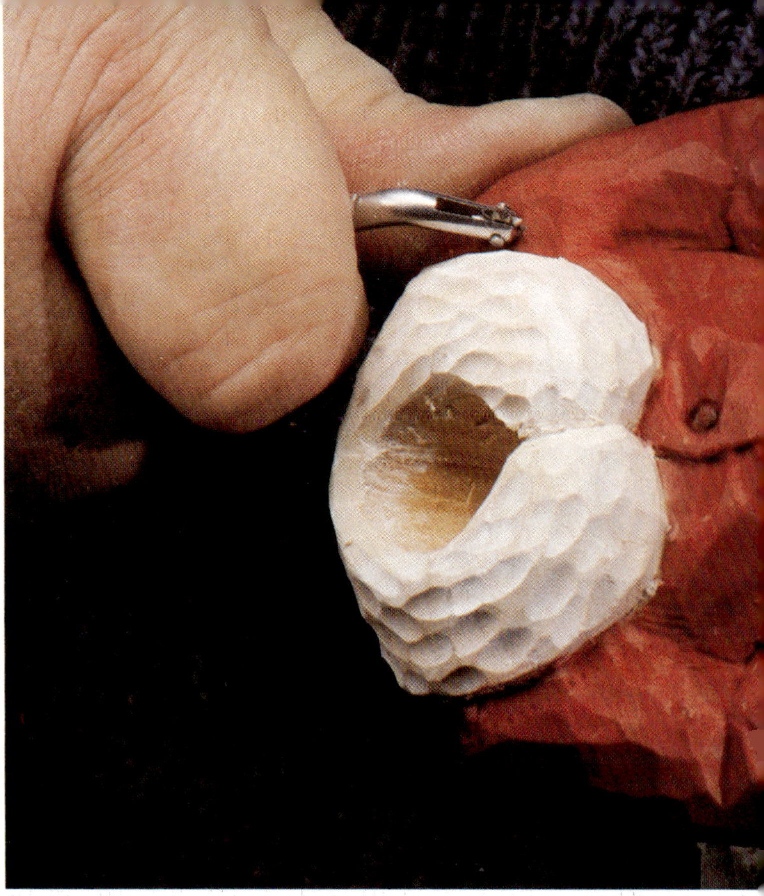

Now that the coat is painted, I remembered what I forgot!! The coat needs stitch marks. Fortunately, it is not too late. I use a tracing wheel. Holding the painted figure in paper towel, I go over the shoulder and down the front.

Take a little more red paint and go over the newly marked stitches to make them show up more clearly.

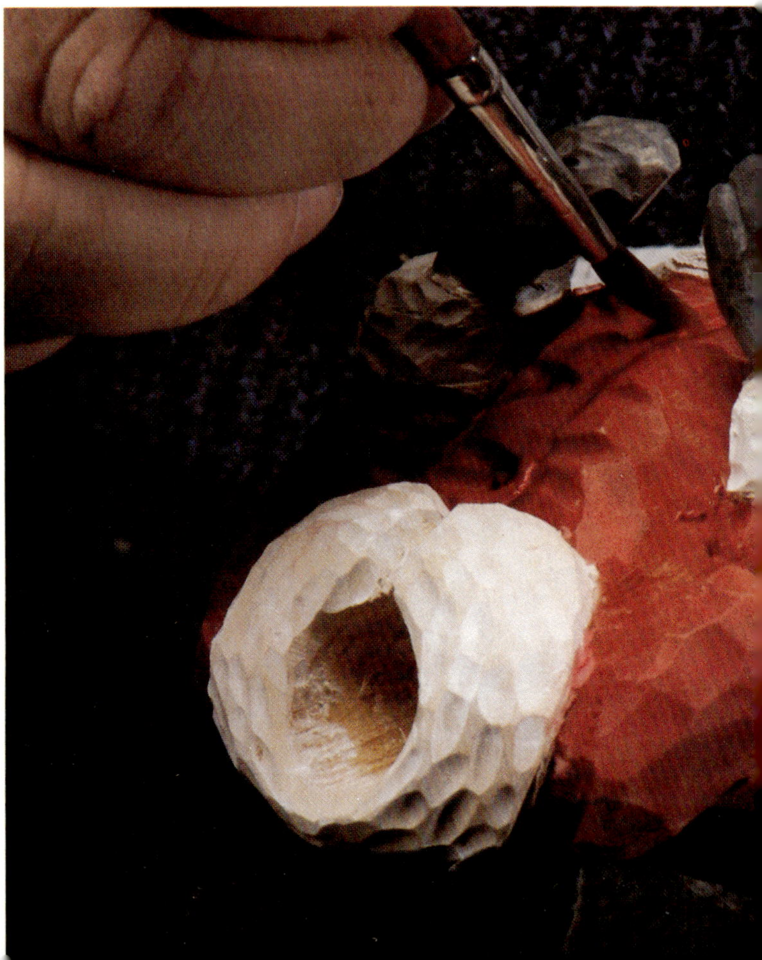

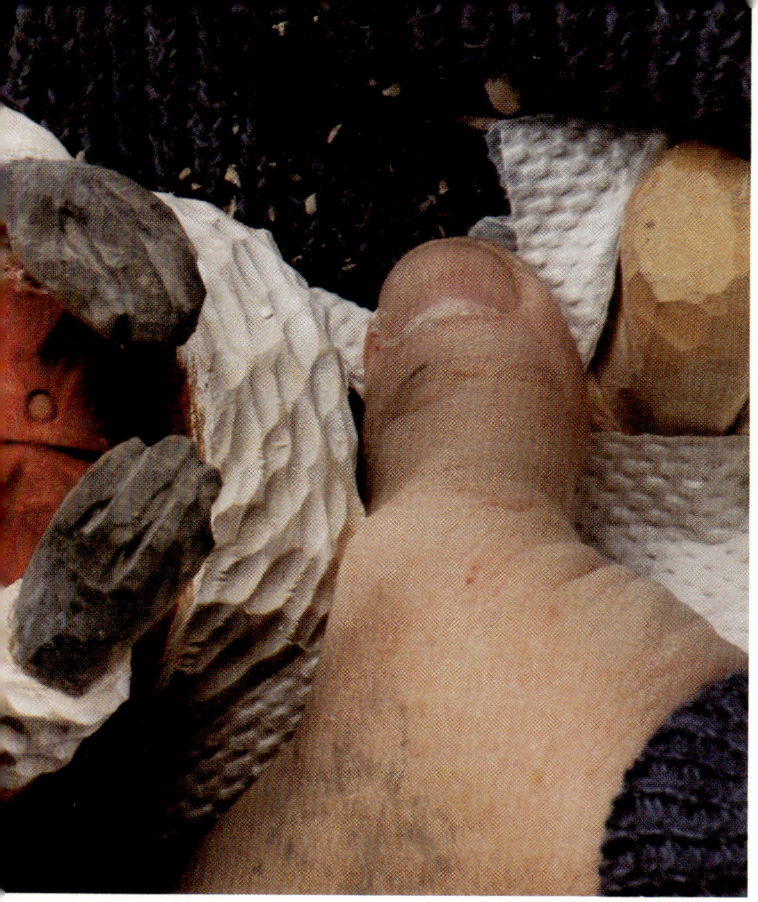

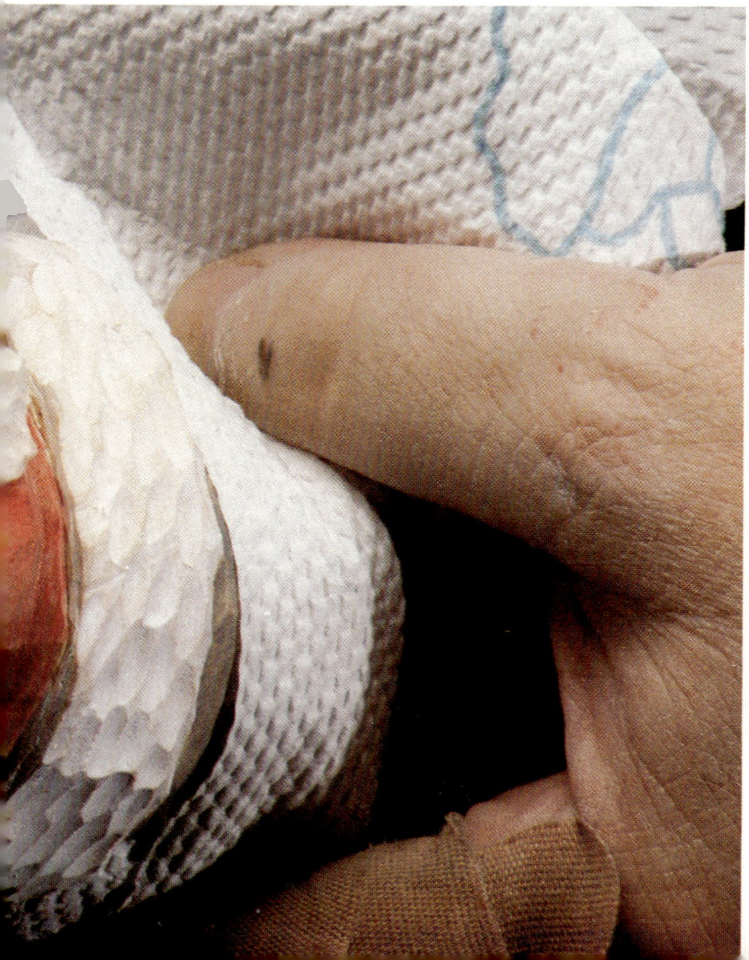

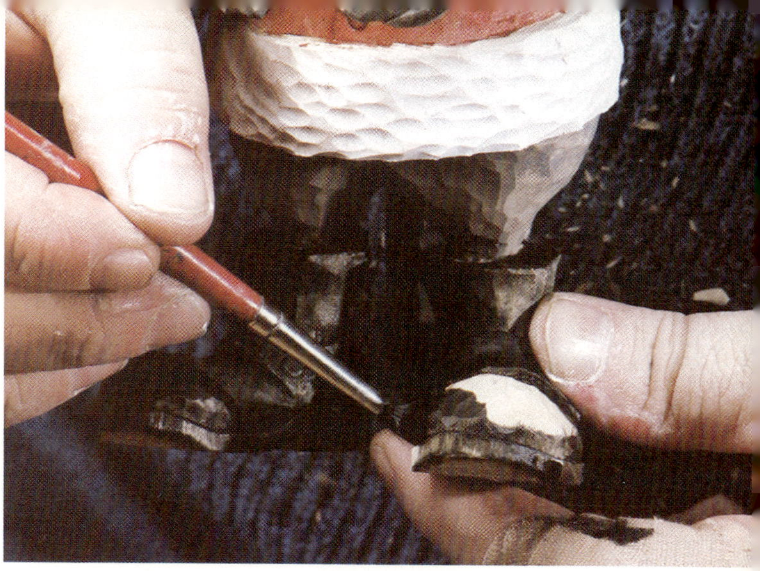

Return to the black to paint the boots.

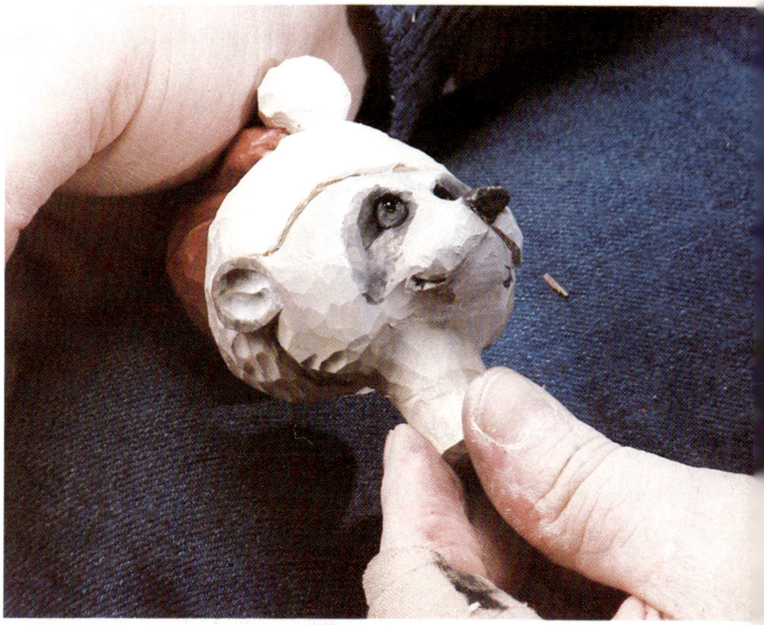

Add some intense black to the pupil of the eye...

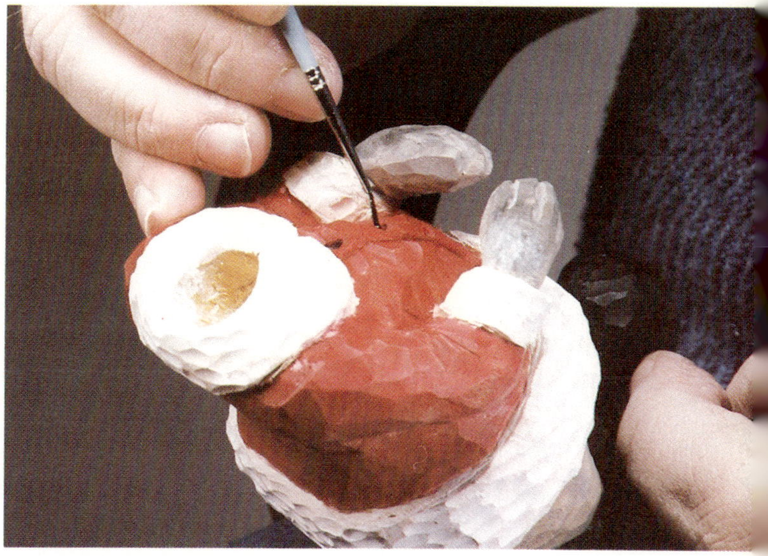

and to the buttons.

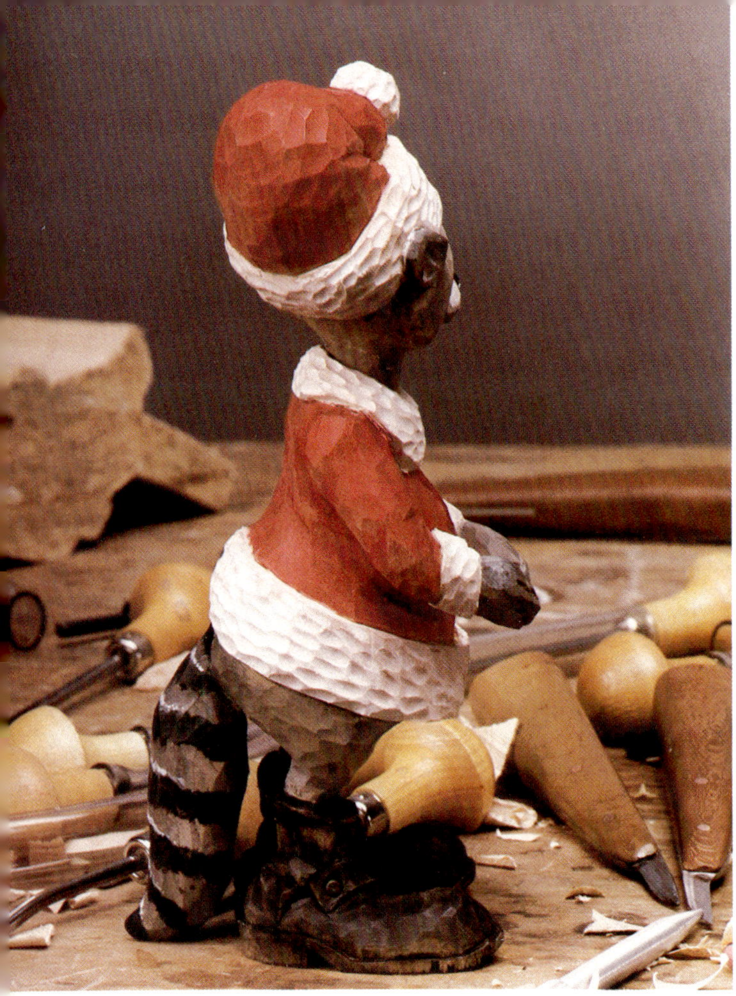

The painted raccoon Santimal.

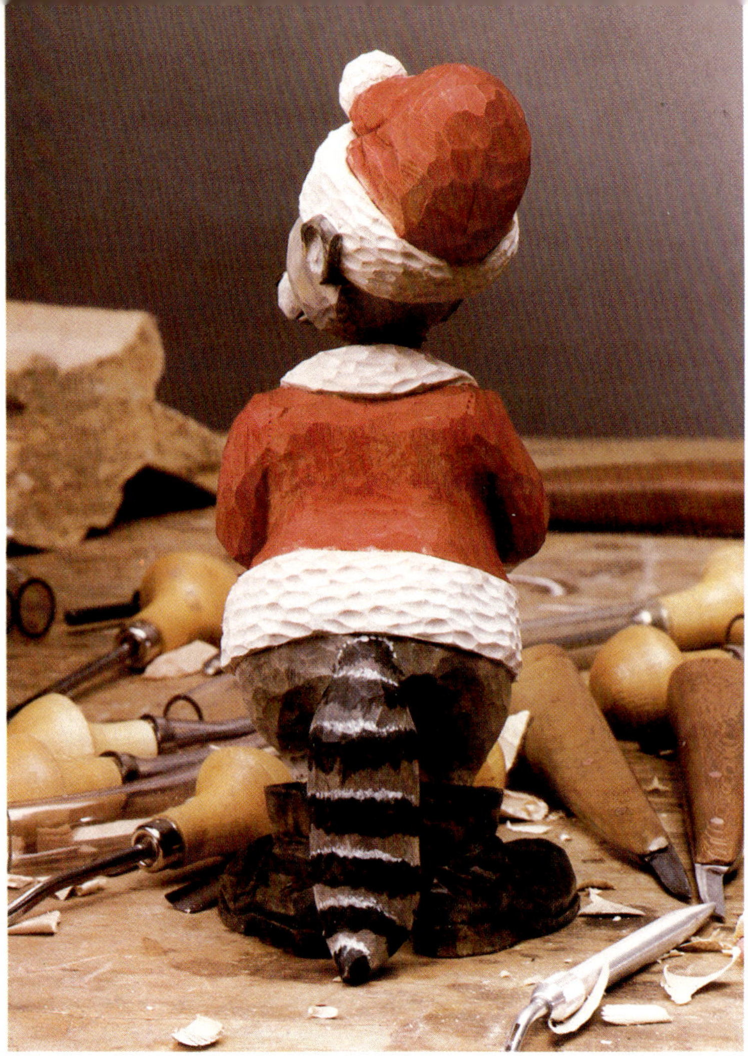

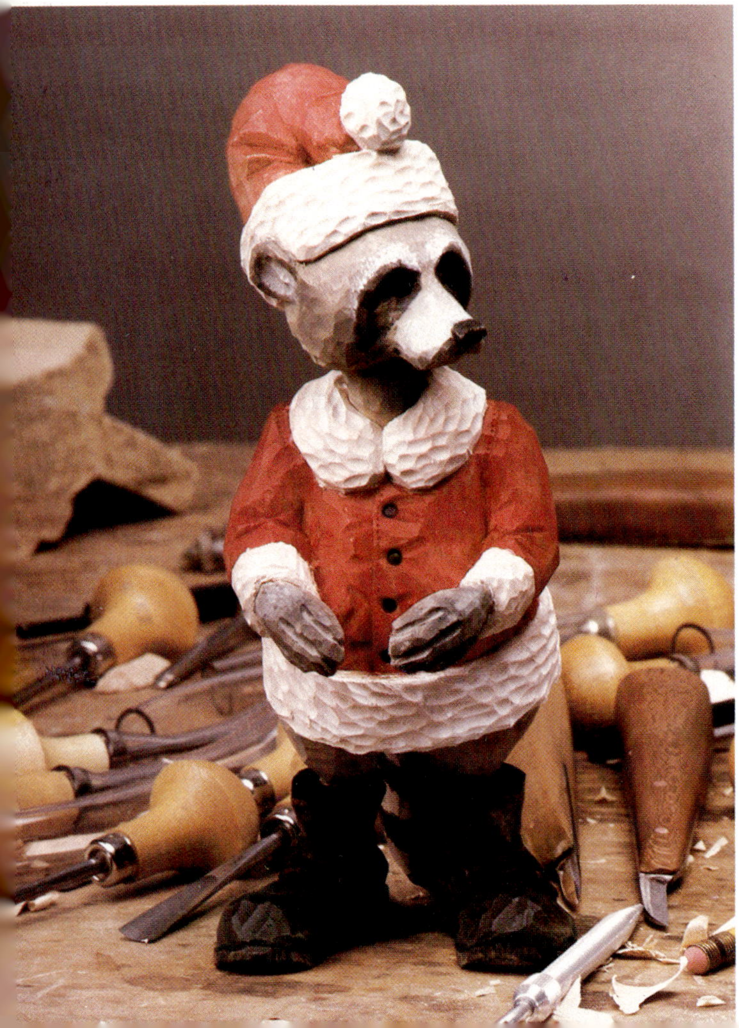

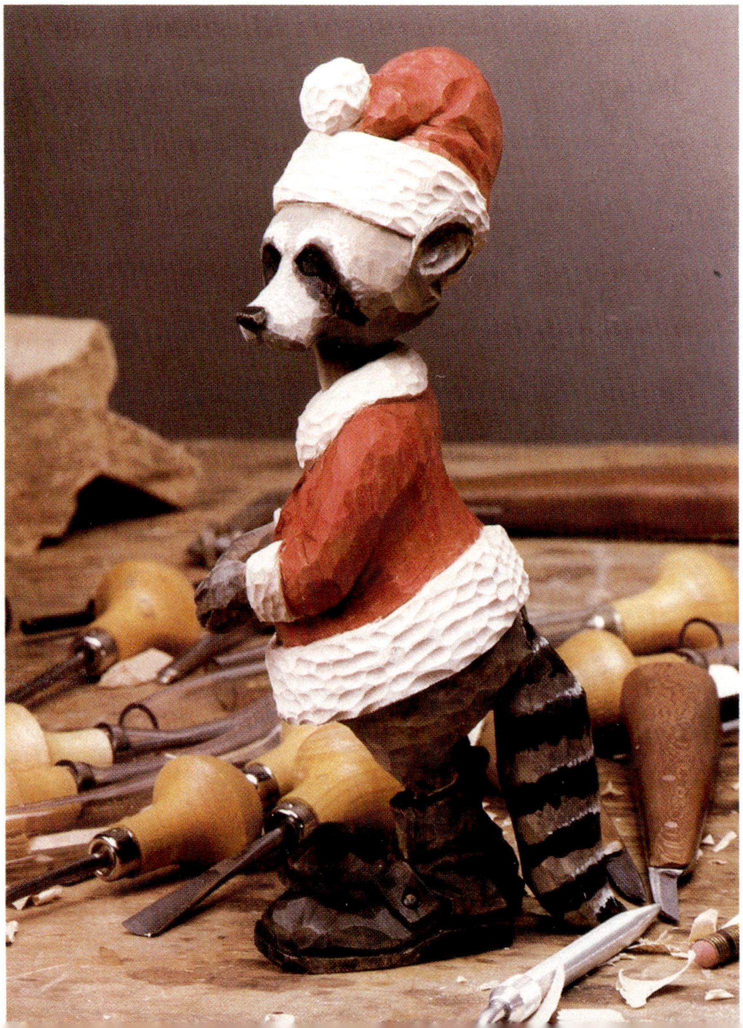

Santimal Gallery with Patterns

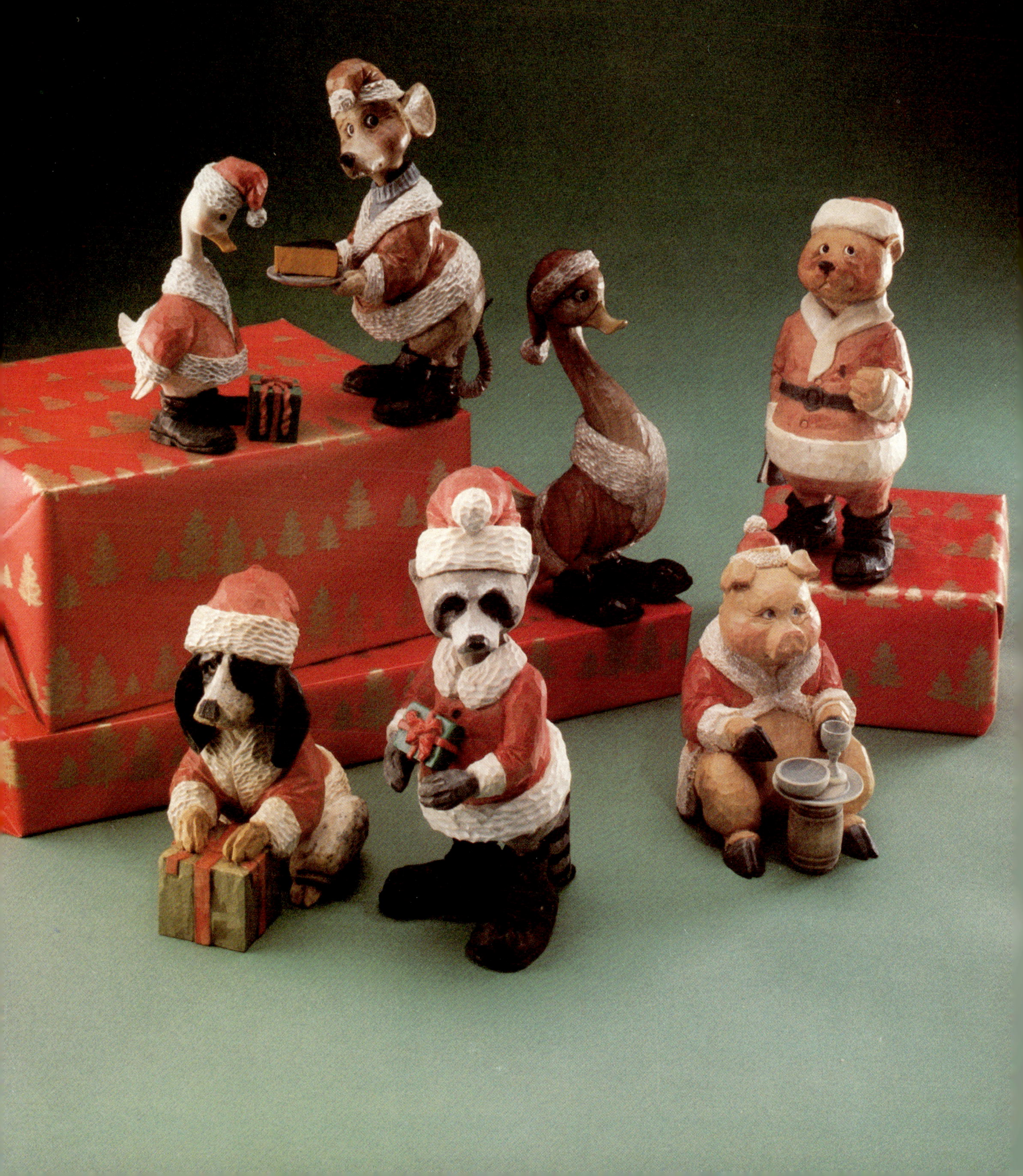

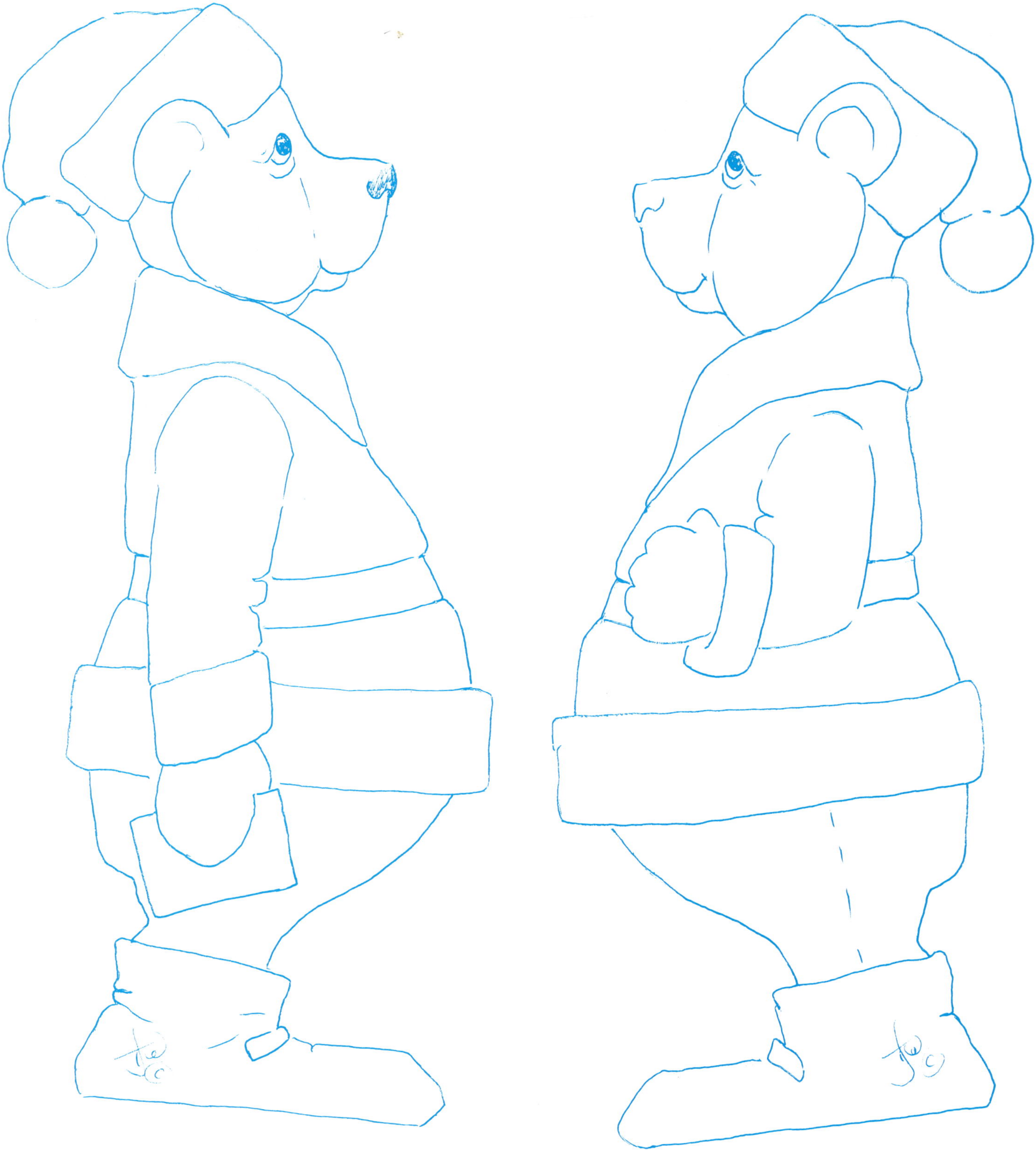

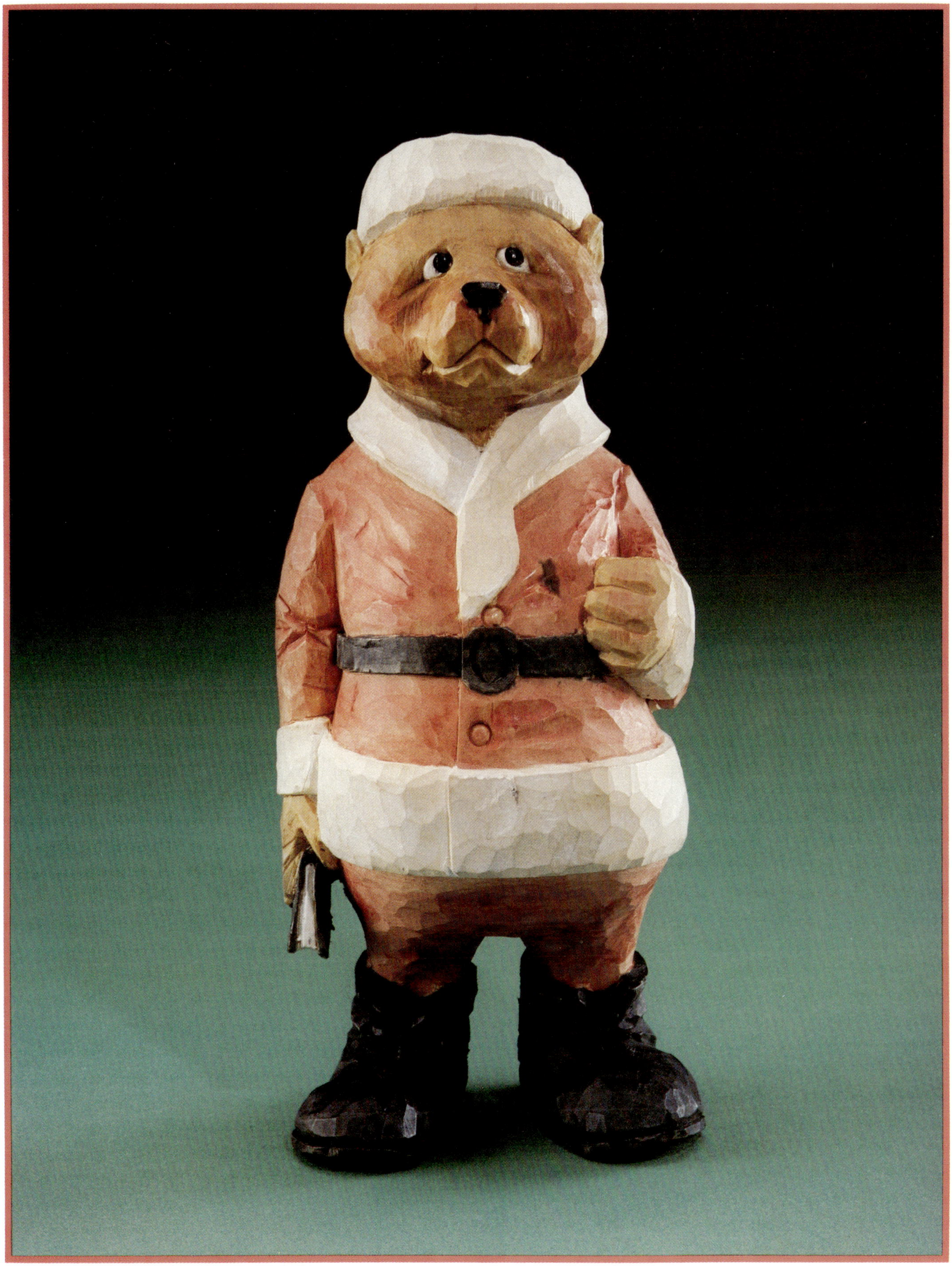

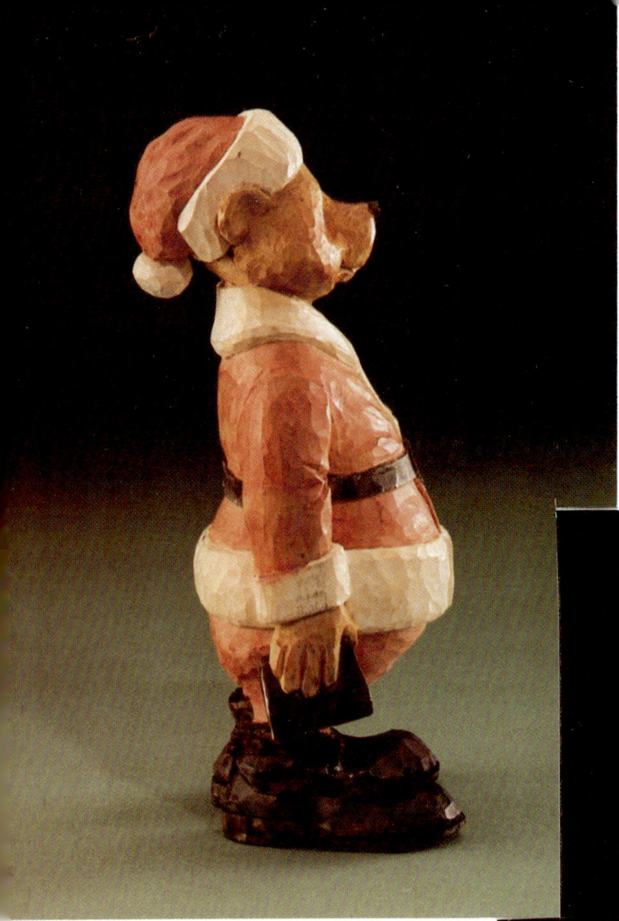

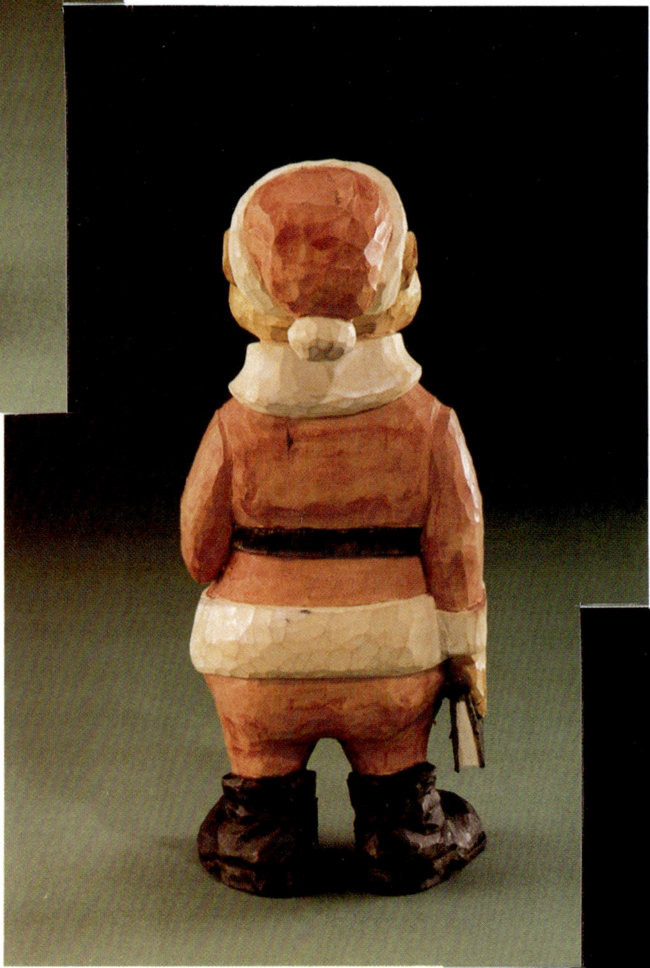

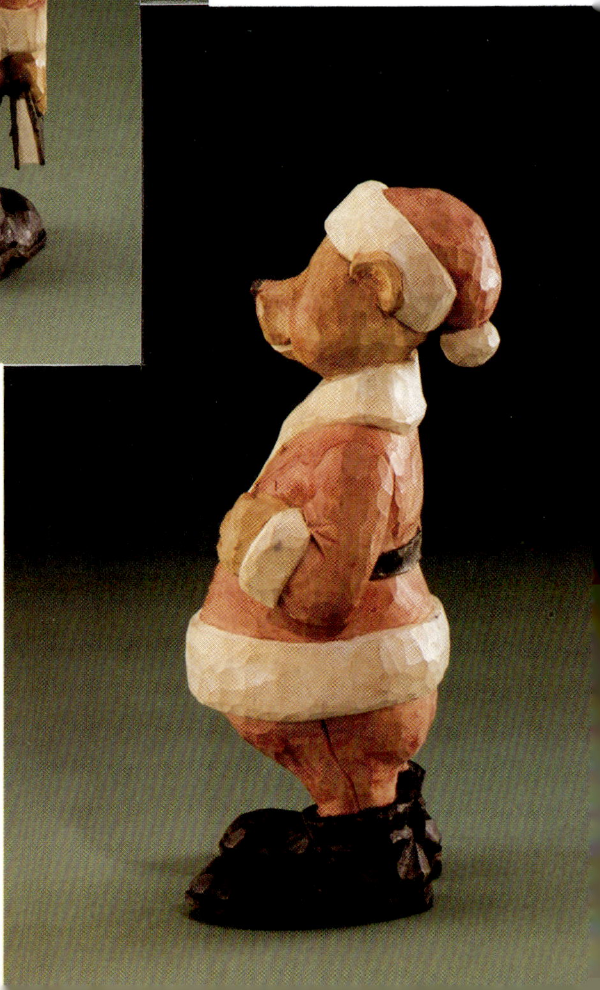

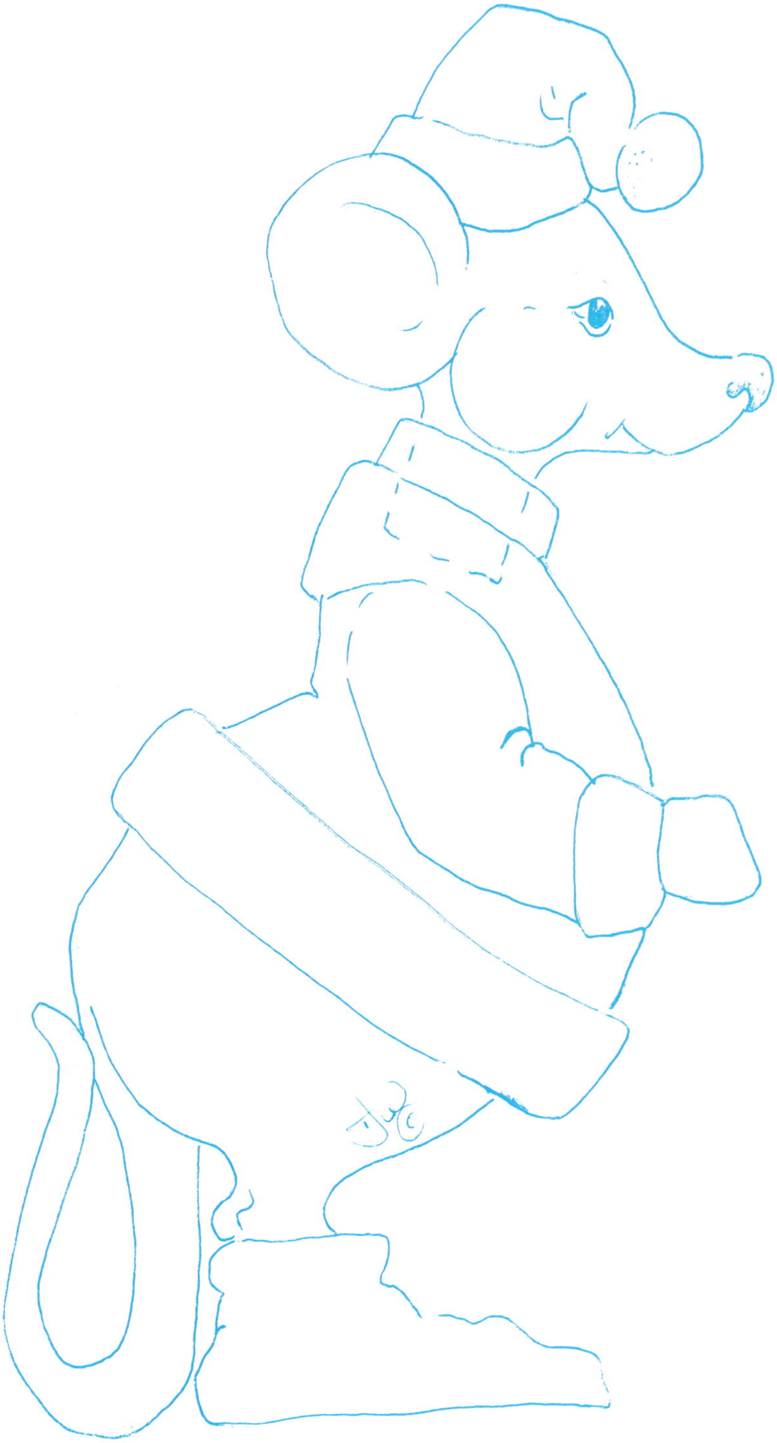

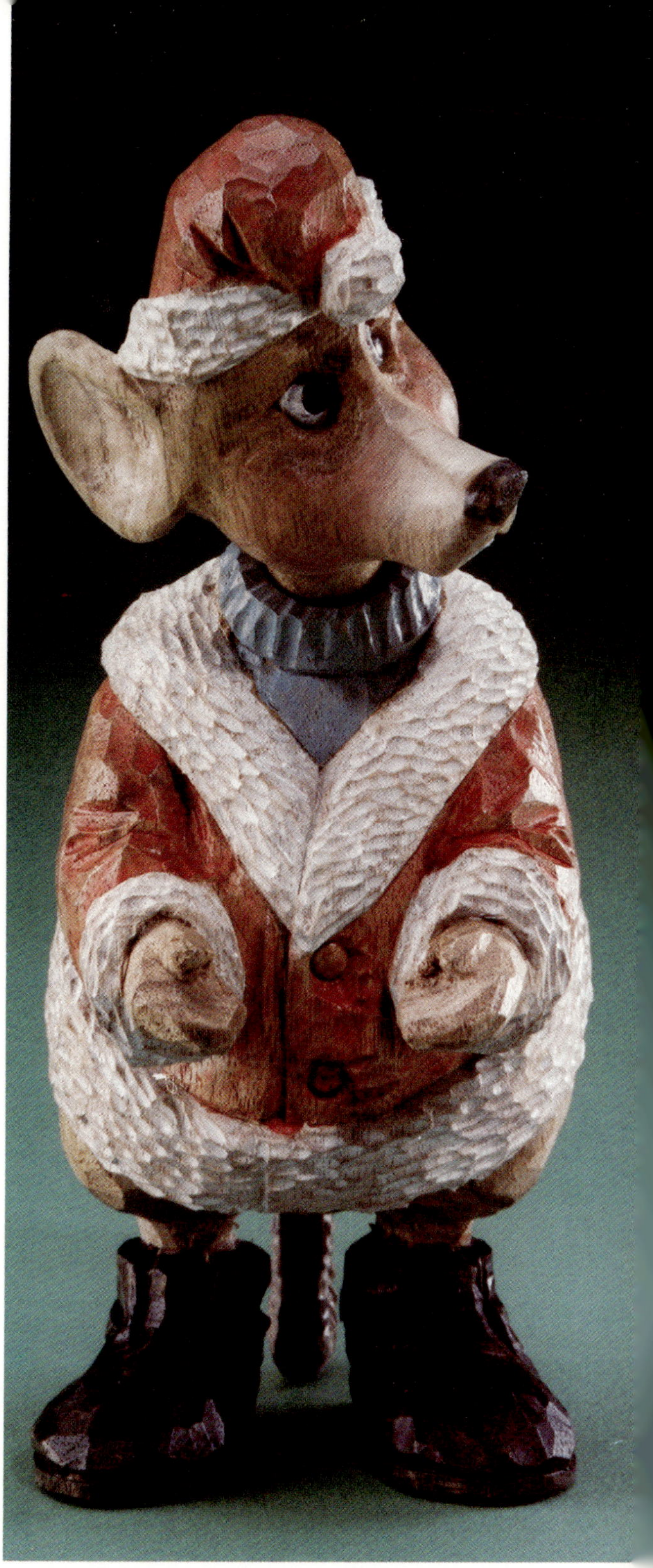

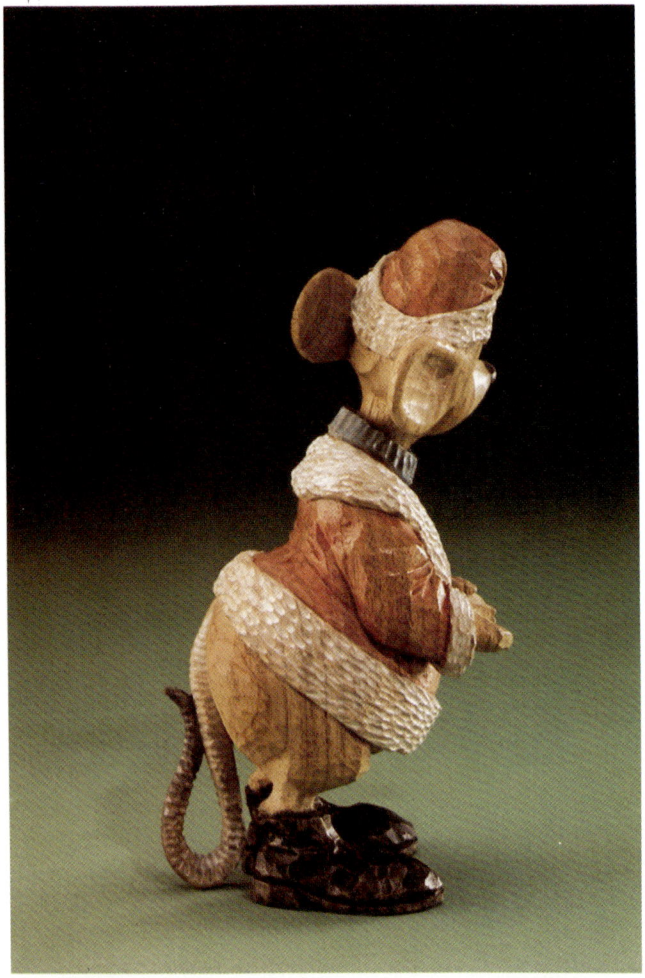

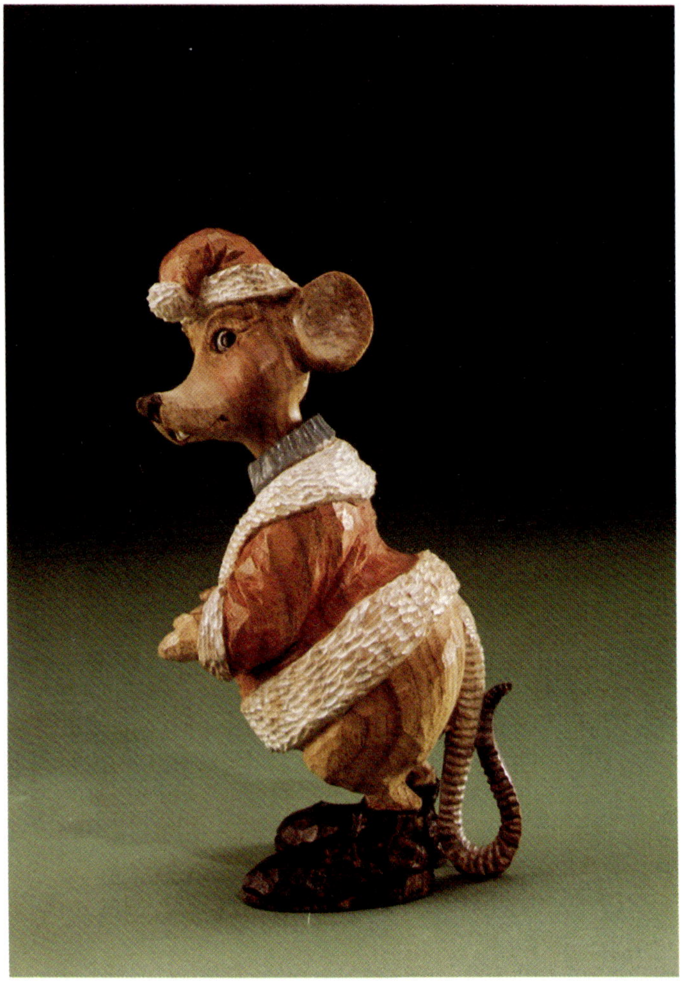

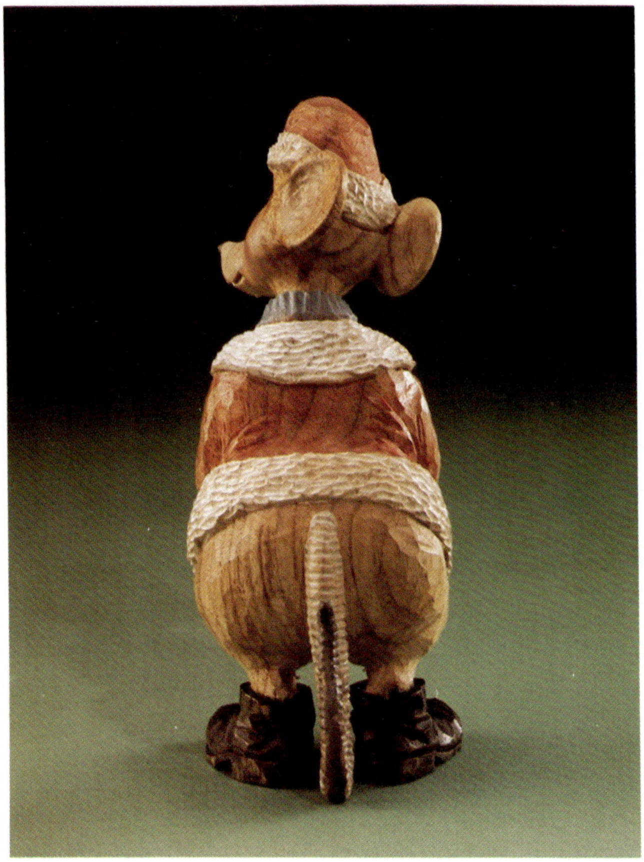

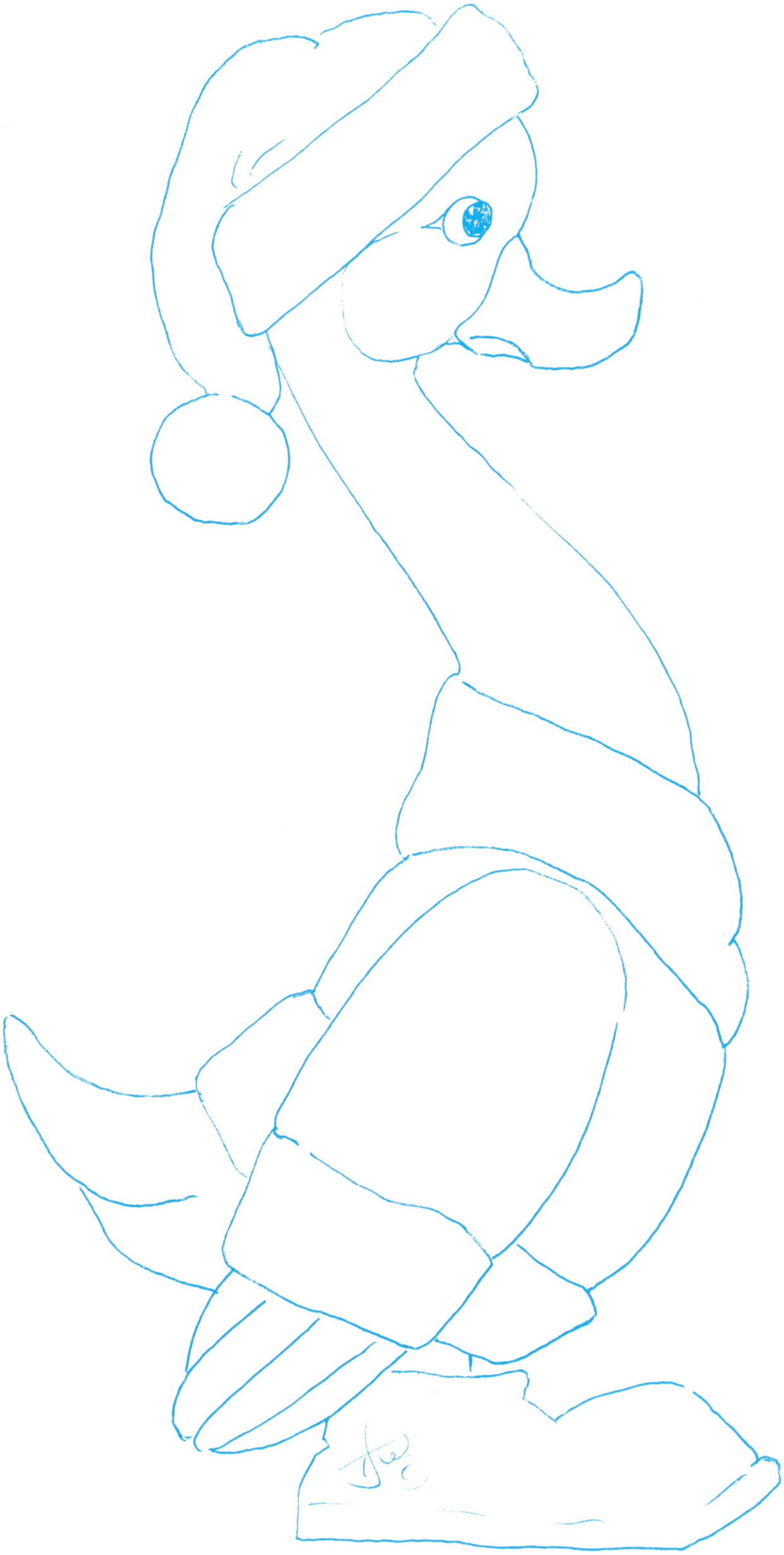

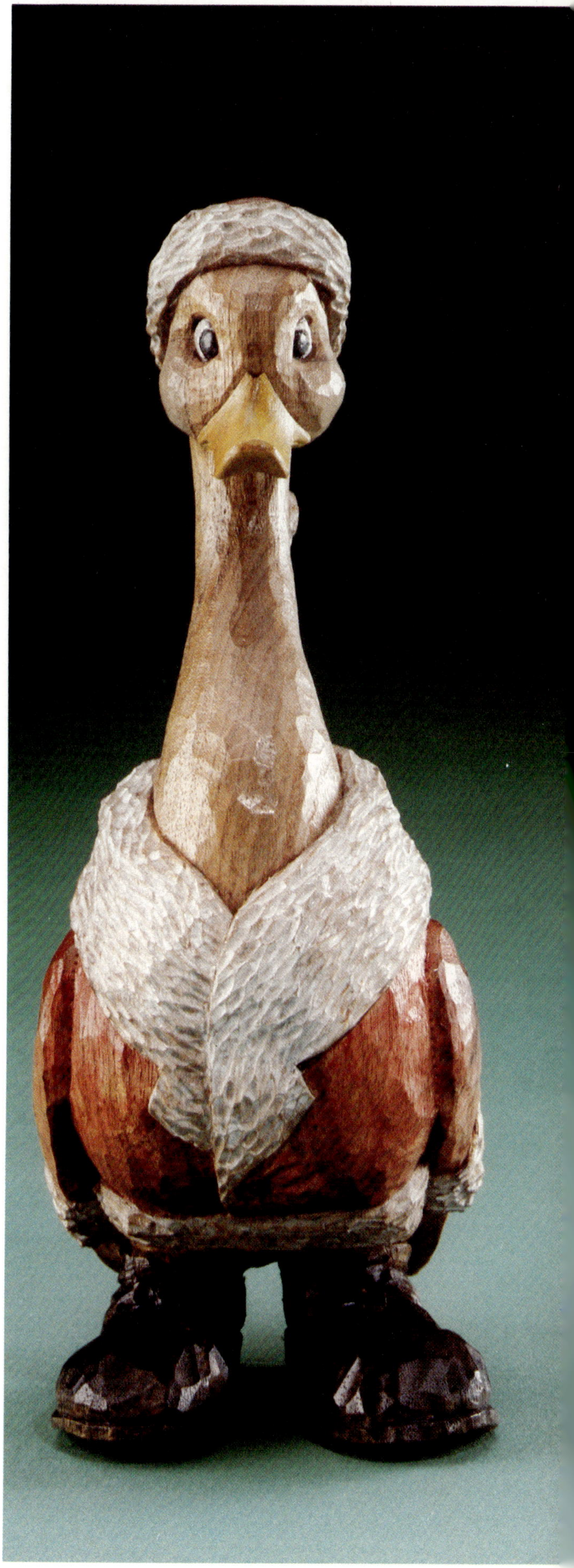

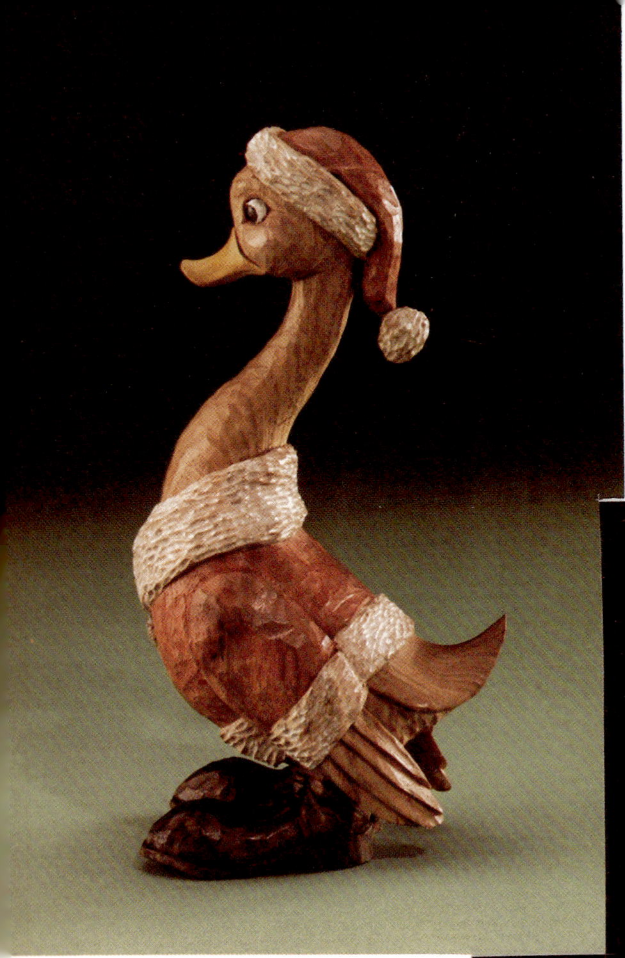

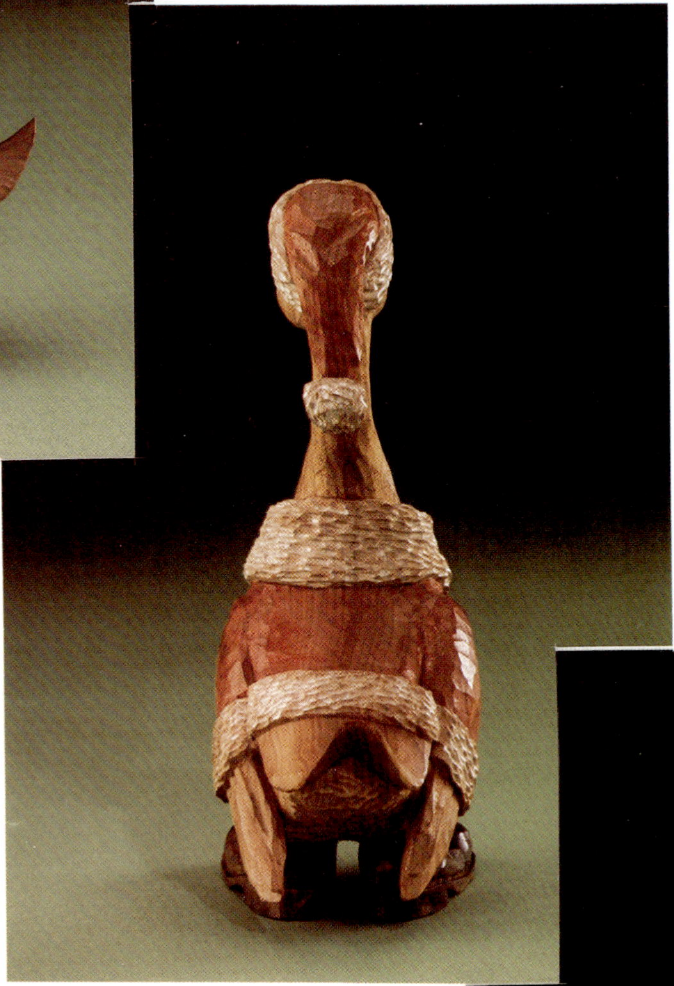

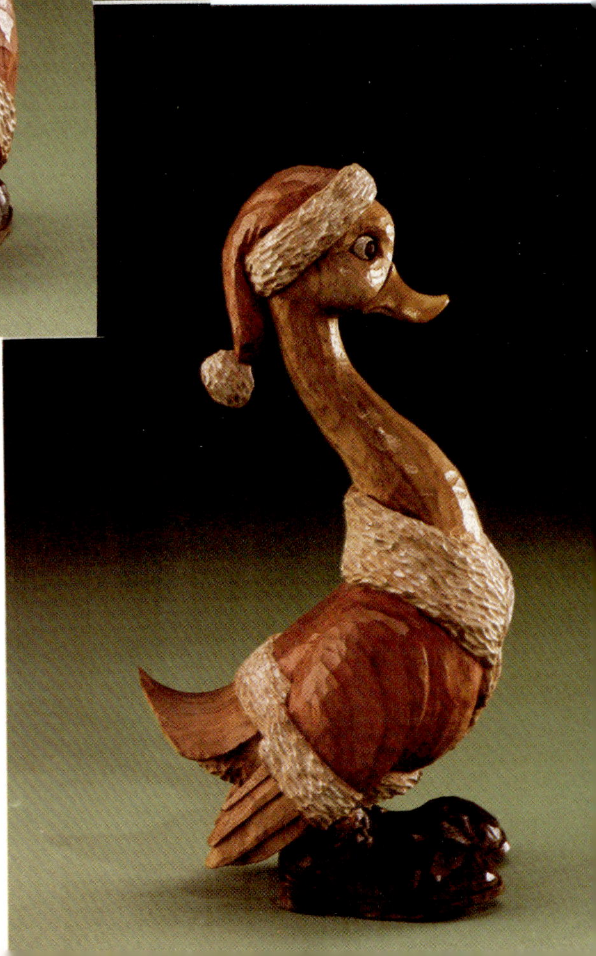

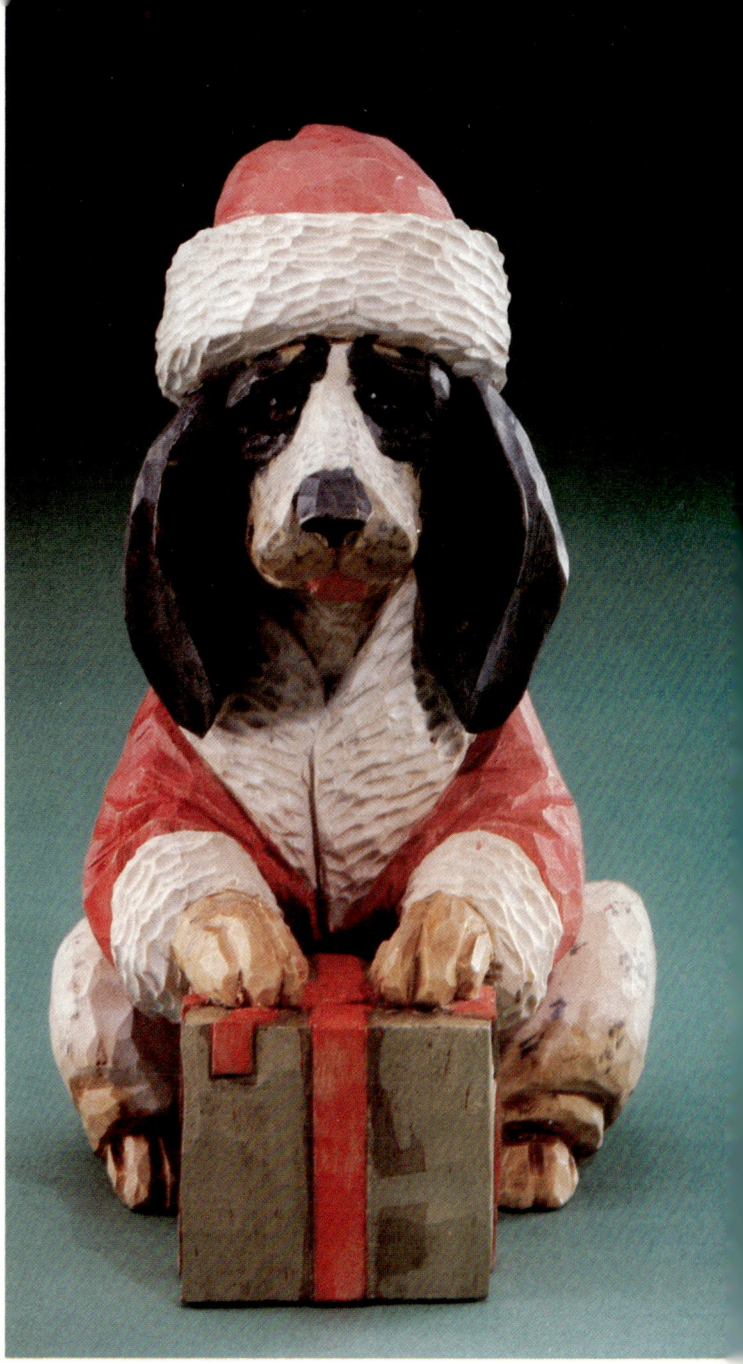

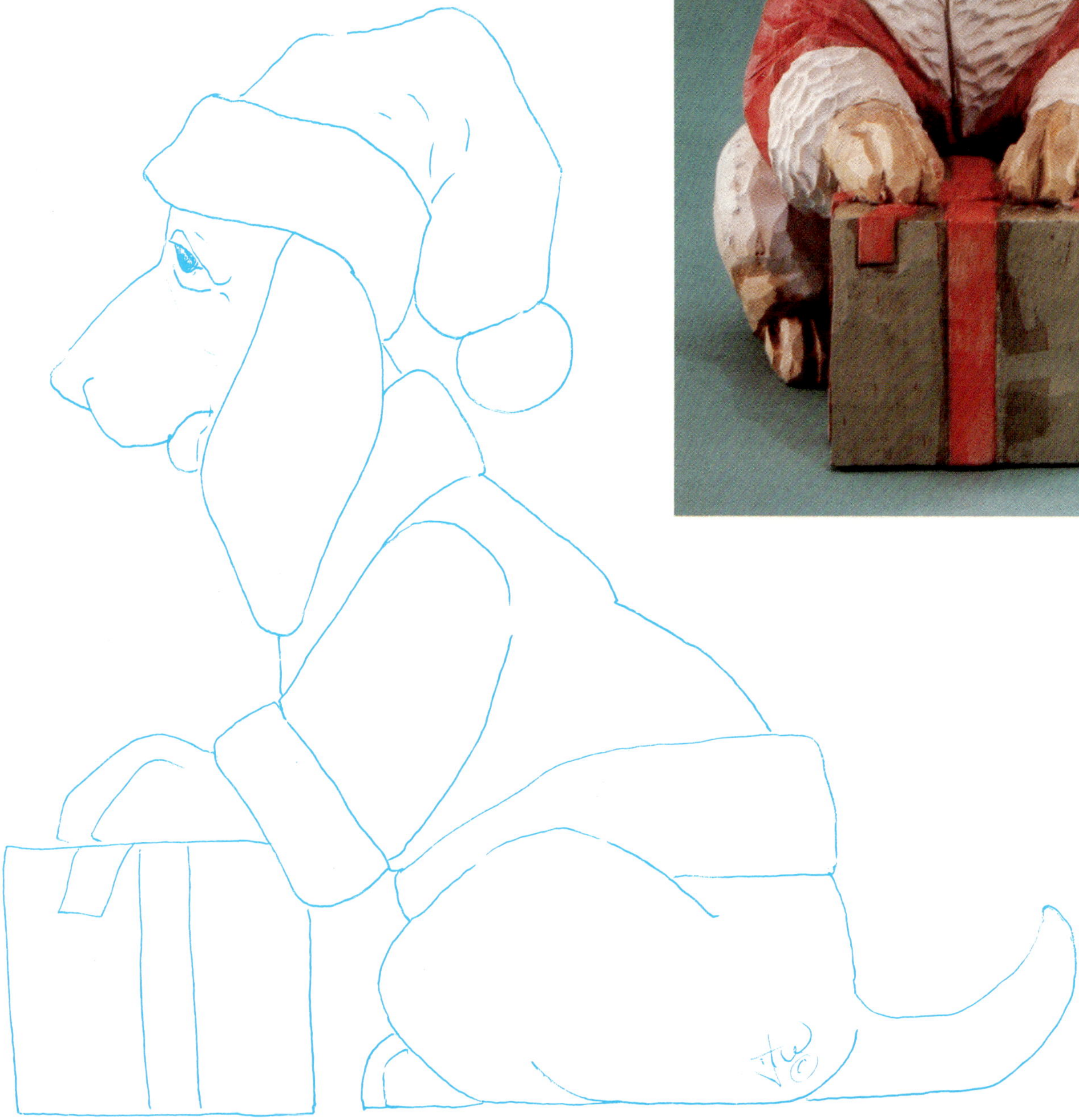

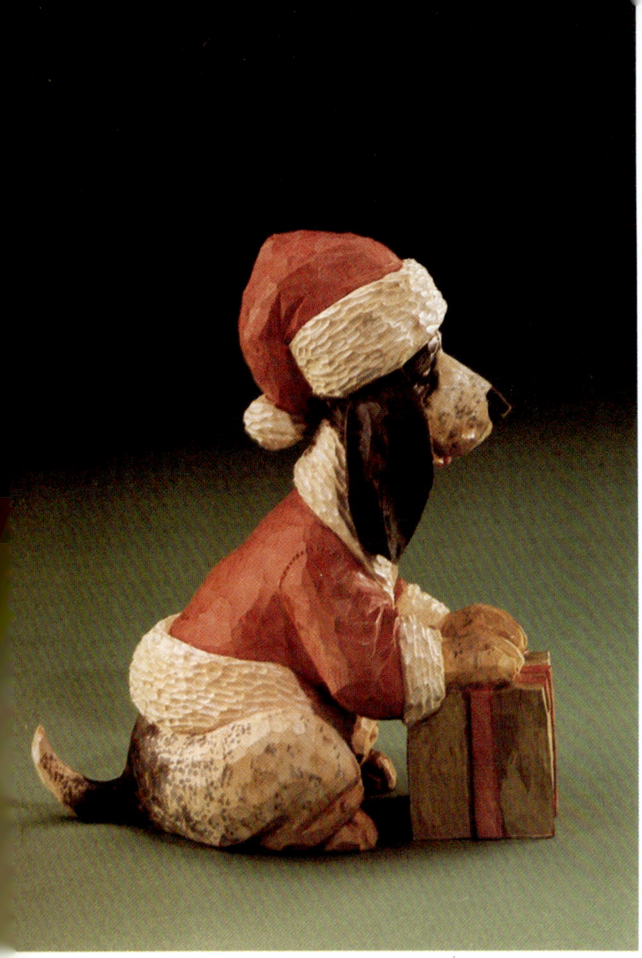

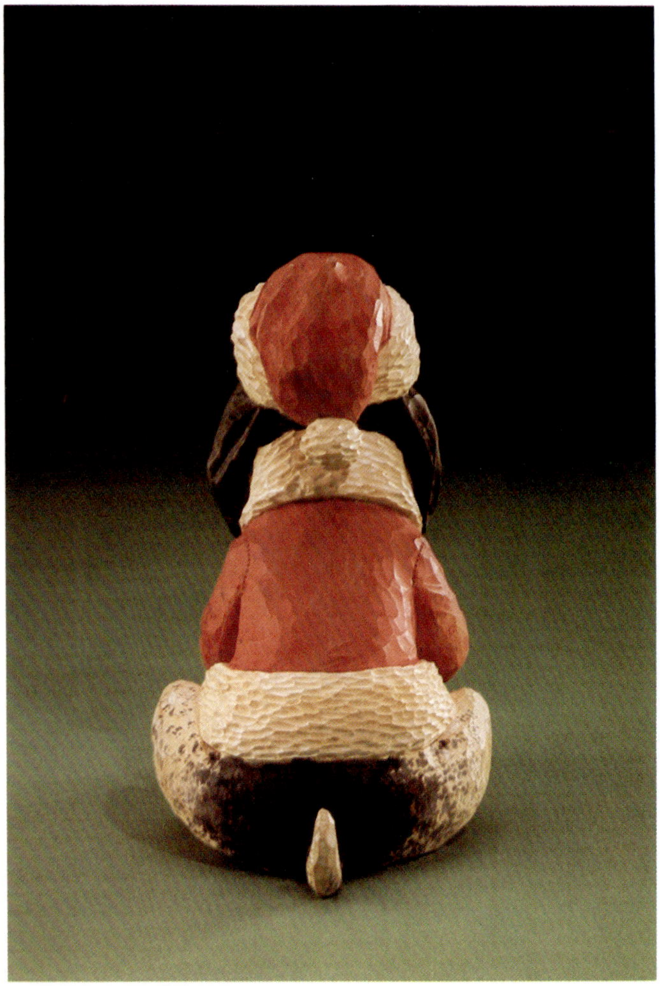

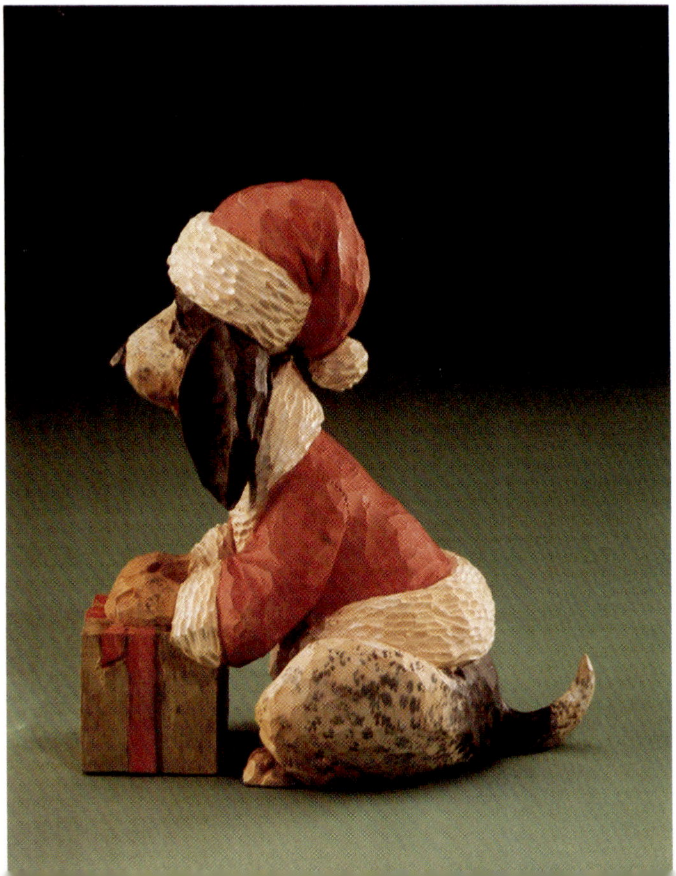

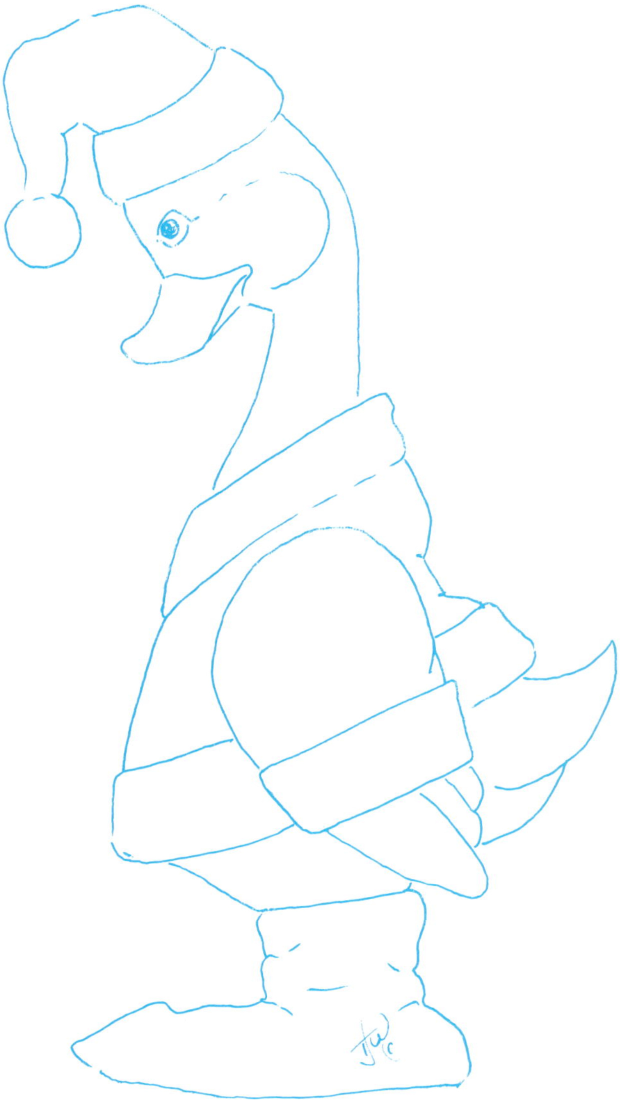

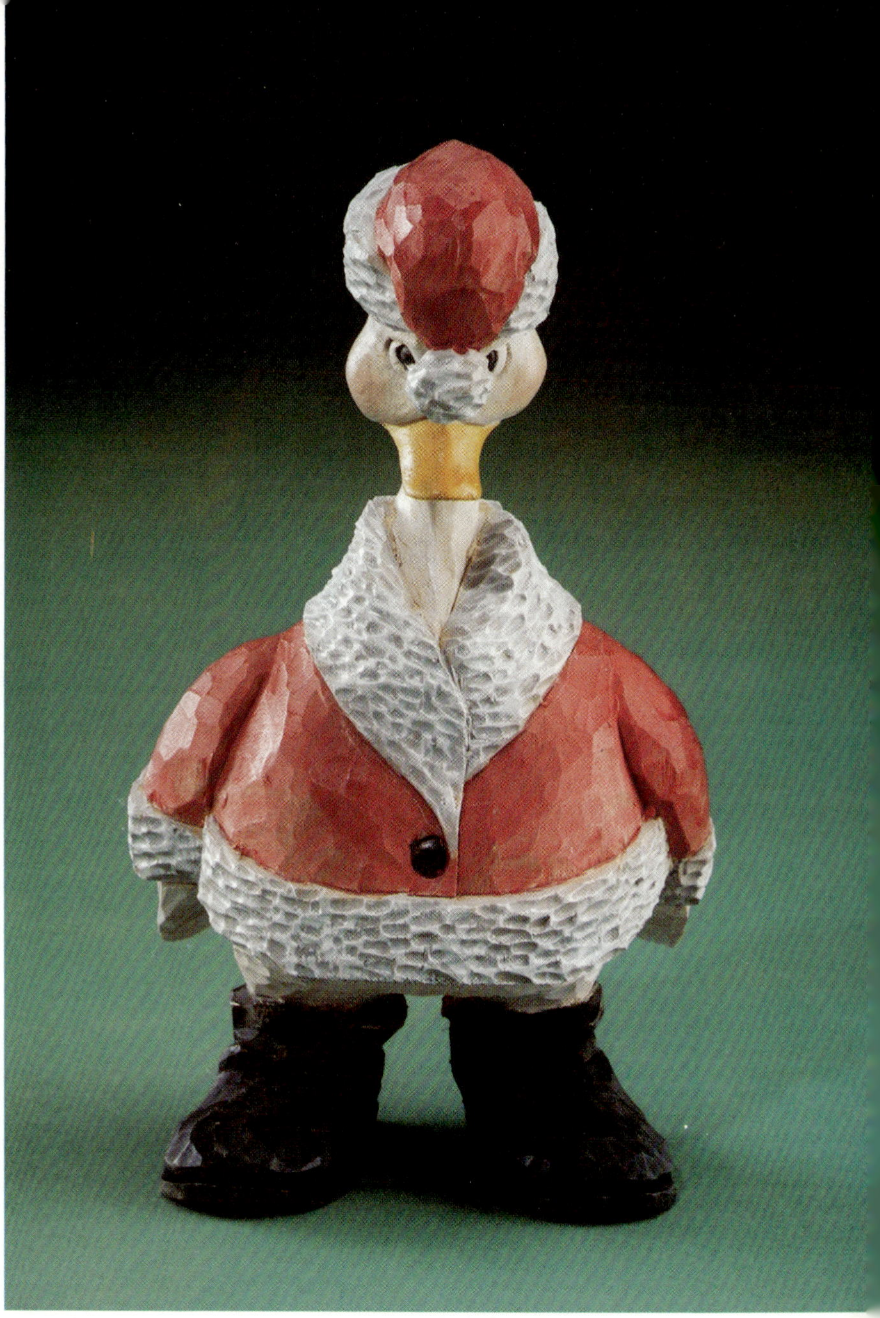

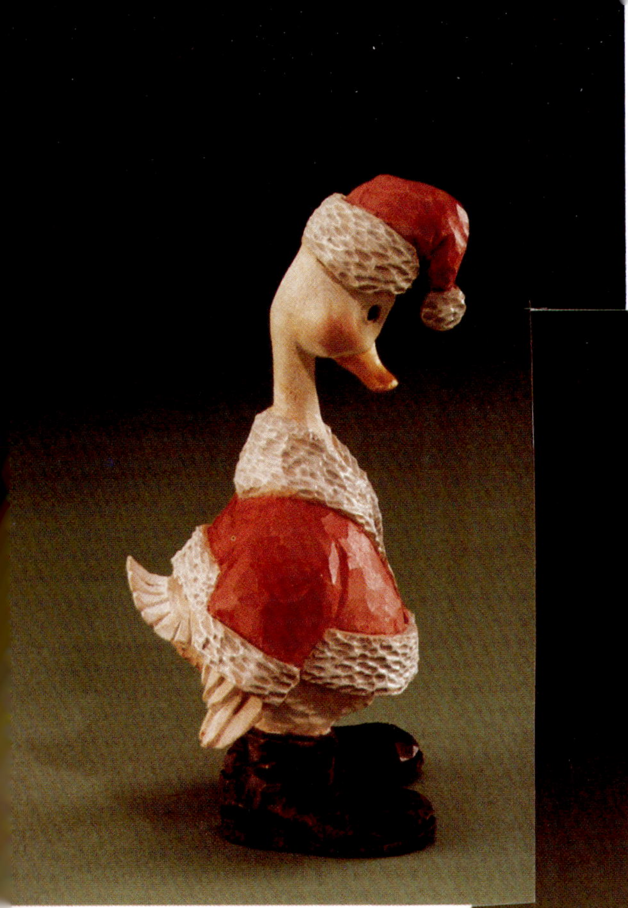

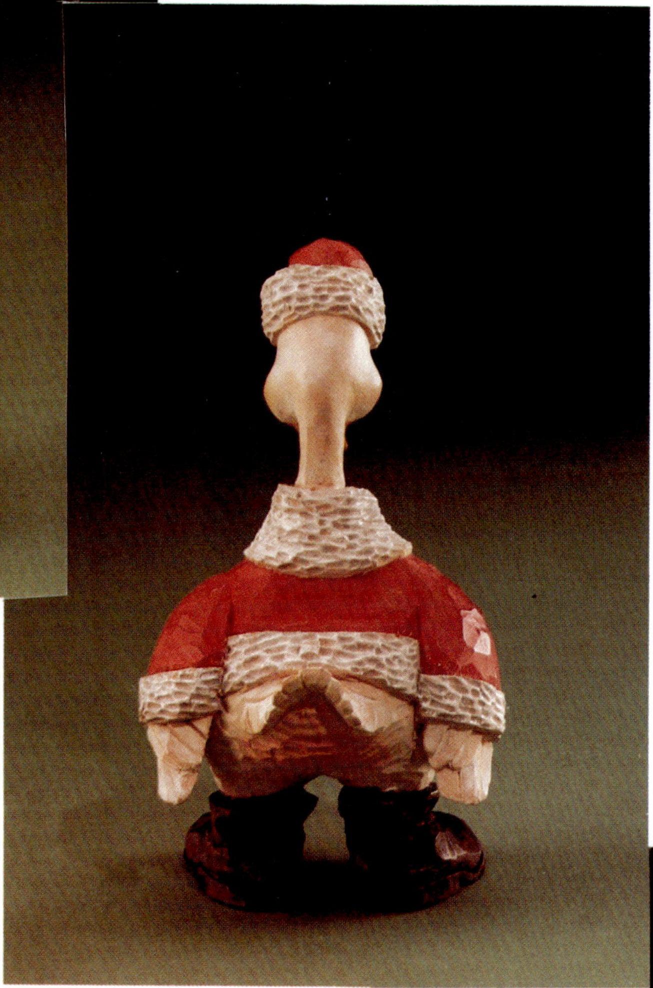

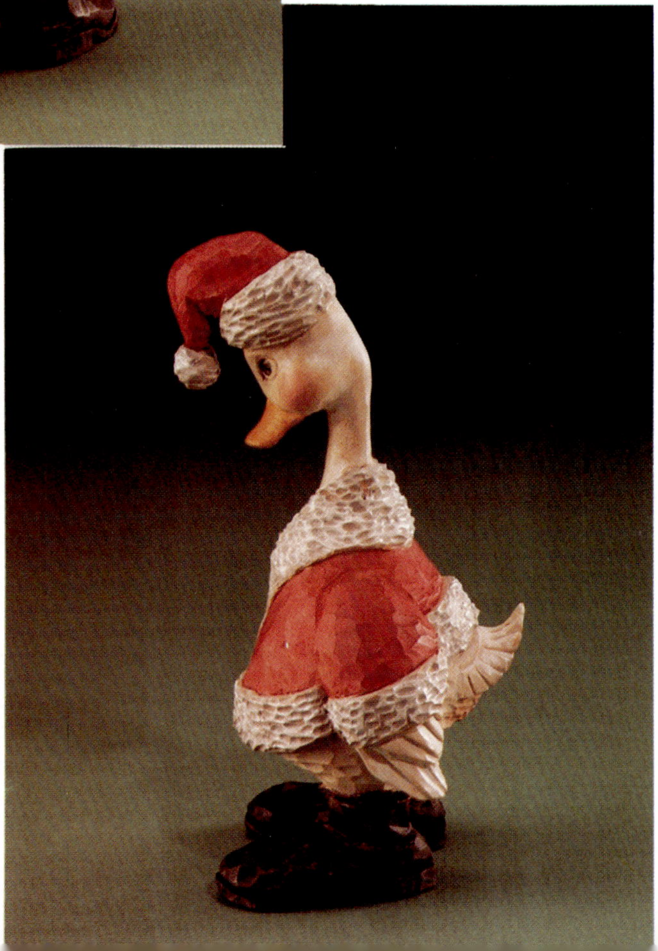

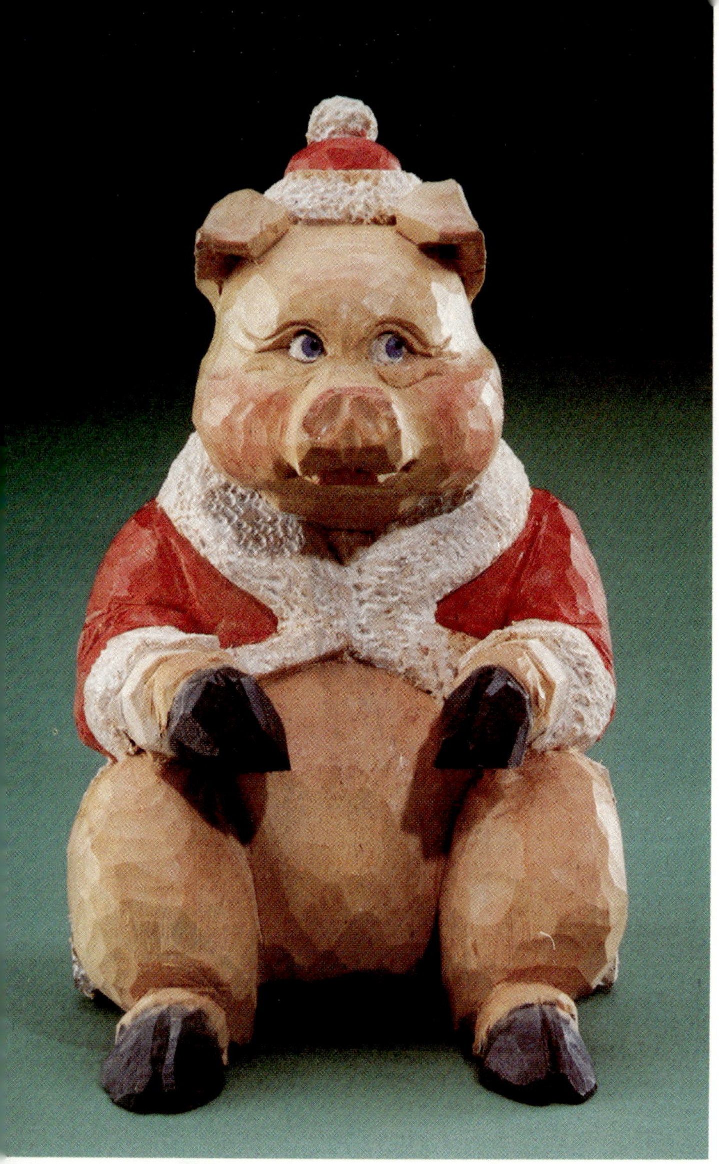

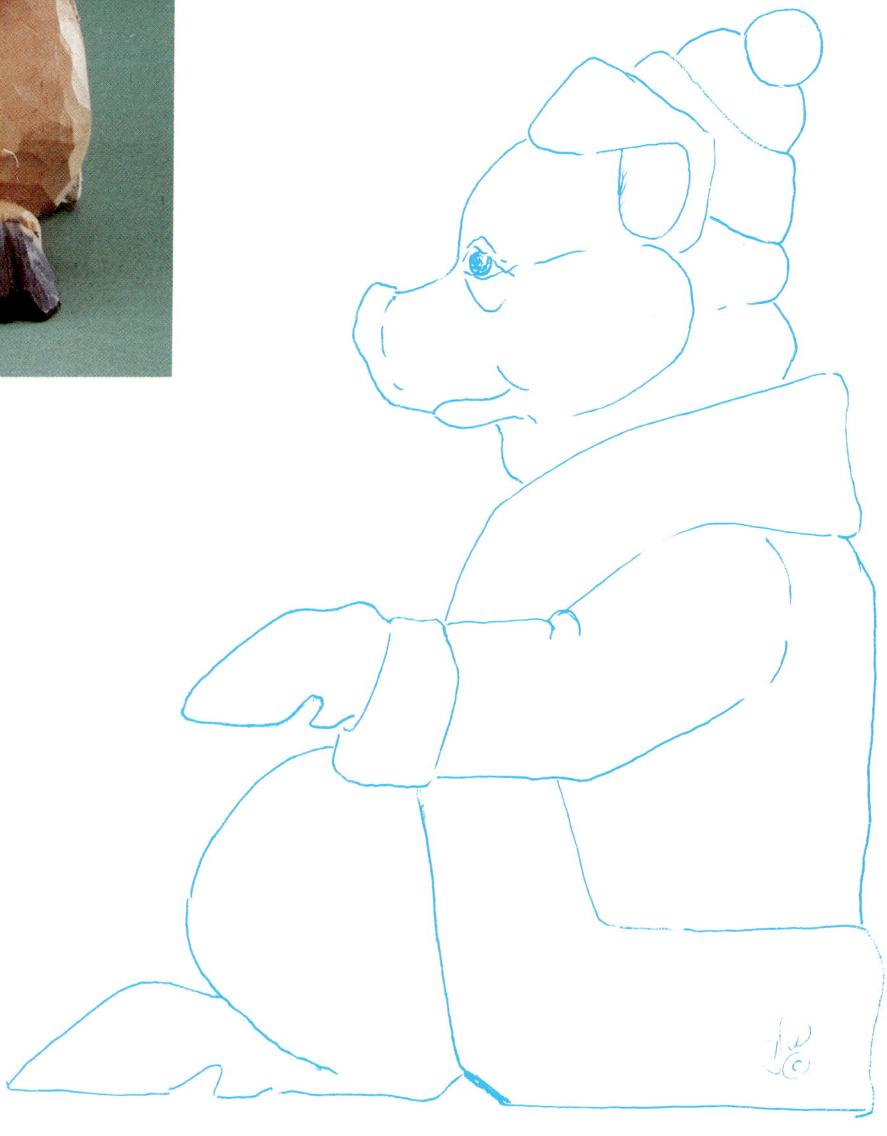

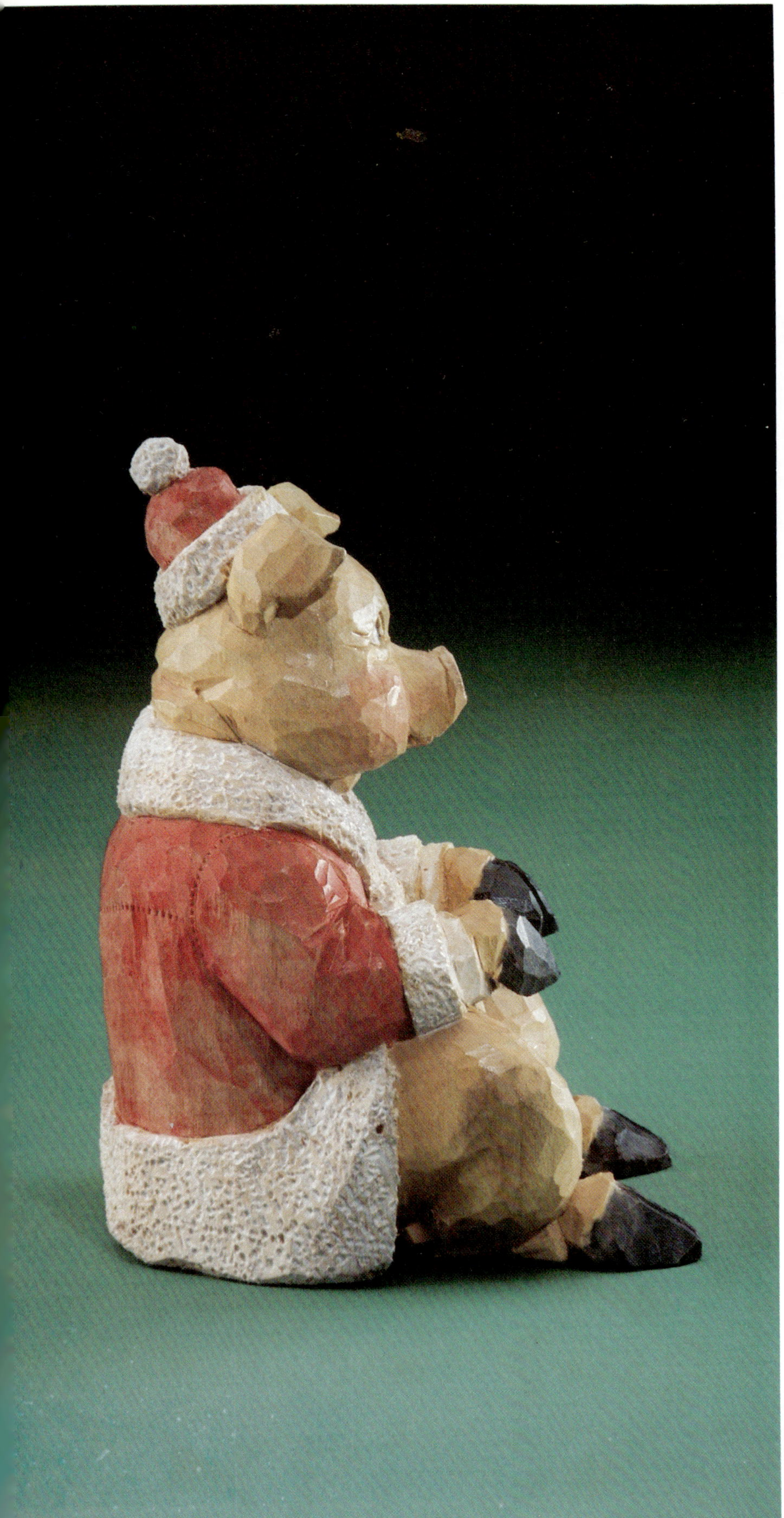

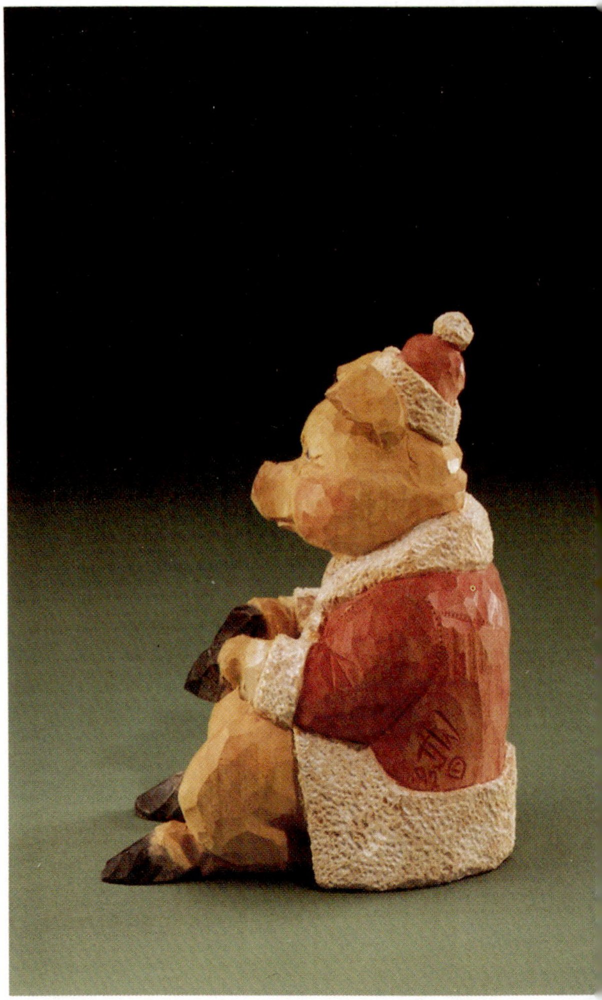

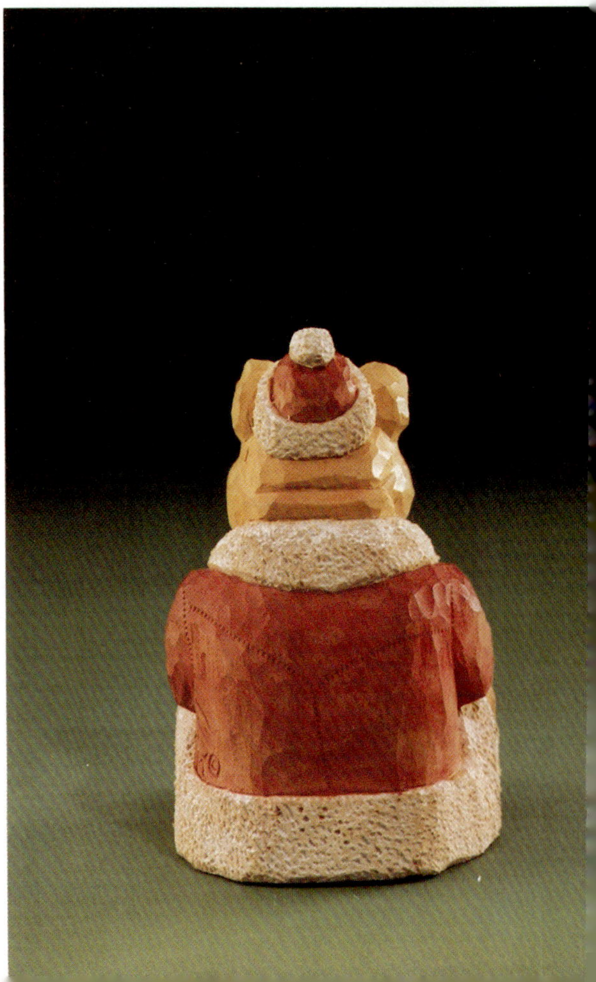

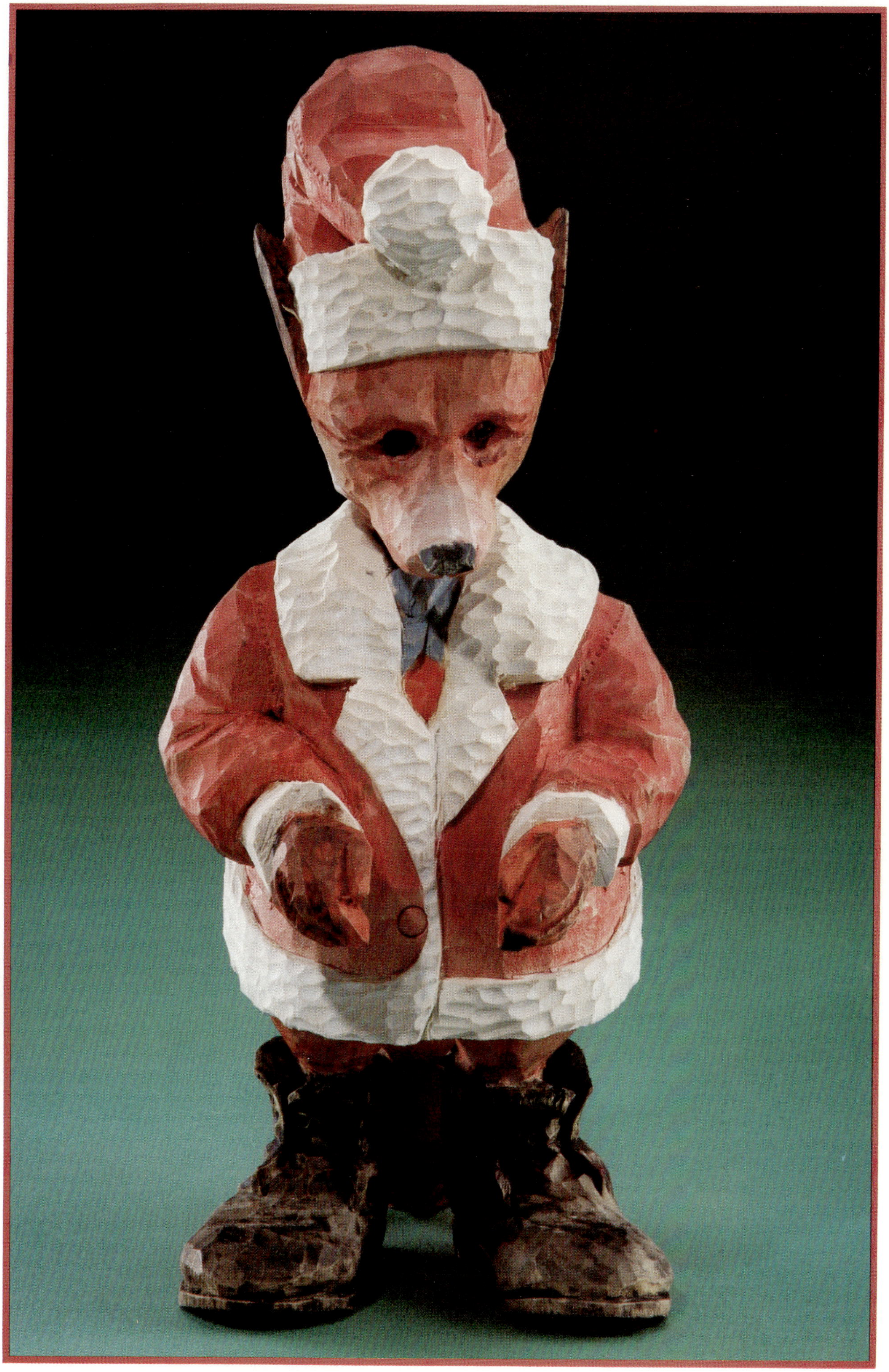

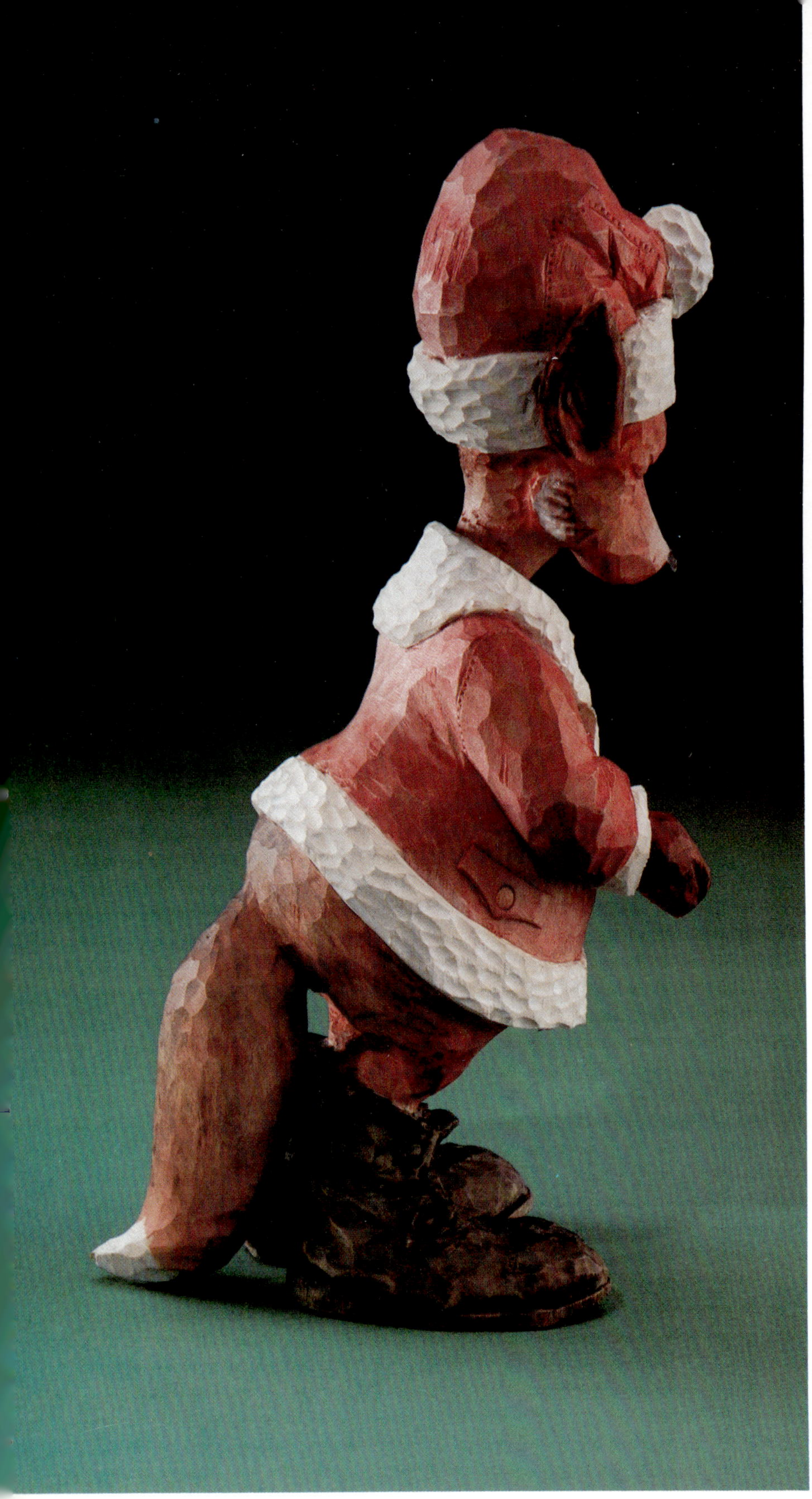

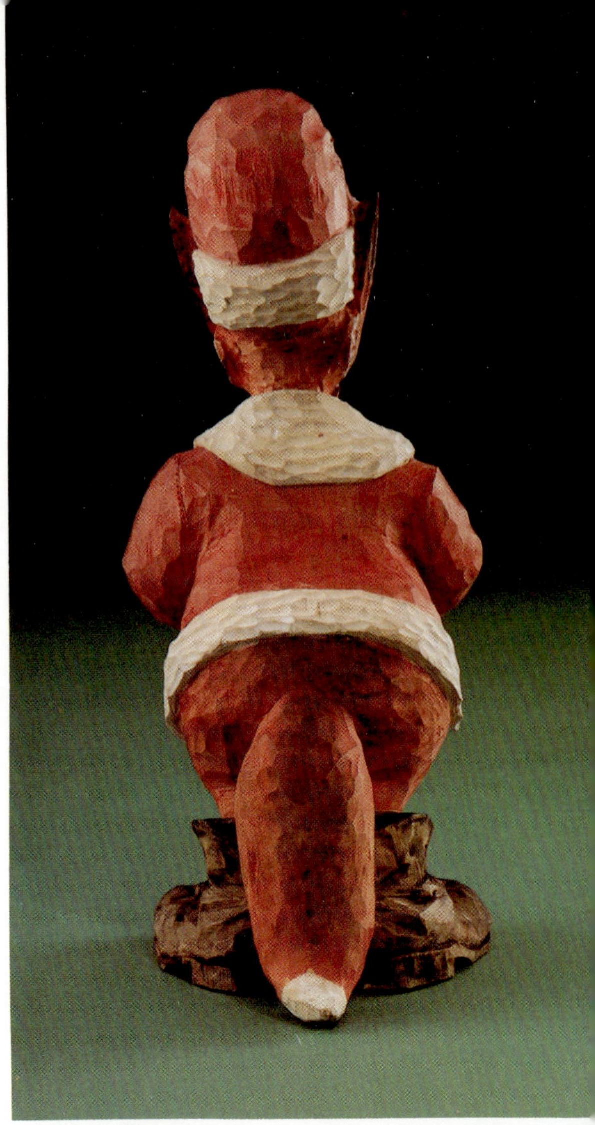

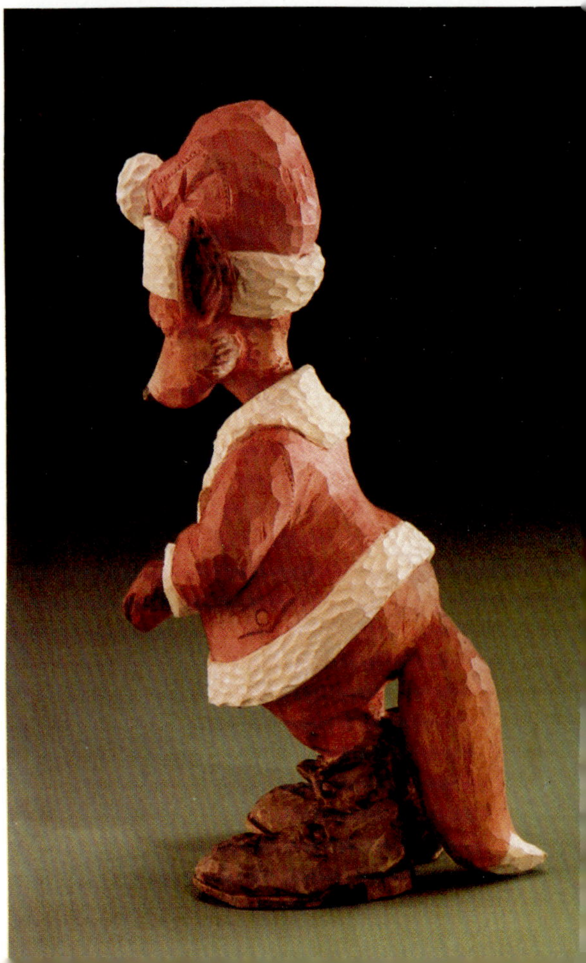